Normative Subjects

Normative Subjects

Self and Collectivity in Morality and Law

MEIR DAN-COHEN

UNIVERSITY PRESS

Oxford University Press is a department of the University of Oxford. It furthers
the University's objective of excellence in research, scholarship, and education
by publishing worldwide. Oxford is a registered trade mark of Oxford University
Press in the UK and certain other countries.

Published in the United States of America by Oxford University Press
198 Madison Avenue, New York, NY 10016, United States of America.

© Oxford University Press 2016

First issued as an Oxford University Press paperback, 2019

All rights reserved. No part of this publication may be reproduced, stored in
a retrieval system, or transmitted, in any form or by any means, without the
prior permission in writing of Oxford University Press, or as expressly permitted
by law, by license, or under terms agreed with the appropriate reproduction
rights organization. Inquiries concerning reproduction outside the scope of the
above should be sent to the Rights Department, Oxford University Press, at the
address above.

You must not circulate this work in any other form
and you must impose this same condition on any acquirer.

CIP data is on file at the Library of Congress
ISBN 978-0-19-998520-3 (hardcover); 978-0-19-093624-2 (paperback)

For Ishai and Talia

CONTENTS

Acknowledgments and Provenance ix

Introduction 1

Part I Construction and Revision

1. Constructing Subjects 11
2. Socializing Harry 46
3. Revising Our Pasts 55
4. Regret, Luck, and Identity 93

Part II Value and Humanity

5. Individuals, Citizens, Persons 117
6. Dignity and Self-Creation 138
7. A Morality of Crime and Punishment 165

Part III Collective Subjects

8. Collective Personhoods 183
9. Sanctioning Corporations 197
10. Freedoms of Collective Speech 209

Notes 233
Index 251

ACKNOWLEDGMENTS AND PROVENANCE

This book consists of previously published essays, though the essays have morphed a good deal in their transition to what now are the book's ten chapters. In revising the existing material, I have reduced redundancies or at least indicated them by cross-references, have highlighted common themes, and have added new material in the interest of increasing overall consistency and coherence. The resulting product is something of a hybrid between a collection of essays and a "real" book. As a compromise, the book does not fully realize the advantages of either of these formats, but with luck it may offer some of the benefits of both. The book covers a larger variety of subject matter and discusses a broader range of ideas than a monograph would be able to accommodate, and it keeps the chapters sufficiently freestanding so that they can be read selectively and out of order. At the same time, there is, I hope, enough unity and continuity to promise some added value to reading the entire book in sequence and to make such an effort worthwhile.

The original essays have been written over a long period of time, and during this time, the world, including its philosophical and legal aspects, has not stood still. This creates some awkwardness in regard to the scholarship on which I draw, which especially in the older pieces is plainly not up to date. I have tried to mitigate this deficiency by acknowledging some salient recent developments and sources that bear directly on the arguments. But since the revisions have taken anyway more time than I had planned, I have not made a systematic effort in this regard, and so the deficiency remains. I don't believe that this is a very serious drawback, though. Whatever this book is, it is most definitely not a reference book. And if there is any merit in the essays now turned chapters included herein, this is the kind of merit one hopes would be able, at least for a while, to withstand the winds of change, scholarly or otherwise.

The sources for the book's chapters are as follows:

Chapter 1, *Constructing Subjects*, is a substantially revised composite of "Constructing Selves," in *Morality, Ethics, and Gifted Minds*, Don Ambrose and Tracy Cross, eds. (New York: Springer, 2009), and "Between Selves and Collectivities: Toward a Jurisprudence of Identity," *University of Chicago Law Review* 61 (1994): 1213.

Chapter 2, *Socializing Harry*, is a slightly revised version of a comment on Harry Frankfurt's Tanner Lectures, published under the same title in Harry Frankfurt, *Taking Ourselves Seriously & Getting It Right*, Debra Satz, ed. (Stanford, CA: Stanford University Press, 2006), 91.

Chapter 3, *Revising Our Pasts*, is a substantially revised composite of "Revising the Past: On the Metaphysics of Repentance, Forgiveness, and Pardon," published in *Forgiveness, Mercy, and Clemency*, Austin Sarat and Nasser Hussain, eds. (Stanford, CA: Stanford University Press, 2006), 117; and "Skirmishes on the Temporal Boundaries of States," *Law and Contemporary Problems* 72 (2009): 95.

Chapter 4, *Regret, Luck, and Identity*, is a slightly revised version of "Luck and Identity," *Theoretical Inquiries in Law* 9 (2008): 1.

Chapter 5, *Individuals, Citizens, Persons*, is a slightly revised version of "Law, Loyalty and Citizenship," *Routledge Companion to Philosophy of Law* (New York: Routledge, 2012).

Chapter 6, *Dignity and Self-Creation*, is a revised version of "A Concept of Dignity," a talk given at the Human Dignity and Criminal Law Symposium held at the Hebrew University in Jerusalem on January 5–6, 2009, and published in *Israel Law Review* 44 (2011): 1; it also contains material from "Dignity and Its (Dis)content," Introduction to *Dignity, Rank, and Rights*, the Tanner Lectures by Jeremy Waldron, Meir Dan-Cohen, ed. (Oxford: Oxford University Press, 2012); and from "The

Authority of the Self," comment on Jeremy Waldron, "Dignity, Rights, and Responsibilities," *Arizona State L. J.* 43 (2011): 1159.

Chapter 7, *A Morality of Crime and Punishment*, is a revised version of "Dignity, Crime, and Punishment: A Kantian Perspective" in *Foundational Texts in Modern Criminal Law*, Markus D. Dubber, ed. (Oxford: Oxford University Press, 2014), 101, containing material from "Defending Dignity," published in my *Harmful Thoughts: Essays on Law, Self, and Morality* (Princeton, NJ: Princeton University Press, 2002), 150; and from "Thinking Criminal Law," *Cardozo Law Review* 28 (2007): 6.

Chapter 8, *Collective Personhoods*, is a revised version of "Epilogue on Corporate Personhood and Humanity," *New Criminal L. Rev.* 16 (2013): 300.

Chapter 9, *Sanctioning Corporations*, is a revised version of a paper published under the same title in *J. Law & Policy* 19 (2010): 15.

Chapter 10, *Freedoms of Collective Speech*, is a revised version of "Freedoms of Collective Speech: A Theory of Protected Communications by Organizations, Communities, and the State," *Calif. L. Rev.* 79 (1991): 1229.

In writing these essays I have greatly benefited from responses by friends and colleagues, and I recorded my indebtedness in each of the published pieces just listed. But in the course of converting these materials into their present shape I acquired two new debts of gratitude, which I happily acknowledge here. The first is to Arden Koehler, a Berkeley philosophy major who had finished her undergraduate studies, and on her way to graduate school was available for a while to lend me a hand. Though hired as a research assistant, her title was later changed to "editorial consultant" to better match her actual contributions: providing detailed (and terrific) substantive comments on the various texts, as well as making insightful proposals about overall organization, and helping identify and eliminate redundancies, gaps, and inconsistencies. All of this doubtlessly delayed the book's publication by quite some time, but not by nearly as much as it would have been delayed had I insisted on doing full justice to all of Arden's sound suggestions and objections. Not the least of Arden's contributions was to line up a worthy successor, Shannon

Doberneck, who with a similar background and trajectory to Arden's, took over seamlessly when Arden had to leave, and has provided first-rate assistance, at the substantive as well as at a more technical level, and saw the project to its conclusion. I greatly appreciate the opportunity I had to work with these two outstanding young scholars, and I am grateful for their invaluable help.

Introduction

Legal philosophy and its neighboring fields—moral and political philosophy—are mostly occupied, naturally enough, with normative issues and the terms that frame them. These fields address questions regarding what to do, rather than the other fundamental philosophical concern, with what there is. But the separation between these two kinds of issues is only partial. What to do depends in many ways on what there is; for example, it is sensible to open an umbrella when it rains. As this example also illustrates, the presence of certain factors, such as rain, is highly relevant to some normative matters, but not at all to many others. One factor, though, is pertinent to all: the subject with regard to whom these matters arise. Rain or shine, the subject is always there. What we do depends on what we are. Consider, for example, such key normative terms as responsibility, autonomy, and dignity. To be responsible is to be answerable for oneself; to be autonomous is to govern oneself; to have dignity is to be the locus of moral value and so to demand and attract respect toward oneself. So what precisely we are responsible for, how far our autonomy extends, and what merits respect, all crucially depend on what the human subject, or in what has become the common nomenclature the self, is, and where its boundaries lie.

This ubiquitous connection between *is* and *ought* has of course not gone unnoticed. Many have tied their reflection on practical matters to one or another conception of self. Consequently, the intersection between practical philosophy and the study of self is populated by a heterogeneous array of views that differ from each other along the normative dimension as well as in the conception of self they espouse. Though this variability defies easy summary, we can get an overview of the range most relevant to the present book by limiting our attention to the liberal tradition. Here the schematic picture that emerged over time and came into focus in recent years consists in a juxtaposition between a consequentialist, mostly utilitarian school of thought, and a deontological, mostly Kantian one. Their points of departure, respectively in Bentham and Kant, can be contrasted both along the normative dimension and in terms of their conceptions of self. On the normative side we find a primary concern for aggregate welfare in the one case and for individual autonomy and dignity in the other. As to conceptions of self, the contrast is between a naturalistically conceived organism driven by the twin motives of pleasure and pain, as against an abstract noumenal self that resides in a metaphysical netherland of things-in-themselves.

As this snapshot of the liberal landscape reveals, liberalism contains its own critique: its normative program is split between two conflicting normative visions, grounded in opposing conceptions of self. Moreover, though Kant's noumenal self can be seen as a radical response to the utilitarians' naturalized vision of humanity, Kant's alternative, with its esoteric metaphysics, is not satisfactory either, and at any rate has not been widely accepted even by followers. How do we proceed? One option is to continue the intramural strife, supposedly until one of the parties prevails or some mutually satisfactory accommodation is worked out. But pending such resolution or as an alternative to it, we can change the terms of the discussion by fixing on a conception of self that for the most part lies outside of this discussion and at any rate has not been integral to it. The conception of self that informs this book, call it the *meaning-conception*, is the joint product of two longstanding and multifaceted philosophical strands, the constructivist and the hermeneutical. The view that "man has no essence" and must create his own, though originating at least as far back as the fifteenth century,[1] was given new impetus and significance in the twentieth in such influential and otherwise diverse schools of thought as existentialism, postmodernism, and communitarianism. They all converge on a conception of human beings as self-creating: through our actions and practices, individual and collective, we define our identities and draw our boundaries. Such constructivism with respect to human beings poses an ontological challenge: what must people be like for self-creation to be a viable option? The other strand on which I draw, the hermeneutical viewpoint regarding human beings, implies an answer. Many thinkers have alternately spoken of the self in dramaturgical, literary, or more broadly semiotic terms. We can recognize in these metaphors and imageries a common thread: like plays and novels, human beings are constituted by meaning and are amenable to interpretation. In conjunction, these two strands convey an important insight that provides this book with a central theme: that the meanings we create, create us. In what follows I explore this theme in different ways and different contexts. Let me briefly highlight some of the main points.

According to a dominant picture, studying our normative engagements requires an antecedent understanding of their human subjects. Subjects come first; the norms that guide or bind them come second. The conception of self I explore suggests a shift or an addition of focus. It draws attention to the role of our various normative engagements not just in responding to a preexisting self but also in shaping it. The result is an emphasis on a reciprocal relationship between law and morality on the one side and the composition and boundaries of the self on the other. Viewing a conception of self as a point of origin of normative investigations is relatively familiar. But how are we to reverse this procedure? This is less familiar territory, and so we need some cognitive aids. One such device, which I've discussed on other occasions, and to which I return in Chapter 1, is provided by the dramaturgical version of the meaning-conception of self, especially its central notion of *role*. Role theory has of course had a long and somewhat turbulent career in sociology; even so, it has not been exhaustively mined for its philosophical significance. Roles consist in structured clusters of norms that serve as constituents of human identity and in light of which human conduct becomes intelligible. The notion of a role thus provides a metaphor that combines the constructivist and the hermeneutic themes just mentioned.

The notion of role also serves as a bridge to the book's second central theme. Individual human beings are not the only subjects on the normative scene. There is also an array of collective entities—such as organizations, corporations, communities, and states—that form a significant category of subjects of morality and law. How do these collectivities relate to the individual actors? The notion of role offers a simple answer. Roles are not just the constituents of individual identities but are also the building blocks of these collective formations. Thus, roles also serve as theoretically handy templates for depicting the internal relation between the subjective and the intersubjective, or the individual and the collective facets of human life. However, a conception of role equal to this dual theoretical task requires that we draw a distinction between two types of roles regarding the way roles participate in the construction of self. The distinction is between *proximate* roles, with which their bearers identify so as to make them constituents of their identity, and *distant* roles, performed without such identification and so lacking the same significance for identity and self. Recognizing this variability helps articulate contrasting modalities in terms of which individuals and collectivities interrelate, as well as to distinguish types of collectivities within which such proximity or distance in occupying a role is enacted.

A second heuristic I find helpful in guiding reflection about the self involves an analogy between people and states. Talk of people as exercising autonomy, bearing responsibility, and enjoying inviolability within the prescribed boundaries of the self conjures up a political imagery and brings to mind such notions as self-government, sovereignty, and jurisdiction, in terms of which the existence of states and the significance of their territorial borders are commonly understood. Applied to the self, such political imagery provides an antidote to a dominant conception of human beings as physical objects and natural kinds. Though we are prone to objectifying (in the sense of treating as objects) both states and individuals, the objectification in the case of states is more visible, and once observed, easier to undo, thus paving the way to a corresponding modification of our conception of people and the role that the analogous normative terms play in their lives. I introduce the analogy in Chapter 2 as a further elaboration of the constructivist theme.

But where there is construction, there is also room for revision, and here too, analogizing the boundaries of the self to those of the state is revealing. Chapter 3 discusses several practices—such as apology, forgiveness, and pardon—that are designed to help us escape the shadow of a grim past. I argue that these *revisionary practices* serve this end by redrawing the temporal boundaries of a subject, individual or collective, in a way that resembles the redrawing of a state's territorial border. The notion of revisionary practices is directly tied to the thought that who we are is a matter of the norms and the meanings that link us to certain objects and events. These norms and meanings can change, and with them our boundaries change too. In this sense, our past is not fixed, or what amounts to the same thing, we are not fixed relative to the past. This gives us some leeway with regard to the effects that past events have on our lives.

But, I argue, that leeway is limited. If who we are is the cumulative product of the meanings we have embraced or enacted over time, there must be a limit to what we can revise through revisionary practices while retaining our identities. This last consideration assumes center stage in Chapter 4, which deals with the perennial problem of moral luck, and the related issue of regret. I argue that the notion of luck applies only to relatively peripheral aspects of our lives. Contrary to what some writers maintain, there is no such thing as *constitutive luck*—that is, luck in the constituents of one's identity—since this kind of luck would have no bearer: there would be no one whose luck, good or bad, this would be. And this suggests a corresponding limitation on what one can coherently regret: beyond a certain point, wishing that defining aspects of one's life were different is to entertain the vacuous wish that someone else existed rather than oneself.

Whereas Part I of the book focuses primarily on the subjects of morality and law, both individual and collective, Part II pays greater attention to substantive normative matters with which these subjects engage. Chapter 5 provides a transition between these two focal points by tying the meaning-conception of self to a broad map of the practical domain as a whole. The argument proceeds from the observation that the clusters of meanings and norms constitutive of human identity form nested structures consisting of variable levels of abstraction or resolution. Consequently, meanings and norms that diverge at a high level of resolution can converge to form unities at higher levels of abstraction. This helps distinguish, and relate, different phases of human identity. More specifically, to be an individual, a citizen, and a person, is for one and the same human being to occupy different rungs on the ladder of abstraction. The same hierarchy of abstraction also provides a key to how the main subdivisions of ethics—prudence, law, and morality—relate to each other and to us. In Chapter 6 I take up one segment of this map, by considering some moral implications of the two earlier themes: human self-creation and the meaning-conception of self. The result is a pitch for a revised conception of Kantian dignity as the master value in a universal morality to which other normative systems, specifically law, are answerable as well. The most significant legal field that is answerable in this way to a morality of dignity is criminal law. In Chapter 7 I argue for a "moralized," dignity-based conception of criminal offenses, and correspondingly of punishment.

This view of dignity as the keystone to morality and to law raises the question of how dignity extends to our collective life, which I take up in Part III. In Chapter 8 I argue that the different modalities, discussed in Chapter 1, in terms of which individuals and collectivities interrelate, suggest a split answer. Some collectivities participate in defining their members' identity, and so partake of their dignity, whereas other collectivities are impersonal, instrumental formations that ought to be treated as such. In this vein, I argue in Chapter 9 that the dignity-based constraints that are central to the treatment of individual offenders by criminal law do not apply when imposing criminal sanctions on corporations. Chapter 10 makes a similar point with respect to freedom of speech. Here too I caution against a persisting failure to recognize the variability among the subjects of law and morality, and the tendency to proceed, explicitly or tacitly, as though all collective entities could be reduced to individual actors or be assimilated to them. We must recognize instead that collectivities engage in communications that are irreducible to those of any particular individuals, and that the protections due to these communications vary with the type of collectivity and its relationship to its individual members. These last two chapters are case studies of a larger point, regarding the need to adjust our normative stance to the multiplicity of types of subjects. In particular, due attention to impersonal social formations, of which business corporations are a prime example, reveals a large area in which maximizing aggregate social welfare is not hampered by deontological constraints designed to protect individuals' autonomy- or dignity-based rights.

As I said at the outset, this book belongs to a broad area that is variously referred to as practical philosophy, as normative theory, or by kindred other labels, and is at any rate concerned in one way or another with issues of value and policy. This calls for a caveat I have sounded on other occasions as well. As I see it, theories in this broadly defined area can only attain a certain degree of rigor and clarity for which they strive by offering a partial and selective vision, and are subject to an emphatic and all-important ceteris paribus clause. They must be promulgated accordingly in a spirit of theoretical pluralism, acknowledging from the start the potential value of other theories even as one tries to display the merits of one's own.* Flagging this attitude should help mitigate two adverse consequences of a more ambitious and exclusive conception of theory in these areas. One adverse consequence concerns the impact theory has on the world. When it comes to such fraught fields as morality, politics, and law, there is a danger of turning theory into ideology. The two are close kin. The difference these terms mark is mainly a matter of our attitude to the clusters of ideas that compose them, rather than a matter of the ideas themselves. When we grant a system of ideas exclusivity and regard it as calling for implementation, we treat that system as an ideology. Theories,

---

* Not the least of John Rawls's contributions is the indefinite article that opens the title of his seminal book.

by contrast, are only expected to inform judgment, not replace it.* The other negative outcome of an excessively ambitious and exclusive conception of theory is its stifling effect on the project of theorizing itself. We can be more experimental, tentative, even playful in our theoretical reflection when we bear in mind that theories are designed to impact the world, if at all, only cumulatively, filtered through a thick layer of practical judgments exercised by individuals in their own lives and by practitioners in various offices, and tempered by these actors' implicit canons of reasonableness and common sense.†

---

* Given the predominantly Kantian orientation of the studies that follow, the repercussions of this metatheoretical attitude with regard to Kant's moral theory are particularly pertinent here. Some criticize Kant for excessive rigorism that yields unappealingly extreme positions, while others feel compelled by his arguments or his authority to swallow the toads. Both are mistaken. Here, too, laudable theoretical rigor may turn into fanaticism when adopted as an extratheoretical, all-things-considered practical view. (Kant himself would most likely disagree—but, then, he was not a graduate of the twentieth century.) It should be noted, though, that the larger the toads, the louder their croaking in opposition to the theory that breeds them. But a theory's congruence or conflict with our convictions and intuitions is not decisive. In particular, even in the game of *reflective equilibrium* (another or Rawls's important ideas), a counterexample does not refute a theory, but only motivates further refinement of the theory or the exploration of other ones.

† These canons are likely to be in part the product of theory, making the availability of and exposure to multiple and incommensurate theoretical points of view all the more important.

PART I

Construction and Revision

1

Constructing Subjects

I. MODALITIES OF HUMAN CONSTRUCTION

This chapter is part summary, part elaboration of some themes I've pursued in the past, and so may feel redundant to old readers and cryptic to new. Even so, it should be useful to both groups in providing a comprehensive if sketchily drawn picture of some foundational matters that bear in more or less direct ways on other parts of the book. The title of this chapter alludes to the book's title, and so to the subjects of morality and law. But *subject* is ambiguous. It designates not only these two fields but also the entities addressed by their norms. Who are the subjects of morality and law in this second sense? A straightforward answer points to human beings: we, and we alone, are norm-bound and norm-following beings; we are, in short, normative subjects. *Constructing* is also ambiguous: it depicts the normative subjects under consideration both as doing the constructing and as the products, as what is under construction. To think about human beings in constructive terms is to apply to them, to us, a variant of an approach that ranges over many other putative constructs as well. One can be, and one or another philosopher quite likely has been, a constructivist about anything, including, at the limit, about everything. Constructivism with respect to humanity is, however, distinguished by the reflexivity involved when we create ourselves.

What is the connection between the view of human beings as normative subjects and as self-creating? On the version of the constructive view

I favor, the connection is quite tight. By pursuing our goals and promoting our projects, and so while abiding by the various norms that guide us in these endeavors, we do another thing as well: we determine the composition of the self and draw its boundaries. The constructive view thus complicates and expands our normative agenda. Absent a stable, antecedently given human subject, subject and norms engage in a dynamic reciprocal relationship in which neither side provides a starting point or a resting place relative to the other. The recognition that we are the products as well as the authors of our practices and norms confronts us with a double challenge: not just what to do, but also what to be. And so in devising our behavior-guiding norms we must glimpse their effects on who we are as well: what subjects will emerge from a system of activity generated by a particular set of norms?

In confronting the constructive enterprise head on, it is natural to resort to the same norms that guide us in regard to the more familiar questions concerning how to act. Just as we choose what to do in light of what best suits our values and serves our interests, so supposedly we can also choose what to be in those terms. But a moment's reflection reveals the difficulty. It is best seen by considering a cluster of norms (by which I mean values, evaluative attitudes, practices, and the like) that are *personal*, in the sense that they take human beings as their objects, and so depend for their content and application on the composition and boundaries of the self. Responsibility, autonomy, and dignity are prominent examples. What precisely we're responsible for, how far our autonomy extends, and what merits respect, all crucially depend on what we take the self to be. Now since personal norms track the boundaries of the self, on the traditional view their scope can be determined by studying those boundaries. The constructive view denies this option: personal norms participate in constituting the self, and thus the boundary they track is in part their own creation. To be sure, specific ascriptions of responsibility or affirmations of autonomy or expressions of respect are supported by a preexisting vision of the subject: she did it, we say, or it's her own life, or her body. But when we probe such statements, philosophically or in cases in which they prove particularly contentious, it turns out that they rest on the sedimentation of myriads of similar statements in the past. If we wish to go beyond precedent or are forced to do so, what can we appeal to?

The idea of construction, which raises this problem, also provides part of the answer. Building codes in general include imperatives that express the very idea of construction, of creating any structure, rather than those that pertain to the construction of a particular one. A building code for the construction of selves would be no different; it too would include some such general and formal criteria oriented toward what it is for a self to exist. So although the thought that personal norms participate in drawing the boundaries of the self does not by itself tell us where these boundaries ought to lie, one way in which it helps draw them is by introducing an important constraint. Seen as tracking the boundary of one and the same entity, personal norms must be coextensive; they must have the same scope. To see the significance of this point, consider our attitude toward responsibility. Responsibility often carries with it burdens, and so we are tempted to evade it. One way to do so is by enacting a more minimal, narrowly circumscribed self. For example, when we learn that the law applies some of its most draconian measures to what we take to be the operations of will, we may respond by contracting the will's domain and instead describe various types of actions in a deterministic vocabulary designed to place them at the periphery of the self or even completely outside its boundaries. Awareness of the coextensiveness of personal norms, however, alerts us to the risk inherent in this maneuver. Evacuating regions of the self in order to escape the burdens of responsibility has as corollary the contraction of the scope of our autonomy and dignity as well. The opposite is also true. People may incline to stake out claims to expansive autonomy and to wide-ranging grounds of respect. But here, too, they must recognize the potentially undesirable constructive implications: since these claims involve expanding the self, they entail the assumption of greater responsibility as well.

Returning now to the reflexivity of human construction, we encounter yet another ambiguity: the "we" of the reflexive formula, the subject and so also the product of construction, can be construed distributively or jointly, leading to two contrasting strands in the constructive view.

The distributive interpretation yields *self-constitution*—the view, associated with modernity's vision of the autonomous individual, according to which each individual is the author of her own identity. The joint interpretation, by contrast, yields *social construction*—the view held by intellectual movements critical of modernity—such as existentialism, postmodernism, and communitarianism—that social practices, discursive and otherwise, shape our selves. Though much ink has been spilled over these seemingly oppositional trends, we should bear in mind that they signify two modalities of the same underlying idea, that of human self-creation.[1] This affinity between the two trends is easy to miss: on the surface, by positing *society* as shaping the individual self, social construction appears to deny what self-constitution affirms, namely the reflexivity of human construction. However, a peek below this surface discloses a different possibility. Holding the reflexivity of human self-creation constant, we can ask: what kind of thing is the self assumed to be if self-creation, of whatever brand, is to be a significant option? One negative answer follows immediately: when we think of humans as creating themselves we are not thinking of them as creating their organisms, and so we don't conceive of ourselves directly and primarily in biological terms.* A more affirmative answer points to a broad tradition of thought that is congenial to the idea of human self-creation. Many thinkers have alternately spoken of the self in dramaturgical, literary, hermeneutical, or more broadly semiotic terms.[2] Relatedly, human life in all its manifestations is seen as the proper subject matter for interpretation. These imageries and metaphors conceive of the self as belonging to a different order from that of physical objects or natural kinds, an order populated instead by such things as novels and stories, plays and roles, and more broadly signs and texts. The common thread is that of content or meaning as constitutive of human beings, and as providing the medium within which self-creation takes place. Now within this system of ideas, the difference between self-constitution and social construction is muted, since the contrast between individual and

---

* For some this by itself may of course be a reason to reject the constructivist approach.

society, on which this distinction depends, is effaced. Instead, *individual* and *society* point to the concatenations of meaning constitutive of human life conceived at different levels of abstraction. On the resulting picture, human self-creation is not exclusively localized in the individual, nor is it exclusively social in any significant way. It rather runs the entire gamut of sites of meaning that define human life, from the individual to the universal, with *social* vaguely designating the vast and variegated terrain in between.[3]

The reflexivity of human construction entails a symmetry between the agents of construction and the products. The thought that *we* create *ourselves* thus suggests a corresponding ambiguity between a distributive and a joint interpretation of the plural pronoun in regard to the output of construction as well. The result is a division between two categories of normative subjects: individuals, like you and I, and collectivities, such as families, states, corporations, and many others.* Furthermore, by reading the reflexivity of construction backward, as it were, from the products to the constructors, this proliferation of potential subjects further complicates the idea of construction: there are now two types of candidates for doing the construction, individual and collective, as well as two types of subjects being constructed. The resulting combinatorial options ramify. For example, one may hold that all the possible permutations are in fact realized, and that individuals and collectivities construct and are also constructed by individuals and collectivities alike. Or one may alternatively entertain a more restrictive picture, say one in which only individuals do the constructing: of themselves, distributively, as well as of the collective subjects in which they participate. Here too, the term *society*, to which the expression "social construction" alludes, is either a generic reference to all collectivities, or else names just one vaguely defined collectivity among many others, all of which potentially answer to the joint interpretation of the *we*, and all of which may play a role on both sides, the

---

* This formulation elides the all-important questions concerning the relationship between morality and law in regard to their respective subjects. I say something about these issues in Chapters 5 and 8.

constructing and the constructed, of human self-creation. The division between self-constitution and social construction thus turns out to mark two particular options within this multifarious matrix.

The distinction between the distributive and the joint senses of *we*, and the resulting proliferation of subjects of construction (in both their active and passive capacity), points to an age-old preoccupation of philosophers and social theorists: what is the relationship between these types of subjects, individual and collective—or, more grandiosely, what is their ontological status? For the most part the tendency has been to give priority to one type or the other, by opting for one or another version of either individualism or collectivism. Privileging individuals often follows the tattered banner of methodological individualism. Treating collectivities as aggregates of individuals has been subjected to sustained and well-known criticisms, which I need not rehearse here. However, this approach can be criticized not just for its deficient account of collectivities, but also for an inadequate conception of individuals: taking individuals as society's basic building blocks ignores the role played by various social formations in shaping the self. The contrasting approach—implicit, for example, in communitarian writings—encounters the opposite problem. By giving primacy to collective entities, it threatens to reduce individuals to social or communal artifacts. An apparently easy way to avoid both an individualistic and a collectivist reductionism would be to adopt a dualist approach that treats individuals and collectivities as equally primary and mutually irreducible. Such dualism, however, would seem to foreclose the possibility, urged by communitarians and other collectivists, of a deep connection and indeed an internal relation between the individual self on the one side and at least some collectivities on the other.

We can view these considerations as presenting a challenge that the three approaches I've distinguished—individualist, collectivist, and dualist—fail to meet: a conception of human constructivism that maintains an internal relation between individuals and collectivities while avoiding individualist or collectivist reductionism. What's the alternative? A possible way of meeting the challenge worth exploring is to think of individuals and collectivities as made up of the same materials; as sharing the same building blocks, as it were. What would these materials or building blocks be? Broadly speaking, an answer has already been given in terms of the idea of meaning as constitutive of human life as a whole. We can, however, sharpen our focus, as well as give the idea of construction greater normative traction, by looking more closely at one familiar variant of this theme. Social thinkers of various stripes have long toyed with the idea that the social construction of the individual self can be interpreted in terms of a conception of self as constituted by social roles. In a parallel vein, others have depicted collectivities as structured composites of roles.[4] The variant of these approaches that I propose combines these two strands into a unitary account that is not reductionist in either the individual or the collective direction.[5]

II. CONSTRUCTION AND ROLES

Roles

The notion of a social role is familiar enough that we can introduce it summarily. Roughly, a social role involves a patterned set of norms defining rights, responsibilities, and more generally expectations regarding behavior by the role-holder as well as by others toward her.[6] We can distinguish in a role two aspects: a formal aspect, consisting in the norms that form the role's *script*; and a material aspect, consisting in the actual patterned behavior that conforms to the script and realizes it. Relatedly, roles can be connected so as to form relatively stable and recognizable clusters in two ways, formally and materially. A formal connection among a cluster of roles exists when the scripts of the member roles systematically make reciprocal references to one another. A material connection among roles exists when the actual role-performances are systematically connected. There are accordingly two ways in which roles can be synthesized or unified into composites. A formally integrated cluster of roles forms a collective entity (or a collectivity for short); a materially integrated cluster of roles forms a self.

Starting from the latter, consider an example. I am a parent and a law professor. What makes both of these roles mine? A natural answer (pun intended) points to the spatiotemporal trajectory of a particular living organism. A further question, however, arises: which one? Well, mine, of course. The difficulty is that, notoriously, it is no easier to account for the mineness of the organism than for the mineness of my roles. In both cases, in order for the answer to lead to a self we need to understand the question as in the first place posed by one, that is as posed in the first person by someone whose awareness of some bodily movements as actions realizing certain meanings by comporting with some norms—hence as potentially amounting to the performance of certain roles—is part of what constitutes her as the self that she is. Thus, the "mine" in question in regard to the roles, no less than in regard to the body engaged in their performance, is not one of possession but one of identity: the two roles I mentioned, parent and professor, are mine in the sense that they are among the constitutive elements of my identity on a par with my body, rather than their being mine due to their relationship to a particular body.

Consider now the formal synthesis of roles to form collectivities. Notice first that many roles, such as those of painter and freelance writer, do not participate in forming any collectivity at all. They are defined exclusively in terms of some task to be accomplished or some objective to be realized. Call them *functional roles*. But other roles, such as those of parent and professor, are collective: in addition to tasks to be performed they include an *affiliation*, such as to a family in the one case and to a university in the other. What does my affiliation as a parent or professor consist in? The answer lies in the scripts of the respective roles. The script of my parental role makes systematic reference to my children and my spouse, just as the scripts of their roles reciprocally refer to mine. These coordinated formal connections form the D-C family. Similarly, the script of my role as law professor includes reciprocal references to the dean, colleagues, students, and staff, thus forming together the coordinated formal cluster known as Berkeley Law. What guides the coordination among a bunch of roles so as to constitute a collectivity? When are roles merely functional and when do they become collective? The answer points to some normative orientation—call it a *mission*—in light of which the interconnections among the roles are defined. The mission may but need not be goal-oriented; the various roles may instead be expressive of some values or other meanings. Nor need the mission be explicit. Though in many cases, such as a state's constitution or a corporate charter, the mission is contained in a formal document, in other cases it is not.

The resulting picture amounts to a kind of *role atomism*, in which roles are the common building blocks for both individuals and collectivities. Or, shifting the metaphor to better suit a conception of human life as a skein of meanings akin to a text, we can see roles as providing the vocabulary of the self, a vocabulary that captures both the distributive and the joint employment of the *we*. So understood, role-atomism invites reflection on human self-creation in terms of modular units of signification and meaning by which all normative subjects, individual and collective, are constituted.

Before we proceed any further, two cardinal issues must be addressed. The first concerns the scope of the role-atomistic approach: how much of human life can be credibly associated with one role or another? In one sense, the answer is: as much as we want. *Role* is a theoretical term whose content depends on its place within the theory we construct. All human goings-on can be seen as falling within some role, and whether they should be so seen is a matter of the theory's overall adequacy and fruitfulness.* Still, we do come to the construction of a theory with some pretheoretical expectations, not only regarding the theory's overall shape but also regarding the content of its main terms. At least rough compliance with such expectations is what gives a theory its plausibility, itself an important theoretical desideratum. Seen in this light, the claim that all of human life can be reduced to the performance of one role or another may seem implausible. Surely there are things one does, such as scratching one's back, that are performed outside the perimeter of any social role. But reflection on this trivial example actually teaches the opposite

---

* In particular, which clusters of norms are designated as a role (or, put differently, how do we individuate a role) is part of a more specific role theory, one I don't purport to provide.

lesson. Numerous roles include provisions regarding the propriety and the permissible methods, if any, of scratching. The role of an audience at a lecture, for example, is rather liberal about the action, whereas that of lecturer is more restrictive, permitting only a discreet scratch in extremis. Not even this degree of latitude is given, however, to a Buckingham Palace guard, nor for that matter to Her Majesty the Queen herself when in ceremonial circumstances; neither would be allowed to perform a back scratch no matter what. Methods of scratching are equally prescribed. A permissible discreet scratch at a dinner party must be administered manually—using an implement, such as a fork, is decidedly out of the question—whereas the opposite instruction applies to an Arapesh first-time father, who is allowed to scratch himself only by using an implement, a stick in this case.[7] But while many roles regulate scratching, not all scratching, it might appear, falls within any role, so that there would still remain cases of lawless scratching after all, viz., the scratching performed in the privacy of one's room. However, even here social norms impinge, allowing the role-theorist to subsume the conduct in question under some role, familiar or ad hoc. Though using an implement such as a ruler would be in order here, one can use one's cat only on pains of appearing bizarre. Appearing to whom? Well, to oneself, and counterfactually to everyone else. In this sense, and for better or worse, one is never alone.

The inflationary use of roles I propose amplifies, however, the tension I've already mentioned between self-constitution and social construction, thus giving rise to the second cardinal issue we need to address. Roles are social units. And although *society*, as already indicated, is a vague term ranging from the companionship between two people to humanity as a whole, it always pertains to the intersubjective, and so is supra-individual. Isn't then subsuming all of human life within one role or another to stifle or nullify individual constructive freedom? In addressing this question, it should be made clear at the start that roles (at least as I understand them) consist in bundles of norms, to the exclusion of any coercion that often "backs up" various norms. Appending to norms coercive threats obviously complicates the picture and compromises freedom.[8] But the normative guidance the roles themselves provide must be seen as appealing in some sense to the individual's own will and as mediated by it. Accordingly, roles leave substantial room for constructive individualism of two kinds: both in regard to which roles one occupies and as to how one performs one's roles.* But though both freedoms can be in principle quite extensive, they are not unlimited. On the view I expound, individual self-constitution is indeed bounded by exigencies of intelligibility, which are intersubjective and thus supra-individual. Whether these exigencies are better seen as constraints on human freedom or as one of its enabling conditions is a much debated question; but either way, these exigencies must be acknowledged and specifically their influence over the two kinds of constructive freedom just mentioned must be recognized. I will illustrate each.

As to freedom regarding the roles one occupies, consider an impressionable young man who is inspired by reading Don Quixote to emulate the legendary figure. But though he can buy a scrawny horse, get the proper attire and a spear, and roam the land in search of adventure and injustice, he would not be a knight-errant for all that. Corresponding exigencies of intelligibility pertain to the degrees of freedom in enacting a role. There is obviously a large variation in latitude that different putative roles leave their bearers. But ascertaining this variation and assessing it requires that we (and this includes the role-bearer) appeal to intersubjective and so supra-individual factors. Recall the role of back-scratcher and compare it to, say, that of a physician. Intuitively, the former leaves its bearer much less elbow room, so to speak, than the latter. But pondering the example raises doubts: doesn't the scratcher, who appears to be confined to a single role-related action, have in fact indefinitely many ways of performing it, each way consisting in a slightly different configuration of fingers, patterns of moving them, and so on? The example of back-scratching is of course artificial and contrived. But now think in this connection of a musician, say a violinist, whose behavior is tightly controlled

---

* Freedom regarding which roles one occupies is not limited to existing roles but must allow for the opportunity to invent new ones. This raises a range of issues I don't enter here.

by a highly prescriptive, detailed script, consisting in large part in the musical score. The discretion left to the performer by the score consists in the minutest variations in the placing of fingers and the pace of moving them within an infinitesimally narrow range, similar in kind to the range of options we have just lampooned in regard to scratching one's back. And yet for the violinist the discretion turns out to be all-important, as it is entirely responsible for the gradation of musicians all the way from the virtuoso to the hack.

Role-Distance

But if everything is a role, doesn't it follow that nothing is? Role theory, of whatever brand, extends to life as a whole a dramaturgical imagery. But this extension creates a puzzle from the start. The imagery of the theater draws its meaning from an implicit contrast between the goings-on onstage and off. But to treat the whole world as a stage is to dismantle the frame that keeps the theater apart, and so appears to undermine the metaphor by depriving the dramaturgical setting of its distinctness. Modeling our understanding of human beings on the theater is sometimes designed to make a point that survives the dismantling. Especially when we recall the origin of "role" in *mask*, the main objective of role theory may be to accentuate a dividing line between a true inner self, on the one hand, and people's external comportment in social situations, on the other. In this vein, the actor in the theater is supposedly marked by such a division, for example, between Laurence Olivier's self and his demeanor when playing Hamlet. But this construal of the theatrical imagery is not available within a thoroughly constructivist conception of self. Such a conception leaves no room for an asocial, "true" inner self that is engaged in enacting roles without being fused with them. Retaining the theatrical imagery within a constructivist frame is possible, however, if we draw a distinction within the domain of roles between different ways in which roles can relate to the self. Although every facet of human life can in principle be subsumed under some role, not all roles are the same.

The first step in this direction is the observation that to conceive of the self as constituted by roles is not to think of it as a mere assemblage of roles. To form a self, the roles must be integrated in some fashion. What does the integration consist in? The answer I suggest is metaphorical: the roles must form a dovetailing, interrelated, and interacting arrangement that we can imagine as possessing a certain "density" or as forming a "core." But as this imagery suggests, people can also occupy roles that are more tenuously connected to the elements forming that core; the ties may become too distended to still count such roles as integral parts of the self. We colloquially mark this possibility by contrasting the *personal* and the *impersonal* as two different styles of demeanor and interaction. Within role-theory this contrast is best captured in the sociological notion of role-distance, which denotes a mode of enacting a role without identifying with it and so without fully integrating it into the self.[9] Identification with a role or detachment from it need not be fixed: the distance between a person and a role can shrink or expand; it can fluctuate over time. It is also not the case that some roles must be worn tightly, whereas others are kept at a distance by all their takers. Still, a certain degree of uniformity in the style of enacting different roles exists, and so some generalization regarding role-distance is possible: certain roles are more likely to be enacted at a distance than other roles. Moreover, these uniformities have a normative side; for example, it seems less appropriate to be a detached parent than a detached bank-teller. Where does this normative difference come from? The most straightforward answer points to the roles themselves: the distance appropriate for the enactment of a role is itself one of the role's normative aspects, part of its script. So it is meaningful, though not altogether accurate, to speak in general about *detached* or *distant* as opposed to *nondetached* or *proximate* roles. We act in a personal capacity when we enact a proximate role, and impersonally when enacting a distant one.

What are the markers and incidents of proximity or distance? Of the many factors that come to mind, two are particularly salient; they concern, respectively, sincerity and motivation. An example I have used on other occasions effectively illustrates both features. Suppose that someone helps

Sam's four-year-old child to cross the street just as Sam happens to walk by, and so he says to the benefactor, "Thank you for helping my child." Contrast this episode with another familiar display of politeness: the AT&T operator who concludes each exchange with a customer by proclaiming: "Thank you for using AT&T." Consider sincerity first. Even though Sam thanks his child's helper strictly in the capacity of parent (after all, the benefactor did not render any help directly to Sam), the thanking in this case would be generally interpreted as conveying a genuine sense of gratitude. This is in keeping with a common understanding of how a norm of sincerity ordinarily undergirds our speech acts. As Professor John Searle observes, "it is linguistically unacceptable (though not self-contradictory) to conjoin the explicitly performative verb with the denial of the expressed psychological state."[10] Specifically, in our example, it would be unacceptable to say, "Thank you, but I'm not really grateful." However, when we turn to the operator's thanking, we discover the opposite, and equally instructive, oddity. It would be quite ludicrous for the overly zealous telephone operator to say, "Thank you for using AT&T," and then add, "and I really mean it." The oddity would not disappear even if the particular operator happened to experience a sense of gratitude, born perhaps of a belief that his own livelihood is secured by the customer's patronage. Evidently, the norm of sincerity does not belong in this language game.

A similar contrast between the two roles illustrates the difference in motivation. In conveying their thanks, both the parent and the operator act in compliance with their respective roles' requirements. Why do they do so? Why do the parent and the operator comply with their respective roles' demands? Again, the question I consider is not in the first place psychological but normative: the claim is that different standards of appropriate motivation apply in the two cases. One way to see the difference is to notice that in the parent's case, the thanking will be taken to reveal the parent as a polite person. It is likely, for example, that Sam would respond similarly on other occasions and in different roles; e.g., he would be careful to thank a helpful salesperson in a store. The thanking in both instances is personal and so internally motivated, just because or in the sense that the display of politeness in both instances issues from an undifferentiated core of the self, which is constituted in part by the two respective roles and is activated or displayed in their performance. Not so in the case of the operator: we would expect no consistency between his demeanor when buying in a store and the gratitude he expresses as operator. Whether rude or polite on other occasions, the operator would be sure to use the polite refrain over the phone. Correspondingly, since this role is external and impersonal, it is not expected to exert a motivating force all by itself; it must be aided by some inducement that links the role's requirements to its holder. The most common one is of course payment: the operator appropriately performs the role's demands in order to be paid, whereas monetary inducement would be out of place in the parent's case.

The metaphor of distance suggests gradation, and relatedly, identification can come in degrees. So the two kinds of roles we've contrasted are better seen as the polar ends of a continuum than as a binary distinction. This raises a question concerning identity. If roles are constitutive of the self, then a binary opposition would seem to be more apt: shouldn't there be a clear answer to the question what is me and what is not? I will not try to do full justice to this important query but only dull its edge by enlisting for this purpose the conclusions reached in Derek Parfit's seminal study of personal identity.[11] Like most philosophers who deal with this topic, Parfit is concerned for the most part with temporal identity, whereas our present inquiry primarily raises issues of what we may call *compositional identity*, concerning the composition of the self and its boundaries at any given time. The two issues are closely related, however. Now on Parfit's view, temporal continuity is a matter of degree, so that an earlier self can be more or less connected to a later one; there is no deep fact of the matter as to whether two temporally bound selves are stages of a single one or not. The same scalar picture applies to compositional identity as well. The question whether something is a part or an aspect of me does not present a genuine binary option, and it need not have a single correct answer. Parfit suggests that we can nonetheless preserve the binary logic that he associates with the concept of identity, by legislating a clear-cut if somewhat arbitrary criterion in light of which binary determinations concerning personal identity over time can be made. Doing so, he maintains, is harmless as long as it is also held that, our ordinary beliefs to the contrary notwithstanding, "identity is not what matters." He advocates accordingly revising the prevailing attitude toward the self by diminishing the normative significance we attach to its identity. But we can also move in the opposite direction: retaining the ordinary normative significance we attach to our identity, temporal as well as compositional, while allowing that a looser concept of identity is appropriate in this case, one that accommodates a degree of fluctuation and indeterminacy.

Distance and Collectivities

As we have seen, not just the self is constituted by roles, but so, though in a different way, are collectivities. The division between proximate and distant roles accordingly has implications for collectivities as well. Specifically, this division maps onto a traditional distinction in social theory between two kinds of collectivity, *community* and *organization*.[12] The mapping depends on the observation that like all roles, collective roles can be enacted with proximity or distance. Moreover, when the collective role is a composite of a functional aspect and an affiliation, these two elements may be enacted at a different distance. In terms of my earlier example, I may identify with my role as law professor, while keeping my affiliation with Berkeley Law at a distance. This disparity in distances is related to the fact that the functional side of the role of professor, consisting of such tasks as research and teaching, can be performed without great disruption while its holder moves between different universities. One's attachment to any particular university may thus be contingent and tentative, consistently with a full identification with one's role as professor. Not so in the case of a parent. Here both the affiliation with the family and the functional role of, say, raising children are widely regarded as proximate.* Though different

---

* In saying this I don't mean to make a substantive pitch for any particular attitude toward parenthood or the family. That parenthood is "widely regarded" in this way is only significant for expository purposes.

combinations of proximity and distance in the enactment of collective roles is thus possible, when it comes to the classification of collectivities, the affiliation dominates, and yields the division just mentioned: communities are the formal union of proximate affiliation roles, whereas organizations are the formal union of distant affiliation roles.

The telephone operator is a member of an organization, AT&T in my example, simply in the sense, and by virtue of the fact, that he holds a detached role in that collectivity. For this reason, he in principle must be paid (or otherwise impelled) if he is to perform the role's requirements. But don't those who do the paying (or impelling) have to do so willfully, out of identification with their roles, and thus exemplify a communal type of participation in AT&T? The answer is negative. It is not really necessary for anyone at AT&T, including those who see to it that the operator performs his tasks, to identify with their roles. The organization may consist entirely of detached roles, all of which depend on some external source of motivation. The same point can be made in terms of the collectivity's normative orientation, what I have called its mission. To say that an affiliation is proximate, or that a collective role calls for identification, is to say that the role-bearers, the members of the collectivity, are expected to endorse the collectivity's mission and treat it as their own (or, what comes to the same thing, that the collectivity is defined in terms of a certain normative orientation that is understood to be shared by its members). When affiliations are distant, by contrast, no endorsement by the members of the unifying mission is expected or assumed. In the polar limiting cases, the community's normative orientation is held by all its members; that of the organization, by none of them.

The idea of a collectivity dedicated to the realization of a mission to which none of the members subscribe may look puzzling, but in fact it is a byproduct, or perhaps even just a redescription, of one aspect of a familiar and pervasive phenomenon: our dependence on others to provide for the objects and practices in which we are interested, and thus on a division of labor. When we allude to this phenomenon in the vocabulary of roles, we simply point out that the objectives and values associated with some proximate roles, objectives and values that reflect the bearers' interests and desires, need not be matched by corresponding proximate roles dedicated to satisfying these interests and desires: for example, some people's interest in listening to opera, and so in occupying the proximate role of "opera buff," need not be matched by others' willingness to sing, and so be "opera singers"; and the desire to drive cars need not match the desire to manufacture them.[13] Markets and organizations are the two main devices to close this gap. There is accordingly nothing particularly mysterious about an organization whose members all perform their roles in response to external inducements without subscribing to the objectives their concerted efforts are designed to serve.

As I have already mentioned, role-distance can change over time, and relatedly, the location of a collectivity on the community/organization spectrum may change too. The different distance one can maintain in the case of collective roles toward the affiliation and the functional aspect may contribute to such change. For example, we can imagine, and to some degree observe, a decline in the ideal of the family concomitant with a continued affirmation of a deep personal involvement with the role of parent that has been traditionally associated with the family. People may still enact the parental role in a proximate fashion but within a collectivity that is more organizational in nature, lacking the significance to the members' identity that affiliation with a traditional family is ideally supposed to have. We can also imagine a scenario that is the symmetrical opposite of this case: it involves a community, whose members thus identify with their affiliation, but one in which the functional roles of some or even all members are distant. There is a tension in such a case between the proximity of the affiliation role and the distant functional roles: members' identification with the community may fail to supply sufficient impetus for an adequate performance of their functional roles. The result may be increased resort by the community to external pressures and inducements to prompt the desired role behavior. Such measures, however, may alienate the members from the community, eventually transforming the community into an organization.

III. NORMATIVE IMPLICATIONS

The preceding comments amount to no more than a rough sketch, depicting with very few selective strokes a large terrain. And as with all cartoons, the test for this sketch too is whether its particular combination of sparseness and distortion (the hallmarks cartoons share with social theories) succeeds in drawing attention to important and otherwise less visible features of its subject matter. The intended payoff in this case is normative. What are, then, the normative implications of the preceding comments? In one way or another, other chapters in this book provide snippets of an answer.[14] In the remainder of this chapter, I summarily point out some promising lines of inquiry.

Personal Norms and Distance

I have indicated earlier how what I called personal norms, such as those concerning responsibility and autonomy, participate in constructing the self. We can further explore the constructive significance of these norms by relating them to roles and their variable distance. Consider responsibility first. People are primarily held responsible for their actions, but roles can expand or contract responsibility relative to this paradigm case. Whether a role expands or contracts responsibility corresponds to the role's distance. Under such headings as vicarious and collective responsibility, the occupants of certain roles are held responsible for the actions of others. Such extensions of responsibility signify an identification with the appropriate affiliation, say that of a parent, and through it with the collectivity, the family in this case, of which that role forms a part. Conversely, acting in a role can diminish or extinguish responsibility for one's own actions. Think for example of the "Privileges and Immunities" that exempt government officials from personal responsibility as long as they act within the confines of their official role. Whatever the historical or pragmatic reasons for this immunity, its meaning concerns role-distance.

Withholding personal responsibility for actions performed in one's capacity as an official marks that role as impersonal by signifying a separation of this role from the rest of the self.

A similar point applies to autonomy. Enacting a proximate role is an occasion for the exercise of autonomy in a way that enacting a distant role is not. To act autonomously is to be guided by one's own norms, norms that are internal to one's self. Enacting a proximate role satisfies this condition. My parental autonomy, for example, does not consist in a license to treat my child with unfettered discretion, let alone arbitrarily. To the contrary, the demands of the parental role are often narrowly circumscribed, sometimes mandating a rather specific attitude or course of action. Still, these imperatives do not compromise my autonomy but give it content by shaping or constituting an aspect of my self. Since there is no distance between me and my role as a parent, since I fully identify with that role, the imperatives that pertain to my child's education, or behavior, or welfare, guide me from within. It does not follow, of course, that my autonomy in going about my parental role depends on my doing so cheerfully and enthusiastically. Many parents would flunk this test when getting up to attend to a screaming baby in the middle of the night, and yet their autonomy in performing their parental role is not diminished thereby. One's identification with the role and one's autonomous execution of its demands are not undercut but are put to the test by temptations and pressures that conflict with the role's requirements.[15] The situation in the case of the telephone operator is diametrically opposed. Since the operator is not supposed to identify with his role, the role's imperatives are external to him. Engagement in the tasks of a telephone operator does not purport to express the operator's own will in the way that properly discharging parental duties is ordinarily supposed to be a manifestation of the parent's will.

The normative significance of roles is not limited to such explicit norms as those of responsibility and autonomy, and extends to other personal attitudes and emotions whose normative underpinnings are less obvious. To give one extreme example, even such a quintessentially personal emotion as love is role-bound: for instance, we are under an injunction to love our children and our neighbors. This injunction thus obligates me toward Sarah or Patrick just in case one is my daughter and the other my neighbor. Moreover, these love-guiding norms are tied in the first place to the roles rather than to their individual bearers. This is easy to miss in the case of natural children, where a gap between identity and role is difficult to contrive, but is quite visible in the case of adopted children: obviously, no obligation of love extends to the particular child prior to adoption. Similarly, the injunction to love one's children includes children-in-law. But here the obligation toward a particular individual expires upon the children's divorce. The fact that attitudes such as love are mediated by roles does not, however, mean that the attitudes are delimited by the roles and so does not impugn the personal nature of these attitudes. To be sure, had not Sarah been my daughter or Patrick my neighbor, the obligations of love would not tie me to them. Even so, if these two people do hold the respective roles, the prescribed love is for Sarah or Patrick, rather than for them just qua daughter or neighbor, and is properly manifested in my concern for them outside these roles; for example, in my concern for how they fare in their professional lives. Finally, as in the case of the other norms I've mentioned, the normative connection between love and the roles to which it applies is reciprocal. The obligation to love one's children not only constitutes in part the role of parent as a proximate role, but it also defines in a corresponding manner the role of a daughter or a son, as involving in part a legitimate expectation to be loved by one's parents.

Types of Payment

I have mentioned earlier that the performance of a distant role such as a telephone operator's is appropriately motivated by some external, most often monetary, inducement in a way that performing a proximate role such as a parent is not. But although parents are not ordinarily paid to perform their roles, professors, the bearers of the other nondetached role I have mentioned, are. And it would be foolhardy, not to mention self-defeating, to imply that there is anything untoward in this practice. To see why bearers of nondetached roles can be paid for discharging their roles consistently with the roles' proximity, we must further consider the normative significance of payments. I can best make the point by drawing an analogy between payment and punishment. The two practices are similar in that both involve responding to some behavior by deliberately affecting the agent's welfare, positively in the one case, negatively in the other. (We commonly refer to punishment as a payment, and speak of the wages of crime.) But since deprivations are more morally charged than rewards, it is no surprise that moral philosophers should have given more attention to punishment than to payment. One result of this attention is a fundamental distinction they have drawn between two contrasting accounts of punishment, as deterrence and as retribution: one is forward-looking, designed to affect future behavior, whereas the other is backward-looking, giving the agent her due. Extending this distinction to the case of payment, we can draw a similar distinction between two modalities: payment as *remuneration*, designed to provide an inducement to perform a role's requirements, and payment as *compensation*, seen as a proper response to a performance rendered. Paying for the performance of a proximate role may accordingly be warranted for reasons other than providing an external inducement to perform the role, and so without impugning the internal motivation entailed by the role's proximity.

The analogy between payment and punishment raises, however, a further complication. Even if we understand punishment in retributive terms, anticipating it will likely affect people's decisions; retributive punishment is unlikely to remain motivationally inert. So also in the case of payment. Practically speaking, the two responsive modalities I have distinguished largely overlap. But here a second distinction, this one concerning remuneration, comes into play. Remuneration can serve as an inducement either to perform a role one already occupies or to assume a role in the first place. Continuing with the example of the role of professor, it is altogether appropriate for people to opt for an academic career in part because of the anticipated pay, even if their performance of the role, once assumed, should be internally motivated. The reason for this difference lies in the constructive significance of a proximate role. Part of what it means for a role to be proximate is that it provides its bearer with an internal motivation. But the role has this normative grip only over its bearers; antecedently to assuming the role, it has no claim on them. So no conflict arises between a role's proximity and the availability of external inducements to assume it. Indeed, this point also applies to my other example, the parental role. Money can be a medium for encouraging people to form families, even if once the family is formed, discharging roles within it is no longer properly oriented toward monetary gains.

Distance and Law

Law is an important engine of construction. Fitting law within the role-atomistic perspective suggests a conception of law as a form of social scriptwriting, shaping with a single stroke individuals and collectivities alike. Law performs this activity for the most part in four typical ways.

First, law participates in scripting existing roles: for example, parents are required by law to provide for their children, and public officials are forbidden from accepting bribes. This partially defines the corresponding collectivities: families are understood, in part, as collective entities designed to provide for children's needs, and public institutions are defined in part by an ethos of impartiality and fairness. Second, law creates roles that would not be available otherwise, such as judge or juror. To perform such roles one needs instruction in the relevant legal scripts. Other legally created roles are less formally structured: think of the litigant, witness, or prisoner. Once again, these roles constitute collective entities as well: courts, prisons, etc. Third, the law bans some existing roles—such as thief, arsonist, and hit man—and seeks to eradicate them. The fourth kind of legal scriptwriting consists in the law's effects on other scriptwriters. Many nonlegal roles are charged with writing or modifying the scripts of other roles. This is true especially in hierarchical contexts, as when the management of a business firm devises the roles of employees. Through its influence on these scriptwriting roles, law shapes indirectly the roles that are being fashioned by the extralegal scriptwriters. Such legal "superscripting" occurs, for example, when law sets requirements on employers' structuring of retirement plans, or on the disciplinary proceedings of schools or universities.

Looking at law through the lens of social roles helps draw attention to various aspects of legal control that otherwise remain in the shade, but here I'd like to discuss just one theme. Like other aspects of roles, role-distance can be affected by law. One way in which law bears on distance is through the intermediary of the personal norms, such as those pertaining to responsibility and autonomy, we've discussed earlier. Law at least partially determines these norms, and so participates in calibrating the distance of various roles. But there are other ways of affecting distance through law. Let me mention two. The first is by setting entry and exit conditions of various roles. This is a broad category, ranging over such disparate areas as marriage and divorce, hiring and dismissal, immigration, elections, and many more. In all of these areas, the law sets incumbency conditions for assuming and shedding a role—of a spouse, an employee, a citizen, or a legislator. The significance of these conditions, and hence of the laws that define them, goes beyond determining who will hold a given role and for how long. The ease or difficulty with which a role can be acquired or vacated bears importantly on role-distance. Other things being equal, the more enduring and secure a role, the more suitable it is for being enacted in a proximate manner. The same incumbency conditions also serve as gatekeeping devices in the corresponding collectivities. By influencing role-distance, incumbency conditions help fix or change the nature of a collective entity and its location on the organization/community spectrum. The other type of distance-affecting devices concerns *compartmentalization* and *spillover*. Compartmentalization refers to practices that treat a particular role as separate from other aspects of the self. Spillover describes the opposite approach of indiscriminately attending to or affecting a number of different roles, disregarding the boundary between them. Consider once more the workplace. What is the relation between the dress code at work and the employees' after-hours attire? How strictly role-related is the information a person is encouraged or required to reveal in carrying out different roles? Which aspects of an employee's life may the employer seek to influence or regulate?

Through these and other avenues, law may increase role-distance or decrease it. Whatever its objective, however, the very fact of legal intervention in a role's script may tend to induce detachment. As I've mentioned earlier, my interest in roles is primarily in their script and so in the normative guidance they provide. But when the law tampers with a script, it typically adds the threat of sanction to enforce the change. And external efforts to secure compliance with a role, especially when they assume a coercive form, may trigger resistance and defiance. A possible result is a tendency to disassociate oneself from the source of such intrusive intervention by severing the ties between the predicate role and other aspects of one's self. These psychological speculations have a normative side as well. By employing coercion, law implicitly stakes out a position about the proper attitude to its demands. Coercion is a paradigm external motivation, which avowedly sidesteps the agent's own will and ignores her autonomy.[16] When tied to a role, coercion not only induces but underwrites distance from the role. These potential effects of juridification on the construction of self have their counterpart on the collective level in converting communities into organizations.

Topology of Self

Is there anything general to be said about the comparative merits of proximity and distance in enacting roles? Should we strive for the one or the other? I have touched on these questions already by linking role-distance with the scope of personal norms, such as autonomy and responsibility, and add here a speculative reflection that ties the comparative merits of proximity and distance to the kinds of general structural considerations to which I have alluded at the outset. These structural desiderata are implicit in a familiar cluster of metaphorical evaluative expressions we commonly apply to ourselves and to each other. We often experience ourselves and others as more or less substantial: we describe people as heavyweights or lightweights, as deep or shallow, as complex or simple, as having or lacking heft. Within the imagery I have sketched, it is natural to associate these qualities with the "core" of the self, and so conclude that forming the self's core, proximate roles give us substance and solidity. Failure to occupy proximate roles would result, at the limit, in an "empty" self. Another constructive danger this imagery highlights is the possibility of occupying mutually incompatible proximate roles, resulting in a split or multiple self, one that is lacking inner unity and a center of gravity. Forming a self accordingly requires the availability of a range of mutually compatible proximate roles with which one identifies. But the structural merits of proximity have a downside as well, rigidity and vulnerability to change: greater damage to self results from losing a proximate role than from losing a distant one. A substantial alteration in or loss of any proximate role will have repercussions throughout the self, affecting other constituents of one's identity. Seen in these terms, proximate roles, which give the self substance and solidity, also make it brittle, whereas distant roles are sources of versatility and resilience. One can assume or discard a distant role without significant repercussions in other parts of the self.

This tradeoff between the structural virtues of solidity and pliability and the other contrasting merits of proximity and distance suggests that the optimal topography of the self would contain a gradation of distances or some combination of proximate and distant roles. Put in terms of the collectivities involved, this conclusion underscores the contrasting benefits (and risks) of membership in both communities and organizations. Membership in a community promotes the constructive advantage of role proximity. To be sure, not all roles, and so not all proximate roles, are collective; one can draw meaning and heft from being, say, a poet or a hermit. But collective roles, and so affiliations, are among the most common and significant constituents of identity, and so their proximity is particularly important. This conclusion has special significance in light of the recent ascent of a communitarian ideology, which in effect endorses community as the ideal form of collective affiliation. Communitarians are right to underscore the importance of community, especially in a world in which distance-engendering organizations predominate while many traditional forms of communal proximity have withered. But endorsing community must be qualified by another salient feature of modern life, a high level of change, which suggests a caveat to the communitarian agenda. Where the level of change remains high, forging communal ties—as well as encouraging other forms of role proximity—may become a trap to selves whose resilience will be weakened in the face of inevitable changes, increasing their vulnerability to identity-shattering experiences. The upshot of these considerations is accordingly not the wholesale endorsement of one or another form of collective affiliation; the aim is rather to accommodate change by correlating different social formations and the roles that constitute them with the varying tendencies toward stability or change in different spheres of social life.

Alienation and Bad Faith

Finally, where there are norms, there can be infringement. Role-distance is no exception. One corollary of the normative aspect of role-distance is the possibility of departures, in both directions, from the distance appropriate in enacting a role: a parent may be detached from his role, whereas a telephone operator may identify with his. This draws attention to the relationship between role-distance on the one hand and two terms that figure prominently in the social philosophy of the recent past, *alienation* and *bad faith*, on the other. I consider these notions in partial isolation from the bodies of thought within which they occur, and only to the extent that they can be said to characterize attitudes toward roles. Both notions have a negative connotation and are used to convey disapproval. Of what? Within the picture I've presented, alienation and bad faith can be interpreted as signifying the kind of departure from norms of distance just illustrated, resulting in two contrasting modalities of inappropriate role-distance: alienation marks distance from a proximate role, whereas bad faith marks identification with a distant one.

The notion of bad faith, which I consider first, is mostly due to Sartre, a prominent proponent of the idea of human self-creation.[17] Linking bad faith to the notion of a role is easy, since Sartre introduces bad faith through what has become a classical discussion of enacting a role, that of a waiter in a café. Moreover, as I mentioned earlier, within the broadly hermeneutic tradition on which I draw, the strand most directly relevant to the role-atomistic picture of self I've presented uses a dramaturgical imagery in which the theater serves as a template or metaphor for human life. And as we'll see momentarily, Sartre's discussion of bad faith does indeed use a theatrical imagery to elucidate social roles and their relationship to self. However, Sartre's depiction of the waiter is too tendentious, and his analogy to the theater too impoverished for the example to be able to sustain the conception of bad faith that it is designed to illustrate. Again, in examining Sartre's discussion of this example I don't intend to engage with his position as a whole. My aim is to extract the notion of bad faith from Sartre's ontology and adapt it to the picture of roles as constituents of the self.

Sartre begins his discussion of the waiter by describing in some detail the waiter's demeanor: "His movement is quick and forward, a little too precise, a little too rapid"; and he concludes that "All [the waiter's] behavior seems to us a game. . . . [h]e is playing at being a waiter in a café."[18] Sartre then comments on the futility of the waiter's efforts. Speaking now in the first person on the waiter's behalf, Sartre maintains that enacting the role of waiter

> is a "representation" for others and for myself, which means that I can be only in representation. But if I represent myself as him, I am not he . . . I cannot be he, I can only play at being he; that is imagine to myself that I am he. . . . In vain do I fulfill the functions of a café waiter. I can be he only in the neutralized mode, as the actor is Hamlet, by mechanically making the typical gestures of my state and by aiming at myself as an imaginary café waiter . . .[19]

Now the charge of bad faith is made against the waiter, whom for convenience I will call Jacques, on the ground that he clings to his role in an ontologically spurious way. Sartre juxtaposes the waiter to an inkwell on Sartre's desk. The inkwell, argues Sartre, *is* an inkwell, whereas Jacques *is* not a waiter. Why? The answer that is pertinent to our present concerns points to contingency: whereas the inkwell could not have been a desk, Jacques might have been a carpenter, a gardener, or a judge. To avoid the paradoxical view that Jacques might have been someone else, we must conclude that being a waiter (or, counterfactually, a carpenter, etc.) is a mere contingency regarding Jacques' identity; it is not what Jacques truly is.* So when Jacques purports to *be* a waiter, he ascribes to himself a kind of existence appropriate to the ontological order occupied by such things as inkwells and desks.† He fails to acknowledge that rather than *being* a waiter, he merely plays at being one, in the way that, say, Laurence Olivier only plays at being Hamlet. Jacques exhibits bad faith by being dishonest with himself about what he truly is. The description of the waiter and the theatrical analogy are designed to vividly demonstrate the inherent limitation of the category of role as a potential source of human identity. On Sartre's view, the imagery of roles can take us only as far as the idea of playing at something or other, rather than that of being it. And for the reasons just given, denying Jacques the identity of a waiter (in the deep, constitutive sense here at issue) would leave him in an ontological abyss, buttressing the apparently paradoxical choice of *nothingness* as the stable metaphysical baseline relative to which everything about a human being turns out to be contingent. But a closer look at the example and the

---

* In denying that the inkwell could have been a desk, Sartre does not imply that a white inkwell might not have been painted black. The view that Sartre imputes to Jacques, and that Sartre impugns, is that being a waiter stands to Jacques in the way that being an inkwell (rather than being white) stands to the inkwell. On Sartre's view, bad faith inheres in the pervasive, commonsense attitude, according to which we at once want to affirm this stronger sense of "is" in depicting our relationship to certain roles while also acknowledging the possibility that we might have occupied very different ones.

† In following Sartre's way of setting up the example, we are dealing with an implicit commonsense ontology, and with the kind of humdrum, ordinary beliefs Jacques supposedly shares. This relieves us of the need to engage with the notoriously thorny issues associated in general with modal claims, and specifically saves us the need for the now-fashionable journey to alternate universes that dealing with these issues would otherwise require.

analogy suggests a different lesson, a lesson that will allow us to qualify the notion of bad faith and cast it in a different light.

To begin with, as described by Sartre, Jacques' performance of his role, like an adolescent's, is marred by excessive self-consciousness. However, no such awkwardness characterizes Laurence Olivier's enacting Hamlet. In contrast to the waiter, all of Olivier's Hamlet-motions are smooth and flowing, and his Hamlet-speech is rendered with eloquence and ease. Sartre's depiction of Jacques does not demonstrate that in enacting a role one is no more than an actor, but merely that Jacques is simply a bad actor. Secondly, pace Sartre, an actor who plays Hamlet does not *represent* him, since for all we know Hamlet never existed; never having been present, he cannot be re-presented. Nor, in enacting Hamlet, is Olivier mechanically making the typical gestures of Hamlet. Even assuming that doing so is a meaningful option, Sir Laurence would not have been the great actor that he was had he done so. When Olivier performs the role of Hamlet, and for that matter when Jacques performs the role of waiter, they each engage wit, ingenuity, emotions, and other such human resources and traits in the service of expressing and realizing, through movement and sound, a stretch of meaning. Once we have this picture of acting in mind, we can extend it to the case in which the role played is of an actual figure: nothing in Olivier's performance would change if it turned out that Hamlet did exist and had the biography the play depicts. All that this circumstance would suggest is that the range of resources of the kind just mentioned that are deployed by Olivier in enacting Hamlet resembles the range of resources originally deployed by the real Hamlet in enacting for the first time the meanings Olivier enacts once more. In neither case (of a fictional Hamlet or a real one) does Olivier represent Hamlet, in the sense in which, say, a drawing of an elephant represents an elephant. Rather, Olivier can be said to *transcribe* Hamlet, similarly to the way a copy of a painting transcribes a painting, or a movie made of a novel transcribes the novel.

Third, when Olivier plays Hamlet, he does so in his capacity as an actor. Playing Hamlet is one of the ways of discharging the social role of actor, but not the only way. As an actor, Olivier also plays Othello and Uncle

Vanya, as well as doing a host of other role-related things, such as attending rehearsals and taking voice lessons. And whereas we are not tempted to say that Olivier was Hamlet (in the strong constitutive sense), we do commonly say that Olivier was an actor, in quite the strong sense Sartre is concerned to deny through the example of the waiter and the theatrical analogy.* What is the relationship between Olivier's two roles, the social and the theatrical? The theater provides a striking contrast between the two by separating them in time and space. Suppose you're telling a friend about having watched *Hamlet* on the stage, and the friend inquires about the time and location of the play. The inquiry is ambiguous, making two replies appropriate: mid-twentieth-century London or sixteenth-century Denmark. What is the relationship between the two replies? Plainly, the goings-on on the stage in mid-twentieth-century London *signify* goings-on in sixteenth-century Denmark. The same applies more specifically to Olivier's enacting of Hamlet: Olivier performs a sequence of actions in mid-twentieth-century London, which signify a sequence of actions by Hamlet in sixteenth-century Denmark.

By creating a salient spatiotemporal gap between these two factors in regard to the enactment of the theatrical roles, the theater helps draw our attention to a similar duality that pervades human life as a whole. In "real life," however, this duality is effaced or goes unnoticed because the two spatiotemporal frames coincide: the content conveyed by movements and sounds by virtue of which the movements are deemed actions and the sounds speech is reflexive, in that the content pertains to or signifies the time and location in which the movements and sounds take place. So, for example, in performing the role of waiter, Jacques' gestures and sounds signify his own demeanor and utterances in serving at the very same café

---

* It may appear that ascribing to Olivier a social role of actor aside from his role as Hamlet begs the disputed issue. This is indeed the case. But this is of the nature of an analogy: all analogies beg the questions they are designed to help answer by assuming the validity of the premise in light of which the analogy is drawn. An analogy, if successful, illuminates by clarifying the premise and making it more vivid and more compelling; it doesn't *prove* or *establish* the premise. In drawing an analogy between the waiter and Olivier's playing of Hamlet (thus ignoring Olivier's being an actor), Sartre is making a symmetrically circular use of the same strategy.

and at the very same time in which those gestures and sounds occur. But though such spatiotemporal coincidence between performance and content is necessary to render the role of waiter constitutive of Jacques, it is not sufficient. The spatiotemporal gap between Olivier's performance and Hamlet's shenanigans only serves to dramatize the possibility of performing a role in an impersonal way, that is to say without the role being integrated with the rest of one's self. As applied to Jacques, the theatrical analogy thus allows for the option that waiting is indeed a detached role that does not form part of the answer to a question about who he is. But the analogy also suggests that the opposite may be the case, and that just as being an actor defines in part who Olivier is, so also being a waiter defines in part Jacques' identity.

There is, finally, another figure that is central to the analogy between the waiter and Hamlet and that Sartre ignores: Shakespeare. Here too we need to recognize a duality. Shakespeare not only created *Hamlet*, but in doing so he engaged in self-creation as well: by constituting himself as an author, specifically (among other things) of this particular play. And although Hamlet's travails do not define Shakespeare's life, being their creator does. In this way the theater offers yet another bimodal template in terms of which we can construe what appears to be a unitary ordinary reality. This bit of reality appears unitary not because the division between author and text has no application to it, but because, once again, the two coincide: in serving the café's patrons, Jacques exhibits the reflexivity of self-creation by constituting himself at once as both author and protagonist of (among other things) a waiter's life. And this coincidence incorporates the two spatiotemporal frames, which in the case of the theater distinguish creation and content but which in the case of Jacques merge into one.

As these observations suggest, the perennial appeal of the theatrical imagery lies in the fact that by displaying and amplifying a separation between a number of factors it provides an articulated template that allows us to identify certain aspects of human life that otherwise remain entangled and invisible.[20] Outside the theater, the three factors that are distinct in the theatrical situation—author, actor, and role—and their separate spatiotemporal orientations coincide. Or, stated in reverse, the theatrical analogy points toward this tripartite distinction that we can unravel within the perceived unity of ordinary life. The lesson the theater teaches, accordingly, is not about an ineliminable gap between us and all our roles. By enacting a cluster of roles with which we identify, we become who we are. And in this process we constitute ourselves not only by the resulting content or meaning of our lives, but also as the authors of that content or meaning. Just as Olivier would not display bad faith in pointing to the role of actor as providing (part of) the answer to the question of who he most fundamentally is, Jacques' corresponding attitude to waiting need not be a display of bad faith either. Whether it is depends on the further distinction between proximate and distant roles. Only if the role of waiter is a distant one would Jacques' conceiving of it as partially defining who he is amount to bad faith, since only in that case would his excessive clinging to the role reveal a failure to realize that he anchors his identity in a bit of meaning that is unsuitable for this task and would not contribute to the creation of a stable, coherent, and autonomous self.

This reconstruction of bad faith suggests a corresponding conception of alienation as a contrasting notion. *Alienation* has been used widely, including by Sartre, to designate a wide range of phenomena, not all of which are relevant here. But two principal forms of alienation, self-alienation and social alienation, are. Again, I limit my comments to the light that the role-atomistic approach can shed on these notions. The first beam of light concerns the adjectival part of both expressions, and so also illuminates the connection between them. Alienation from self is detachment from a constitutive, and so a proximate, role;* and when that role is an affiliation-role, detachment from it involves social alienation as well. These considerations link up with another theme in the literature on alienation. Like bad faith, alienation is a negatively charged evaluative term. Why? One salient answer points to loss of meaning. There is an

---

* But can't one identify with a distant role, and at the price of bad faith make it nonetheless constitutive of one's identity? Yes, in a sense in which one obviously *can* add two and two together and obtain five.

obvious connection between this concern and the meaning-conception of self. Within the role-atomistic variant of this theme, roles are the repositories or sources of meaning, and so detachment from a role results in a meaning deficit and an impoverishment of self.

But again, and in contrastive symmetry to bad faith, not every failure to identify with a role and integrate it into the self carries a negative charge and amounts to alienation. For consider George. He never votes in the American elections, does not serve on juries, nor does he ever file income tax returns with the IRS. He doesn't care about baseball or football, and when it comes to soccer, a sport he does like, he never roots for the American team. Moreover, George not only speaks ungrammatical English and makes many spelling mistakes, but he is quite indifferent to these shortcomings. George, you may conclude, is as thoroughly alienated as can be. But you'd be wrong to draw this conclusion, since George is actually a Frenchman residing in France. Noting George's failure to live up to the requirements of the role of American has no negative overtones and so does not amount to alienation. The lesson is simple but instructive. Not just anyone can be alienated from any role. For one thing, one has to be an incumbent of a role in order to be able to be alienated from it. So in order to know whether George can be deemed alienated, we must attend to the predicate role, of American in this case, and specifically to its incumbency conditions. This much is obvious, but not trivial. What makes one an incumbent varies greatly from role to role and can be quite a complicated issue. For instance, it wouldn't make any difference in George's case if American law were to endow him with U.S. citizenship because, say, his grandparents happened to be American. Such purely de jure circumstances would not affect our judgment that without so much as having ever visited the United States, George is not a candidate for alienation from it. In order to be alienated, George must first satisfy more substantial, and less clearly defined, incumbency conditions of this role. But the incumbency conditions are not alone among the role's norms that set preconditions for alienation to be an option: so do also the role's distance-defining norms. In order to retain its critical edge, the charge of alienation cannot be made with regard to distant roles, where detachment from the role is the proper stance.

We can summarize these comments regarding alienation and bad faith in terms of the examples of parent and AT&T operator I've used earlier in this chapter. Given some background assumptions I make regarding the role-distance suitable for these roles, identifying with a parental role (in the strong sense targeted by Sartre's waiter example) does not amount to bad faith, whereas a similar stance by an operator does. Conversely, a detached parent is alienated, whereas a detached operator is not.

2
Socializing Harry

Though the conception of self I pursue draws on many sources, some quite old, one especially prominent source is contemporary: the influential writings on this topic by Professor Harry Frankfurt. His views are frequently in the background of what I say, even when there is no specific acknowledgment. The opportunity to engage with his views directly is, accordingly, particularly welcome. I was given such an opportunity in commenting on Frankfurt's Tanner Lectures.[1] Seen within the context of this book, this chapter considers three main themes. One is a continuation of a theme broached in the first chapter, concerning the constructive significance of ascribing responsibility and of the role played by different social actors in doing so. The second theme, further developed in the next chapter, is an analogy between the boundaries of self and those of the state. And the third, which is picked up mostly in Chapters 5 and 6, links the meaning-conception of self to an appeal to levels of abstraction as the medium or the source of social as well as universal moralities.

There are two main themes in Frankfurt's Tanner Lectures, as there are in his work in general: one concerns autonomy and freedom of the will, and the second concerns the nature of normativity. They can be summarized as follows. First, *we either identify with an attitude, or we don't*. This defines the shape of the will, the extent of our autonomy, and, as he puts it elsewhere, the boundaries of the self. Second, *we either care for something or we don't*. This provides the ground of normativity. My general point is that Frankfurt's focus on individual psychology has to be expanded to take account of the intersubjective or the social. Using the distinction I have introduced in Chapter 1, this suggestion can be best seen as a comment on the *we* in the italicized statements: Frankfurt uses the pronoun distributively, whereas in extending the theory in the direction I propose, the *we* would better serve if used collectively.

Frankfurt's lectures address the shape of the will and the nature of autonomy, but they also treat of responsibility. My main interest is in the latter term. When are we responsible? What are we responsible for? The key to Frankfurt's conception of autonomy, but also of responsibility, is the idea of identification. In his lectures, the connection between responsibility and identification is indicated most explicitly in the discussion of character. According to Frankfurt, responsibility for character

> is not essentially a matter of *producing* that character but of *taking responsibility for* it. This happens when a person selectively identifies with certain of his own attitudes and dispositions, whether or not it was he that caused himself to have them. In identifying with them, he incorporates those attitudes and dispositions into himself and makes them his own.[2]

It's a short step from this account of responsibility for the character traits themselves to a similar account of the responsibility the agent bears for actions that issue from those character traits and in which those traits are exhibited or expressed.

This extension of the theory of responsibility can be applied to a dramatic hypothetical that Frankfurt presents. Frankfurt imagines himself as a loving father who is beset by a desire to kill his son. "The desire," he says "is wildly exogenous; it comes entirely out of the blue," and "is ordinarily safely repressed."[3] But now consider the harrowing situation in which the repression is unsuccessful and in which the desire does prevail. This in fact happened in the case of *Regina v. Charlson*.[4] The defendant's ten-year-old son entered his father's study. For apparently no reason, Charlson hit the child over the head with a heavy mallet and threw him out of the window. Fortunately, the child was not killed. At his trial, Charlson successfully pleaded *involuntariness*: he was suspected of suffering from a brain tumor, and he alleged that this explained his behavior. A claim of involuntariness amounts to a total denial of responsibility equivalent to the statement, "I didn't really do it." Now on the conventional understanding of involuntariness, this claim is read with the stress on the word *do*. The inquiry is: was an action involved here? And this we tend to interpret as raising a question of control: could Charlson have acted otherwise? Was compliance with the law an option for him at the time?

The difficulty with this conventional interpretation can be seen starkly if we compare *Charlson* with another case, *State v. Snowden*.[5] Snowden was involved in what appeared to be a minor quarrel with a woman outside a bar. At some point, he claimed at his trial, she kicked him. In response Snowden took out a knife and stabbed her to death, inflicting more than ninety wounds over her entire body. Snowden's explanation of this response was simple: when kicked by the victim, he flew into a rage and lost control; in his own words, "I blew my top." On his version of the events, his action was no more up to him than Charlson's was up to Charlson. But, I think not surprisingly, Snowden's defense was unsuccessful; he was convicted of first-degree murder. Now when interpreted in terms of the idea of control, the difference in result between the two cases is puzzling. Can it be said beyond reasonable doubt—which, after all, is the standard of proof in a criminal trial—that Snowden could have contained his temper, reined in his fury, and subdued his murderous impulse? Indeed, on Frankfurt's view this counterfactual inquiry would be misguided.[6] Frankfurt's approach suggests instead that we reorient the inquiry by reading the claim "I didn't really do it," implicitly made in these cases, with a different intonation, accenting the "I." Applied to Charlson, the claim is, "It was not really 'I' who brought about the injury; it was the tumor." In Frankfurt's terms, Charlson refuses to identify with whatever prompted his murderous outburst and to take responsibility for it. He "banishes" these promptings by placing them outside the boundaries of his self, or to reverse the metaphor, he draws his boundary so as to leave these promptings outside. Either way, the control such promptings exercise over Charlson is "external" and "tyrannical." This would explain why he was indeed acquitted. Frankfurt's approach also explains why we don't seem to be particularly perturbed by whether or not Snowden was able to contain his rage and subdue his outburst. On Frankfurt's view, as far as responsibility is concerned, the fact that Snowden couldn't help but act the way he did is neither here nor there. The difficulty, however, is that as it stands Frankfurt's own account may exempt Snowden of responsibility as well. On this account, the maneuver attempted by Snowden closely resembles Charlson's. By saying that he blew his top, Snowden can be understood to convey his refusal to identify with this irresistible rage; like Charlson, he too would rather draw the boundary of his self in a way that leaves the fury outside. If such dissociation were successful, it would, after all, keep him, as it did Charlson, out of jail. But at least as far as the jury in this case was concerned, the maneuver failed. What are we to make of Charlson's success in defending himself against criminal charges and Snowden's failure?

The basic insight that greatly contributes to our understanding of these cases seems to me the connection indicated by Frankfurt between responsibility and the boundaries of self. But when it comes to the ascription of responsibility, Frankfurt's approach must be supplemented in order to account for the difference between the two cases. The crucial point is that the self's boundaries are not drawn unilaterally, not only from within. The shape of the self is at least in part the product of what we may call *constructive practices*, including those of law and morality. Central among these practices are those of ascribing or withholding responsibility. As the cases suggest, the drawing of the self's boundaries may involve a process of negotiation, in which the agent participates, but over which she has no unilateral control. Through the jury, society plays an active role in drawing the defendant's boundary. On this view, the verdict in *Snowden* amounts to a determination that, unlike a tumor, rage is internal to the self, a regrettable yet legitimate component of one's character and personality, and so something for which one bears responsibility.

Although questions of responsibility arise on innumerable other occasions as well, the criminal trial provides a particularly visible and stylized setting for the kind of negotiation involved. The normative stakes in drawing the self's boundary are also particularly high in this context.

Defendants are typically eager to draw their boundary narrowly so as to escape the nasty ramifications of legal responsibility. This need not be just strategic posturing on their part: the phenomenology of withdrawal or flight from responsibility is altogether familiar and real. The prosecutor, eager to pin down responsibility to advance law enforcement and carry out justice, can be prompted by equally genuine indignation and resentment to advocate drawing the self's boundary widely. These momentary pressures and concerns of the trial should not, however, be allowed to eclipse the long-term and more general normative incidents of the self's boundary. The latter are obviously more complex than the immediate, momentary ones, but the political context from which the boundaries metaphor is drawn provides a useful, if simplified, analogy that affords a glimpse of the main considerations. A state's boundary settles at once the scope of both its sovereignty and responsibilities. Replacing sovereignty with autonomy, the more apt label for an individual's self-rule, we get a picture, alluded to in Chapter 1, in which autonomy and responsibility are coextensive, both defined by the boundaries of the self.[7] To abdicate responsibility by contracting the self's boundary is accordingly also to forfeit part of one's autonomy, since by evacuating potential responsibility bases we also give up regions of autonomy and self-rule. Moreover, responsibility is itself a two-sided concept. The moral and especially the legal context focus for the most part on forbidden behavior and thus bring to mind responsibility's negative side, as a source of blame and a basis for sanctions. But questions of responsibility also arise concerning credit due for positive actions and events. By defining the scope of one's responsibility, the boundaries of the self thus determine not only the extent of one's vulnerability to blame and punishment, but also the sources of satisfaction and gratification, of praise and reward. Drawing the self's boundary is a delicate balancing act, in which both the momentary and the long-term perspectives play a part, and in which conflicting considerations and difficult tradeoffs apply. I will not expand any further these cursory remarks on the nature of this process and will instead briefly comment on the connection between the ascription of responsibility, which Frankfurt does not explicitly consider, and the assumption of responsibility, which he does. I do so by relating this connection to another, I think particularly moving, point in the lectures.

Frankfurt speaks of harmony within the self, a congruity between higher-order attitudes and lower-order ones, and links this state to Spinoza's ideal of "acquiescentia in se ipso" ("acquiescence to oneself").[8] If the self's boundaries are drawn, as I suggest, through social practices in the public domain, and in a process that involves something like a negotiation between the agent and others, another kind of harmony or dissonance comes into view. The negotiation may end in agreement, as it apparently did in the *Charlson* case, where society, represented by the jury, came to accept the defendant's dissociative maneuver and drew the boundary accordingly. There is, however, the possibility of a breakdown in negotiations, with each party insisting on a different version as to where the borderline is drawn. *Snowden* may be such a case. I say *may be*, because more than one scenario may unfold. One possibility is for Snowden to persist in the face of the conviction in denying his responsibility. Either in proud defiance or in embittered self-pity, he'll consider himself the victim of two external forces that ruined his life: his rage is one, a cruel and uncomprehending jury the other. There is another possibility, though: Snowden may come to accept the verdict. This means that he will now align the boundary of his self as he conceives of it with society's. Contrition and remorse are mechanisms through which such harmony between Snowden and society can be restored. A single version of his self, rather than two incompatible and competing versions, will emerge.

But what does it mean to speak about two competing versions of one and the same self? It may at first appear that there's got to be a fact of the matter as to where a thing's boundary lies. In a case of disagreement, one party—either Snowden or the jury—must have gotten it wrong. But this appearance is dispelled by the constructive conception of the process by which the boundary is drawn. Antecedent to the negotiations, there is no fact of the matter; the process fixes the segment of the boundary that is under dispute. It may be felt, however, that once the process is over and the boundary fixed one way or another, there can be only one self.

Refusing to acknowledge it at this point amounts to ignoring the facts. It is an advantage of the metaphor we're using that it does not force this conclusion on us either. In the international arena from which the metaphor derives, indeterminacy of borders is all too familiar. There need not exist a single authority whose judgment is accepted by all. Hence different and incompatible versions may persist, though often with more or less disastrous consequences. These further implications of applying to the self the idiom of boundaries seem to me altogether apt. The self's boundary is the product or reflection of normative determinations regarding a person's responsibility, autonomy, and the like. Such putative determinations can be made by the person herself as well as by others, acting in various pertinent capacities. These determinations often converge. However, when they do not, no recognized supreme authority need exist to settle the dispute, and so, as in the case of the state, different versions of one and the same self may persist.

Let me now indicate some implications of this attempt to socialize Frankfurt's theory for the second theme of his lectures, the issue of moral authority. Here again my interest is in the kinds of practices that the cases I've mentioned illustrate: not just ascribing responsibility, but blaming and punishing. Can Frankfurt's approach account for these as well? According to Frankfurt, the authority of morality, and more broadly of all judgments of importance, is grounded at bottom in what we care about; in "the attitudes and dispositions of the individual." "If what we *should* care about depends upon what we do care about, any answer to the normative question must be derived from considerations that are manifestly subjective."[9] This view, I take it, parallels the one that was held by Professor Bernard Williams, that only internal reasons exist. On Williams's version of this view, we cannot charge another person with a failure of rationality by reference to some objective values or standards, as long as these values and standards are not included in that person's "subjective motivational set."[10] Both views imply a sense in which blaming others is pointless, unless they too care for what one cares about—unless their will is aligned in the relevant respect with one's own. But Frankfurt's view has the further and more striking implication that one can't really blame others even when their will *is* aligned with one's own. Surely my will has authority only over me. If the authority of morality derives from my will when my will endorses or accepts some moral precepts, morality too has authority only over me. By what right can I invoke its imperatives to blame others?

Put in other words, Frankfurt offers an attractive and metaphysically lean construal of the Kantian view that each person is a law unto himself. However, a question of jurisdiction now arises: even if the laws of two states have the same content, each state can prosecute only the violation of its own laws, not the other's, because each legal system has authority only domestically. According to Frankfurt, if I violate my deep values and convictions, I betray myself; and by the same token, if you violate your values and convictions, even if they resemble mine, you betray yourself. What business is this of mine? By what authority can I condemn you? Of course, I can be mad at you for harming me or the things I love, or disparage you for your hypocrisy or for the weakness of your will. But neither anger nor disparagement is the same as blame. For me to be in a position to blame you for the violation of a moral norm, we must be both under its jurisdiction. One and the same norm must have authority over both of us. Where would such authority come from?

My comments on Frankfurt's first theme indicate the general direction in which an answer may be sought. On Frankfurt's view, the authority of what's important comes from its importance for us. As I noted at the outset, Frankfurt uses the "us" distributively, whereas I propose to use it collectively. Support for this suggestion can be found in another insightful observation in Frankfurt's lecture: "The fact that there are things that we do care about [or, to use Frankfurt's other expression, that things are *important* to us] is plainly more basic to us—more constitutive of our essential nature—than what those things are."[11] What I take to be essential to human nature on this view is that some things appear to us under a certain description or designation, namely as "important." The point as I understand it is that not only do some things appear as "important to me," but also, and crucially, that certain things appear to me as "important." *Important*, however, is a word, specifically an adjective, and what it takes for something to be important is that the adjective apply to it. But to say this is to withdraw exclusive authority from the individual over this bit of content or meaning. My suggestion is that "taking ourselves seriously," as Frankfurt urges, requires that we take seriously the semantics of words, or concepts, such as *important*, that according to Frankfurt's own view play in human beings an essential, constitutive role.

Once again, this is an appeal to an intersubjective context and to our mutual intelligibility. Though we often disagree vehemently about what is important, this is a disagreement in our understanding and interpretation of a single term or concept. All of us are willful subjects of one and the same authority, the authority of *important* and kindred basic normative terms such as perhaps *right* or *appropriate*, whose meanings are embedded in a shared conceptual framework that secures our common human intelligibility. When we blame each other, we invoke this authority, under which we all live. To use again the legal analogy, we are more like lawyers who disagree about the proper interpretation of one and the same statute whose authority they all concede than like the inhabitants of two different jurisdictions whose statutes happen to resemble one another.

3
Revising Our Pasts

Our practical life is for the most part future-oriented, concerned with what to do next. But though the future often presents daunting challenges, the past can raise more intractable ones. When two neighbors disagree about the use of a driveway, it is possible that with some ingenuity and goodwill they may be able to reach a mutually advantageous agreement. But if the source of their acrimony is that one neighbor had already slapped the other or hit him over the head, the prospects for an amicable resolution seem dimmer. Future-regarding conflicts appear at least in some respects easier to settle than past-regarding ones. Since the future is open-ended, there may be room for an accommodation that will make the bone of contention disappear. But a past event is fixed, casting a permanent shadow; it cannot be undone. This predicament of living in the dark shadow of the past is faced not only by individuals, but by collectivities as well. States in particular must often cope with the "dead weight" of history and address grievances whose origins lie in past mischief.

In considering the predicament of the past, we can draw encouragement as well as guidance from recognizing that we are not in fact helpless in coping with past misdeeds. Although humanity's record in this regard is far from stellar, it is not altogether bleak. Not all disputes linger forever, and many grievances, individual as well as collective, have been successfully resolved. Indeed, we have at our disposal a battery of familiar responses to wrongdoing: punishment, reparations, repentance, forgiveness, and pardon come immediately to mind. But although they all serve to overcome the lingering effects of a past misdeed, they do not do so in quite the same way. The first two responses I have listed, punishment and reparations, are in part future-oriented: punishment is designed in part to forestall a repetition of the wrong, and reparations ameliorate an ongoing injury. But the other practices on the list—repentance, forgiveness, and pardon—are distinctly past-oriented: their avowed purpose is to remove or escape the shadow of the past. They raise therefore the predicament of the past in a starker form. For, given the tenacity of the past, how can their mission be accomplished?

In the previous chapters I have discussed and illustrated some aspects of a constructive approach to the self, and correspondingly, to collectivities. In both cases constructive practices are central. In this chapter I introduce and explore the correlative notion of *revisionary practices*, practices that on my interpretation are designed to change the temporal boundaries of individuals and of collectivities alike. I argue that the various past-oriented responses to wrongdoing I have mentioned are designed to redraw our temporal boundaries, and so in effect permit us to revise our pasts.*

In introducing the notion of a revisionary practice, I focus primarily on those practices in which past-orientedness predominates—repentance, forgiveness, and pardon are the most salient—though what I say bears on other responses to wrongdoing, such as punishment and reparations, inasmuch as those too play, at least in part, a similar revisionary role. Despite important differences, repentance, forgiveness, and pardon have much in common. They all pertain to the same object, a wrongdoer, and perform the same function: the cessation of a range of appropriate negative responses triggered by a wrongful action. These practices differ primarily in the subject of this reorientation: the subject of repentance is the wrongdoer; of forgiveness, the victim;[1] and of pardon, an official acting on

---

* By speaking of practices, I only mean to imply that some public criteria exist as to what counts as repentance and so on. It doesn't follow that the practices themselves must consist in public acts. For example, internal, subjective acts of contrition may in principle satisfy the criteria for repentance, though in such a case these acts would obviously have to be communicated for repentance to play its usual interpersonal role (e.g., as a reason for forgiveness).

behalf of society or the state.² Each of these subjects in turn correlates with a distinctive paradigmatic response to wrongdoing: the wrongdoer with guilt; the victim with resentment; and the official with stigma.³ There are many differences between guilt, resentment, and stigma, but what is more instructive in the study of revisionary practices is the common thread: a wrongful act gives rise to a range of negative responses; revisionary practices bring these responses to an end. How can they do so?

The issues I am addressing here are primarily theoretical, not practical. We are looking not for a new strategy, but for a new account. Given that we do in fact occasionally escape the shadow of the past, we want to better understand how we manage to do so. Greater clarity may, however, have a practical payoff as well, in perhaps increasing our rate of success. The first task, discharged in the next section, is accordingly to examine some pervasive conceptions of the predicament of the past and of our common responses to it. As I try to show, the problem has remained largely out of focus, with its difficulty either understated or overstated. Consequently, the most common responses, as generally understood, also appear to miss the mark, by either undershooting or overshooting it. Once the problem is in sharper focus, we can address it more effectively.

I. THE SHADOW OF THE PAST

In the case of the two neighbors, as in the case of two neighboring states, the aspiration is to relieve acrimony and induce peace. But the past altercation stands in the way; it casts a dark shadow. For the peacemaking mission to succeed, we must be clearer about the nature of the obstacle presented, the shadow cast, by the past event. What is the significance of the assault, and why does it mar the neighbors' relationship? The starting point is to observe the obvious. Following the attack, bad feelings will linger, perhaps to the point of prompting further hostilities. But bad feelings do not beset the parties as a common cold might; they are not just brute facts. Rather, there is a normative dimension as well. We judge it appropriate that an assault should provoke *reactive attitudes*, in particular the victim's resentment.[4] Why are negative responses to the misdeed deemed appropriate, and correlatively, what might require their termination?

Understating the Problem: The Reductionist Approach

Some common answers that come readily to mind turn out to be evasions. Especially when in the grip of instrumental rationality, an interest in the present and the future will seem prudent and sound, whereas dwelling in the past, idle and irrational. So the temptation is to convert our past-oriented concerns into present- or future-oriented ones. But by failing to accommodate our ubiquitous interest in the past qua past, such reductionist accounts do not so much explain reactive attitudes as attempt to explain them away. Three putative reasons for our past-oriented attitudes will illustrate the point. The first, and easiest to discard, concerns the enduring results of the assault, such as a broken bone or persisting pain. These results are doubtlessly important, but not quite to the point. Reactive attitudes do not depend on persisting harm and would remain appropriate even in its absence. Moreover, insofar as remedial action plays a role in mollifying resentment, we insist that the action be taken by the offender, not by just anyone. Yet a concern to bring the victim's suffering or loss to an end ought to be indifferent to the source of amelioration.

A second reductionist suggestion highlights the evidence the assault supposedly provides of the wrongdoer's violent character and her disposition toward aggression. Here the past event is taken to signal a defect in the wrongdoer, spelling future trouble.[5] Correspondingly, repentance is said to terminate reactive attitudes in one of two ways, evidentiary or substantive. On the evidentiary side, repentance serves to negate the inference about the offender's character that would be otherwise drawn from the wrongful act. For example, the remorse displayed by the offender subsequent to the wrongdoing alters the significance of the wrongful act in the overall assessment of the offender: she may turn out not to be quite so bad as we would have otherwise thought. Forgiveness and pardon express this reassessment.[6] Alternatively, repentance is said to play a more substantive role in fixing the dangerous defect revealed by the wrongful act, "like repairing that part of a house which contributed to an accident." The path to forgiveness is open because "there has been a replacement of (part of) what was responsible for the suffering with something which promises to be harmless."[7] But neither version is satisfactory. The emotional response that an appeal to a future threat addresses is not resentment but fear—the same reaction that would be invited by an approaching lion or a flood. Reactions to wrongdoing differ markedly from reactions to danger; the present account effaces this difference. Nor are the resulting accounts of what terminates the reactive attitudes convincing. The evidentiary view insists that we assess the offender within a broader timeframe, which includes the subsequent repentance or remorse as bearing on the overall assessment of her moral character. However, such a broader timeframe, a backward-looking one, is already available when the wrongful act is committed: the act can be assessed against the background of the offender's record up to that point. And yet we commonly resent a wrong done by an otherwise good person, just as that person may experience guilt and remorse for a single moral failure despite an otherwise flawless record. The substantive conception of repentance, as repairing the character flaw and so eliminating the danger this flaw poses, fares no better. Reassurance against future danger does not by itself bring the reactive attitudes to an end. For example, the victim may permissibly nurse her grievance even after the aggressive neighbor moves to a distant location and thus no longer poses a threat.

A third account of how reactive attitudes to wrongdoing are terminated characterizes violence, along Kantian lines, as an expression of disrespect. On this view, the victim's resentment is a protest against *ongoing* disrespect by the wrongdoer. Correspondingly, repentance is said to negate the inference from the past wrongdoing that the wrongdoer still disparages the victim. Since the repentant wrongdoer is not "now conveying the message that he holds me in contempt," "I forgive him for what he now is."[8] But this misrepresents the connection between the victim's resentment and the aggressor's remorse. The attitudes of the wrongdoer and the victim are, of course, related: remorse often paves the road to forgiveness and so to a termination of negative attitudes. Still, it is up to the victim whether to traverse this road and grant forgiveness. This account eliminates this choice by making forgiveness automatic or otiose. If the victim's resentment is sustained only by the wrongdoer's ongoing disparagement, then, once this disparagement abates, resentment is deprived of an object; there is nothing left to forgive.[9]

This is not to deny, of course, that past wrongs often have further present and future ramifications that fan the flame of animosity. Arresting or rectifying such enduring consequences of the wrongful act is obviously of great importance and a necessary step toward the restoration of goodwill. Even so, by ignoring the pervasive interest in the wrongful act as such, reductionist accounts induce the illusion that these remedial steps are sufficient, and that reassurance that a past wrong no longer persists and will not recur should all by itself allay bad feelings and terminate acrimony.

The reductionist misdiagnosis of the problem is bound up with a corresponding misunderstanding of the appropriate cure. As I've already mentioned, many of our responses to wrongdoing, such as sanction and reparation, do have a prospective aspect, in that they address in various ways the present and future ramifications of the wrongful act. But by focusing exclusively on this prospective aspect, the reductionist tendency would leave these practices utterly ineffectual in dealing with the distinctly past-oriented dimension of reactive attitudes. This omission is particularly glaring in regard to the predominantly past-oriented revisionary practices, such as repentance, forgiveness, and pardon, that are my central concern.

It is possible, of course, to insist on the reductionist approach to past-oriented grievances and to deny the need for an alternative account by simply dismissing people's reactions to the past as unfounded and silly. The bit of human reality at stake here, however, is too pervasive to be easily dismissed. Perhaps even more significantly, we must recognize a vague and inchoate yet deeply felt yearning that defines our pretheoretical attitudes in this area. The past sometimes weighs heavily on us, and we desire to shake free of it; we wish for a new start. Revisionary practices appear from this point of view as answering to this yearning.¹⁰ Here pardon provides the most compelling metaphor, that of erasing a nasty event from one's record. But when the record consists in the actual sequence of life's events, in our histories and biographies, how can it be amended? How can we pluck an event out of the past and expunge it? And if we cannot, are we to conclude that the aspirations underlying revisionary practices are incoherent, and occasional glimpses of success, a mirage?

Overstating the Problem: The Fixity of the Past

I have so far examined attempts to evade the predicament of the past by converting it into a present- or future-oriented concern. By contrast, when the predicament of the past is confronted head on, it appears intractable, eliciting some rather extreme suggestions for how the past's shadow can be escaped. Upon inspection, however, such suggestions turn out to be mere counsels of despair. Two approaches in particular are noteworthy, one ontological, as it bears on the contending parties' continued existence, and the other epistemological, concerning our knowledge of the past misdeed. The basic idea of the ontological suggestion is simple and stark. To revert to the example of the neighbors, if either of them were to die, discord would come to an abrupt, if sad, end. Though this would resolve the conflict only in a Pickwickian sense, this scenario does in fact provide a model for a serious theme. Reactive attitudes are relational, addressed for the most part by a victim to a wrongdoer, and so require that both parties continue to exist.* In light of this, it has been argued that the change in an offender wrought by repentance may be so profound as to count as a change of identity. The offender's transformation thus deprives the reactive attitudes of their object. A similar suggestion is made in regard to collectivities as well. In particular, the discussion of strife between states sometimes focuses on their conditions of identity: is today's Russia continuous with Tsarist Russia, or today's France with Napoleon's?

---

* To simplify matters, I ignore here the offender's own reactive attitudes, such as guilt.

The assumption animating such inquiries is the same as that concerning the neighbor's death: the condition for release from responsibility or for the termination of a grievance, and so for a cessation of hostility, is that one or the other of the parties has effectively ceased to exist.

As the case of the neighbor's death also teaches, however, such appeals to discontinuous identity are not a promising track. First, an interest in reconciliation arises only among parties who at least view themselves as respectively continuous with the wrongdoer and the victim. To take seriously the notion that one or both parties to a dispute are no longer around is not to effect a reconciliation but to deny the need for it. Second, the conclusion that the wrongdoer no longer exists achieves the abatement of grievances at the victims' expense, as it deprives them of any recourse and nullifies wholesale all claims to remedial steps. Finally, if we allow that as a result of the wrongdoer's change in identity there is no one to resent or attach stigma to anymore, we must also recognize that for the very same reason there is no one to forgive or pardon either. Just as resentment loses its object, so do forgiveness and pardon.* [11]

The other radical response to the predicament of the past has a more epistemological bent. The suggestion is sometimes made that relief from the burdens of the past lies in forgetting; amnesia is allegedly a strategy individuals and societies follow in order to escape an unpleasant past.[12] But this response is no more attractive than the previous. One reason is unreliability: deliberate attempts at forgetting are notoriously counterproductive ("don't think about an elephant") and precarious, easily reversible by anyone who cares to provide a reminder. More importantly, knowledge of the past, and in particular of a grim past, is a valuable

---

* Though ruptured identity is mostly invoked to account for the effects of repentance, thus focusing on the wrongdoer, the same idea can be extended, symmetrically, to the victim as well. If repentance can amount to a change of identity, so supposedly could other practices and events, which might affect the victim in a corresponding way. In this scenario, the erstwhile victim no longer harbors negative attitudes toward the wrongdoer because the connections to the historical self that had suffered the harm have been severed. However, a similar difficulty arises in this case to the one that arises in the case of the victim's changed identity. Offenders often desire forgiveness, which can be granted only by the victim herself. To take the victim's changed identity seriously is accordingly to deprive the offender of the prospect of forgiveness rather than grant him this wish.

source of learning that can help avoid repeating past abominations and mistakes. Foregoing this knowledge is a high price to pay even for attaining a desirable goal.*

But why are such radical responses to the problem of the past deemed necessary? Why invoke the equivalents of death and amnesia as required to escape the past's shadow? In contrast to the reductionist approach, which evades the problem of the past and thus understates its difficulty, these responses tend to overstate the problem and thus overreact. The source of the overstatement and overreaction lies in a simple oversight. Past events are indeed unalterable. But when it comes to wrongdoings and grievances, we are not in fact interested in the past as such. Reactive attitudes are addressed not to the wrongs themselves, abstractly conceived, but to their perpetrators; the concern is with *someone's* past, be it an individual or a collectivity such as the state. And to speak of someone's past is to speak of a relation—namely, that between some events and a subject. The realization that the past is unchangeable pertains only to one of these relata, the events themselves. This does not preclude the possibility that the subject might change, particularly in such a way as to no longer be the subject of these events. The inquiry accordingly shifts away from a fixation with the past and the hopeless task of undoing it, and focuses instead on the subjects of the wrongful acts: how are we to understand the temporal career of individuals and collectivities, and how does this career affect their relationship to past events?

In considering these questions, I begin with an analogy and a detour. Though our interest is in the temporal dimension, I propose to look at the spatial dimension first. My starting point is a phenomenon that is as familiar as it is misunderstood: the territorial borders of a state. Properly construed, these borders and their change provide a key to the account of revisionary practices we seek. It is commonplace that a change in a state's border affects the state's responsibility. I argue that analogous shifts in a

---

* Though amnesia can play a corresponding role in the offender's life, and so, for example, stop guilt, the situation is different from the one involving either party's change of identity, since the offender's forgetting the wrongful act is more likely to exacerbate hostility than allay it.

state's temporal boundary are also possible, bearing a similar relationship to responsibility and consequently to the appropriate responses to a past wrong. I then extend the account to individuals as well: the boundaries of the self, physical as well as temporal, resemble in relevant respects those of the state. The result is a unitary account that applies to individuals and collectivities alike: revisionary practices redraw the wrongdoer's temporal boundary so as to leave the offense outside, thereby rendering any negative attitudes toward the wrongdoer based on the past misdeed no longer appropriate.

II. BOUNDARIES OF STATES AND INDIVIDUALS

Spatial and Temporal Boundaries

Consider a simple example of a change in a state's territorial border. The state of Arcadia has within its border an oil field that leaks into an adjacent lake on neighboring Tasmania's land. As a matter of course, Arcadia bears responsibility for this pollutant: it is required to take measures to reduce the damage, to compensate Tasmania for the damage wrought, and the like. It is equally obvious that this responsibility would expire if Arcadia's border were redrawn so as to exclude the offensive site.*

A few features of this example are noteworthy. First, the example illustrates how a border change can affect responsibility by removing the object that serves as the responsibility-base. It also makes vivid the constructive and hence indispensable role played by the process or action by which the boundary is changed. Good reasons for retracting Arcadia's border may have existed prior to the change, and these reasons are likely

---

* In light of the analogy to temporal boundaries that I wish to draw, two clarifications of this example are in order. First, the border change does not relieve Arcadia of obligations that accrued before the change. The point is only that pursuant to the change, no new obligations will accrue. Second, it is immaterial whether after Arcadia's border changes, the pollutant is joined to another state or winds up in some unowned territory. The latter possibility is less likely on a globe that is mostly divided among states, but this is a contingent, and indeed a relatively recent, situation.

to have prompted the actions, peaceful or belligerent, for making the change. But the reasons themselves, no matter how compelling, are not self-executing. Arcadia's responsibility for the pollutant would persist in face of such reasons unless and until the change in the border is actually made, say by treaty or a UN resolution. Certain events and certain parties have the normative power to affect a state's boundary in the sense that the occurrence of these events or actions taken by these parties simply *mean* or *count as* a border change.[13] Why do they mean this, and to whom do they so count? What are the sources and the scope of this power? Importantly, neither logic nor political practice mandates that these questions have a clear and uniform answer. There is room among states not just for border disputes but also for disputes about the proper means of settling them, without there being a supreme authority able to resolve all such disagreements. There is accordingly room for indeterminacy in the location of a state's border, with different parties accepting different territorial versions of the same state. Note, next, the delicate balance between continuity and change in the Arcadia scenario. To say that Arcadia's boundary has been redrawn implies a change substantial enough to relieve Arcadia of responsibility but not so substantial as to threaten the state's continued identity. Though the region containing the pollutant is no longer part of Arcadia, the state of Arcadia does persist as a viable subject; so saying that *it* is no longer responsible for the pollutant is not an empty or a paradoxical claim. Finally, Arcadia's territorial parts, either before or after the border change, need not be contiguous. Lack of contiguity does not render Hawaii and Alaska any less parts of the United States than, say, Nebraska.

The pollutant is an object, so a geographic border change is adequate for the purpose of removing it from the scope of Arcadia's responsibility. Our interest, however, is not in objects but in events. Instead of the pollutant, consider along similar lines a past mischief committed by Arcadia against its neighboring state. Some time ago Arcadia invaded Tasmania, wreaking havoc on its people. After a heroic struggle, the Tasmanians managed to expel the invaders and regain their freedom. But emotions in Tasmania have since run high, hostility toward Arcadia persists, and occasional calls for retaliatory action are made. These reactive attitudes are the incidents of holding Arcadia responsible for the mischievous acts. Relieving Arcadia of that responsibility would accordingly render these attitudes no longer appropriate. In the case of the pollutant just discussed, redrawing Arcadia's territorial boundary would accomplish such a feat. Can we analogously think of redrawing Arcadia's temporal boundary so as to exclude the invasion? My suggestion is that revisionary practices do just that.

Analogizing the temporal case to the spatial must of course be defended, but before doing so we need some reassurance that the effort is worthwhile. We can gain the reassurance by considering how, when transferred to the temporal case, the features of a territorial border change I have highlighted would lay to rest the difficulties of coping with the past and account for the role that revisionary practices play in this regard. First and most importantly, by redrawing the wrongdoer's temporal boundary, revisionary practices relieve the wrongdoer of responsibility for the wrongful act. In doing so, these practices render reactive attitudes, the ordinary incidents of responsibility, no longer appropriate. Second, these practices are constructive in the sense that the effects on the wrongdoer's boundary and responsibility are brought about by the practices themselves, cumulatively or in some combination, rather than by any antecedent reasons for activating them. This explains the normative significance of these practices beyond their material and psychological effects. By engaging in revisionary practices, various parties exercise normative powers to modify the wrongdoer's boundary. Where do these powers come from, and how do they relate to each other? Though roughly speaking the answer must rest on various parties' special interests in the wrongful act, the third lesson the territorial analogy teaches is that these powers are contestable and vague, so the resulting boundary line may be indeterminate and ill defined. Consequently, the connection between different revisionary practices is loose: they may, but need not, be activated in harmony and converge. As in the territorial case, in the temporal case, too, different versions of the boundaries may coexist.[14]

The fourth feature of the territorial case illuminates the kind of change in the wrongdoer that the revisionary practices involve. Like redrawing a state's boundary to exclude a chunk of land, excluding certain events from the ambit of its temporal boundary is a change significant enough to require the cessation of negative attitudes toward the offender, though not so extensive as to disrupt the offender's identity. Finally, lack of contiguity in the territorial case corresponds to lack of continuity in the temporal case. Discontinuous events can be unified just as disconnected territories can. Conversely, just as dislodging a bit of land by a territorial border change might leave a gap, so might dislodging some events by changing the temporal boundary.[15]

Toward an Ontology of the State

As these parallels to the temporal case suggest, analogizing a change in a state's temporal boundary to a territorial change would provide a way of addressing our distinctly past-oriented concerns. But while excluding the pollutant from Arcadia's geographic scope is easy, isn't this quite unlike excluding a wrongful act from Arcadia's temporal scope? The challenge these questions pose looks especially acute when seen against a particular backdrop—namely, an implicit picture of states as akin to ordinary material objects. In this picture, the geographic borders of states resemble those of other objects that occupy a volume of space or cover some region of the earth. To be sure, such material objects do come into being and eventually expire and in this sense can be said to have temporal boundaries—a beginning and an end. But this notion of boundary is quite unlike the spatial one. The main difference concerns change. Much of the significance that attaches to territorial borders comes from the possibility of redrawing them. Shifts, actual or potential, in states' geographic composition are a central preoccupation of the international political scene. No similar latitude seems available in the temporal dimension, rendering the notion of a temporal boundary, understood as marking the fixed points of inception and termination, relatively sterile and superfluous.

The picture of the state as a material object resonates with us, and its spatiotemporal implications are often taken for granted. But a moment's reflection ought to stir us from such metaphysical slumber. Are states really equivalent, ontologically speaking, to sticks and stones? Giving up this imagery, and attending more carefully to what is involved in a state's territorial change, reveals that the state's spatial dimension is actually quite analogous to its temporal dimension. Changes in both types of boundaries thus turn out to be feasible and to have corresponding normative effects.

When Arcadia's border is retracted, Arcadia is indeed being cut down and reduced in size; its territory has shrunk. At first glance the alteration thus appears to resemble what happens when a tree is trimmed or a rock chiseled. But the appearance is misleading. Reducing the size of a tree or a rock does consist in these physical operations—the trimming or the chiseling—and their resulting material reconfigurations. Reducing Arcadia's size, by contrast, involves no such physical operations and no material change. Everything on the ground remains just as it was. Specifically, the pollutant does not change its location, and its emissions continue to affect the same region as before. What then does the change of boundary consist in? How does it exempt Arcadia from responsibility?

In order to answer these questions, we must pose a more basic one: why is Arcadia held responsible for the pollutant in the first place? The common reply would simply point out that the pollutant is on Arcadian soil. Though this reply is valid and plays an indispensable pragmatic role in ordinary dealings with these kinds of issues, it hides more than it reveals. At a deeper explanatory level, a more informative answer is available. Rather than a state's being responsible for X because X is within its boundaries, it is the other way round: X is within the state's boundary insofar as and in the sense that the state bears responsibility for it. Arcadia's relationship to the oilfield is of course not limited to what happens when the field catches fire or leaks. At other times Arcadia has the right to exploit the field, exclude others from doing so or tax those who do, and so on. To say that the oilfield is in Arcadia is accordingly not to specify the field's geographic location in the same sense as pointing out that it is, say, a hundred miles south of the Rockies. It is rather to indicate that Arcadia's *jurisdiction* extends to the field, and so to allude to a complicated network of institutional and other normative arrangements that in combination constitute Arcadia as a sovereign state. The answer to the question about what a boundary change is and to the question about how it releases Arcadia from responsibility is, therefore, one and the same: a border change ultimately just *is* a reallocation of responsibility and other incidents of sovereignty with respect to a particular object.

How are we to reconcile these two replies—the common, pragmatic one, which views the pollutant's location within Arcadia's borders as the grounds for Arcadia's responsibility, and the theoretical, explanatory one I have offered, which reverses this statement? Correspondingly, how can a reallocation of responsibility for the pollutant be explained by a border change when border changes just are reallocations of responsibility? To see the gist of the matter, consider a variant on the original example. Imagine that in Arcadia's case the usual incidents of the border line do not converge on a single geographic location: some people are allowed to enter Arcadia's territory at one putative "entry point" while others may enter elsewhere; customs are paid at some points but not others; Arcadia bears only partial responsibility for certain goings-on in some scattered territories, whereas others are responsible for the remaining goings-on and the remaining regions; and so on. Obviously, at some point such arrangements would drain talk of a border of all meaning, and any talk of Arcadia as a territorial entity would be empty too. The impracticality of this alternative arrangement, at least in the world as we know or think we know it, is also apparent. This impracticality serves as a backdrop for understanding the pragmatic role of reifying *border* and *state*. Though a state's border is but the reflection of such normative arrangements as I have mentioned, the border provides various norms with a focal point, thus allowing for an easy consolidation of what would otherwise be cognitively and practically an unwieldy jumble of such norms. Correspondingly, border-changing practices such as treaties are devices for inducing in one fell swoop the modification of an entire battery of norms and attitudes considered to be the common incidents of the border's location—a modification that in principle, but probably not in actuality, could be wrought piecemeal, without recourse to the orienting or unifying idea of a border and its change. To cite the location of a border or a change in it as the grounds for judgments of responsibility is to take advantage of the orientation and unification that the idea of a border provides.[16]

The change that leaves the pollutant outside Arcadia's border is spatial, but the foregoing considerations suggest a distinction between two senses of this adjective. *Spatial* can designate a change that takes place *in space* or alternatively a change that *pertains to space*. Trimming trees and chiseling rocks are spatial in the first sense, since they involve essentially the redistribution of matter in space. A change in a country's boundary, by contrast, is spatial in the second sense; it is a change in the network of normative relations, as well as other understandings and attitudes, pertaining to a particular piece of land. Now a similar distinction also applies to *temporal*. In one sense a temporal change would require an alteration in the sequence of events. It is a fundamental tenet of commonsense metaphysics that, unlike the corresponding spatial changes, temporal changes of this kind are impossible. A second sense of *temporal*, however, is that of *pertaining to* or *concerning* time. Changes in the significance we attach to events, in our attitudes toward them, and most importantly, in the norms that relate to them, are temporal in this second, metaphysically innocuous sense.[17]

We can see this parallel between *spatial* and *temporal* in the second sense of these terms by taking a closer look at Arcadia's attack on Tasmania, its neighboring state. The Tasmanians obviously hold Arcadia responsible for the attack. But why exactly is Arcadia responsible? It may appear that by saying that Arcadia invaded Tasmania we have already answered this question, just as pointing out that the pollutant is within Arcadia's territory seems to settle the question of Arcadia's responsibility for it. Being Arcadia's action, the invasion saddles Arcadia with responsibility in this case just as surely as the pollutant's being within Arcadia's territory saddles it with responsibility in the other. But as our discussion of the territorial case intimates, this answer, though not false, is incomplete. When we speak of Arcadia's attack, we ascribe to a collective subject a single action that supervenes on innumerable actions by individuals. A great deal of social theory is an effort to spell out what this relation of supervenience amounts to, and much disagreement persists. But whatever the account, just as in the case of the pollutant, the nasty goings-on that take place on the battlefield amount to an attack by Arcadia only in light of a complicated network of norms and practices—such as those designating the individuals in question as soldiers, specifying relationships of authority, relating their activities to those of other individuals labeled collectively as a government—which in combination constitute Arcadia as a locus of responsibility and other incidents of sovereignty. Here too, as in the territorial case, what happens on the ground—in this case, one bunch of men busily slaughtering another bunch—underdetermines the situation. Only in light of the types of factors just mentioned is it the case that one group belongs to the Arcadian army, and the other to the Tasmanian, that Arcadia is beating its arch-enemy Tasmania in a battle, and that, consequently, Tasmanians harbor resentment and other reactive attitudes toward Arcadia.

And just as redrawing Arcadia's territorial border does not require any rearrangement of material objects, so in redrawing its temporal boundaries, revisionary practices need not interfere with the sequence of events. All the practices need accomplish in both instances is a contraction in the scope or field of application of some norms and attitudes. In the spatial case, changes in norms and attitudes regarding the pollutant add up to relieving Arcadia of responsibility for it. Similarly, changes in norms and attitudes regarding the attack can render Arcadia no longer responsible for it either. The imagery of boundaries captures both of these situations. In the one case, involving an object, we express the change by saying that the object is now outside the state's territorial boundary; in the other case, involving an event, we can say in a similar vein that the event is outside the state's temporal boundary. When revisionary practices have run their course—after sanctions are imposed, reparations and apologies made, and forgiveness is granted—a change in Arcadia's temporal border, one excluding the past misdeed, comes into effect. In contrast to the radical ontological response to the problem of the past, such a change does not amount to a switch in identity that implies Arcadia's ceasing to exist. Rather, this change signals the release of Arcadia from responsibility for the invasion. Consequently, the reactive attitudes toward Arcadia based on that invasion are no longer appropriate and ought to come to an end.

From States to Individuals

I have so far pressed the analogy between the familiar notion of a state's territorial boundaries and the less familiar one of its temporal boundaries, demonstrating how the analogy helps account for the operation of revisionary practices in the collective case. The next step is to extend this account to the individual case. The extension depends on a second analogy, introduced in the previous chapter, according to which the self's boundaries resemble the state's. My present aim is to show how the meaning-oriented, constructive conception of self adumbrated in the previous two chapters supports this analogy, and lends credence and substance to the thought that the boundaries of the self are also determined and changed through constellations of practices and norms. Judgments of responsibility, as well as other personal norms and attitudes, which we commonly validate by reference to the constituents and the boundaries of the self, shape the self and delineate its boundaries. And if the contours of the self, spatial as well as temporal, are the product of such constructive practices, the preceding account of the mode of operation of revisionary practices in the collective case applies to the individual case as well.

In discussing the state I've considered first its spatial dimension, its territory, as the site of sovereignty, and have then drawn a parallel to the temporal dimension. The discussion of the individual self follows a similar pattern, albeit with a terminological shift. We don't usually speak of people's (as distinguished from peoples') sovereignty, or for that matter of their jurisdiction, but use instead a cognate expression, autonomy. But because "autonomy" wears its political connotations on its sleeve, it makes for a smooth transition from the state to the individual's case. The link I have indicated between the state's sovereignty and responsibility is also replicated here. Autonomy and responsibility are two sides of the same coin. To inquire about the analogue to the state's territory in the individual's case is accordingly to ask about the spatial extension of an individual's autonomy and responsibility, which in turn amounts to an inquiry regarding the physical boundaries of the self. The proper field of this inquiry is not biological but social and discursive: the wide range of practices, attitudes, and understandings by means of which individual autonomy and responsibility are fixed and come into play. And as this inquiry reveals, the spatial dimension of the self does not coincide with the contours of the human body and has quite a different shape.

The sense in which the body is a site of autonomy and responsibility is straightforward. Consent is ordinarily required before your body can be touched or invaded by someone else, quite apart from whether the contact affects your welfare in any way. Your autonomy extends to your body for the simple reason that to touch or invade your body is to touch or invade *you*. Correspondingly, and for the same reason, you are responsible for your body as part of your responsibility for yourself. For example, you are responsible for ensuring that your body not impermissibly touch or invade someone else's, and you'll bear some consequences if it does. As it turns out, however, neither of these observations applies exclusively to the body. A similar situation obtains with regard to other objects, namely, the objects you own. Consider invasion first. Trespassing on someone's property is regarded as per se wronging the owner, even if no setback to the owner's welfare is involved. Invading someone's property, like invading someone's body, implicates the owner's autonomy and requires her consent, since in both cases the invasion counts as doing something to the person whose body or property it is. Similar comments apply to responsibility: if trees growing in your backyard present a fire hazard to the neighbors, it is ordinarily incumbent upon you to trim them to reduce the risk.

These examples point toward a family of theories of property that view it as an "extension of self." But this label may mislead. The tacit suggestion is that the self's relationship to the body provides a point of departure and a model for a subsequent "extension" through ownership to other objects. But so used, the idiom of extension implies a prima facie difference between body and property: supposedly, in the case of the self's relationship to the body, extending is not required, whereas in the case of property it is. Why? A likely answer points to a naturalistic conception of human beings, which envisages the relationship of self to body as the identity of any biological organism with itself. But if this were the relevant relationship of body to self, there would be nothing to extend. A self would no more "extend" to, say, a person's house than a horse could be said to incorporate "its" stall. The "extension of self" idiom is accordingly liable to confound the basic insight that motivates it from the start, namely that a person's body as well as her home are sites of responsibility and autonomy, and kindred norms and attitudes, in a way that neither a horse's body nor its stall are. Given the hold that a naturalistic picture of human beings has on us, it might be easier to maintain a mental grip on the distinctly normative underpinnings of our relationship to objects, body and property alike, if in depicting the physical boundary of the self we reverse the "extension" metaphor and start with property as the paradigm case that "extends" to the body as well. In both cases the relationship consists in one's *owning* the respective items. To be sure, our ownership of the body is in a number of fairly obvious senses prior to our ownership of other objects. The naturalistic picture conveys this priority, but at the same time it also misrepresents it and its significance. We get a clearer grasp of what ownership amounts to by giving explanatory priority to our relationship to property over our embodiment, highlighting thereby the role that normative factors play across the board in physically circumscribing the self. Here, too, as in the case of the state, a variegated battery of constructive practices, centrally including those of morality and law, fixes the physical boundaries of the self by determining the spatial scope of norms defining each person's responsibility, autonomy, and the like. Modeling our understanding of the self's relationship to the body on its relationship to other objects results in a unitary account of the self's physical constitution that resembles that of a state's territorial boundaries.[18]

These similarities between the physical constitution of the self and the state's territorial dimension pave the way to a discussion of a corresponding similarity between self and state along the temporal dimension, thus moving from objects to events. Among the events for which we are responsible and by which our autonomy is displayed, actions occupy center stage. Actions involve bodily movements, and so the preceding comments on the physical boundaries of self apply here as well. However, there is more to action than bodily movement. Two additional factors participate in determining which action, if any, a particular bodily movement amounts to or displays: mental states, especially intentions, and circumstances, including a bodily movement's results. And as I argued in the previous chapter, normative judgments, especially regarding responsibility and autonomy, play here too a constructive role.[19] They do so by selectively relating the self to some such factors and not others, thereby including some and excluding others from its ambit.

Let me briefly restate the main points, starting with responsibility for mental states. In order to serve as (part of) my responsibility-base (and, correspondingly, to be bound up with my autonomy), a mental state must of course be mine. But though this much is obvious, the question which metal state is mine in the requisite sense is not as simple as it is sometimes taken to be: we do not think all the thoughts we have. The reason is familiar: our mental space is routinely and inescapably populated by a plethora of wayward thoughts that constantly assault us without, as it were, taking root. For instance, a jingle I hear praising the dietary advantages of a new brand of cereal inevitably resonates in my mind; still, I don't in fact believe in the cereal's merits. Qua subject of responsibility and of autonomy, I do not own any and every going on within the mental space of which I am directly aware. A further process of selection and determination is required by means of which only some of this mental content contributes to the constitution of a self. For example, only by integrating the alleged merits of the advertised cereal with other desires and beliefs, I own up to the thought that the cereal is a good thing; I take responsibility for this bit of mental content. But although I exercise considerable authority in doing so, this authority is not infallible or absolute, and at any rate, others may exercise corresponding authority. This was illustrated by the discussion of the *Snowden* case in the preceding chapter.[20] Accused of stabbing a woman to death, Snowden explains his conduct, or rather tries to explain it away, as a fit of rage. In doing so he seeks to distance himself from the action by disowning the rage that prompted it. But as we have seen, in convicting Snowden of murder the jury exercised a competing authority regarding the location of the self's boundary relative to Snowden's rage, and took a different stance. On my interpretation, the verdict in *Snowden* amounts to a determination that Snowden's rage is internal to his self.

If in regard to mental states the agent occupies a privileged, though not exclusive, position of authority, when it comes to the circumstances and results that define her action, she enjoys no advantage at all. Consider the proverbial hapless hunter who aims at a deer but accidentally hits another man. The hunter's state of mind would have been identical had the target turned out to be the intended deer, and yet due to the error, the hunter is deemed to have killed a man. To be sure, the hunter may not be morally blamed or held criminally liable in this case. But the "strict" responsibility that attaches—after all, we do say that she did kill a man—constitutes the hunter as "killer," and so has weighty significance all the same. Though here, too, the hunter may prefer to draw her boundary narrowly and refuse ownership of the mishap, others, and the law, may take a different view of the matter with no less authority than hers.

The upshot of these observations is this. In analogy to the case of the state, judgments of individual responsibility (and related normative judgments) track the boundaries of the self. These boundaries, in time as well as in space, are in turn fixed by constructive practices, including the very practices involved in holding people responsible. The resulting boundary may be contested, with no rock-bottom facts to rest on, nor an ultimate authority to appeal to in order to settle all disputes. And as in the case of the state, so also in the individual case, what constructive practices do, revisionary practices are able to undo. The cluster of practices we've been discussing, especially those, like repentance, forgiveness, and pardon, that are distinctly past-oriented, bring responsibility to an end by redrawing the temporal boundary of the self. They give rise to a new version of the self from which the wrongful action is excluded, and on which the reactive attitudes no longer have an appropriate grip.

III. MEMORY AND RESPONSIBILITY

The discussion has thus far focused on the ontological aspect of our coping with the past. The primary foil has been the radical and indeed paradoxical suggestion that in order to escape the shadow of the past, a subject must undergo a change of identity, and so, in effect, cease to exist. The notion of temporal boundaries and their revision offers a less extreme and more appealing alternative. This notion has corresponding attractions at the epistemological level as well. Here the foil is the suggestion that in order to rid ourselves of a nasty past we must forget it, thus forfeiting important knowledge. The notion of a change in temporal boundary offers an intermediate possibility here as well. In discussing it, I reverse the order of proceeding, looking first at the individual case and next at the collective case.

Memory and Identity

At first sight, a change in the offender's boundary that excludes the wrongful act renders the appeal to forgetting superfluous. Whereas identity change is offered as primarily an account of repentance, and so concerns the offender, forgetting supposedly accounts for forgiveness, and concerns the victim. A change in the offender's temporal boundary allows the victim to retain full knowledge of the past events, consistent with an appreciation that reactive attitudes toward the offender, as currently constituted, are no longer appropriate. The victim may accordingly still benefit from the lessons of the past while associating those lessons with a version of the offender that is no longer viable. But although forgiveness is in the first place bound up with the victim's epistemological stance, the offender's epistemological position is relevant too, complicating matters. If asked point blank whether she remembers the wrongful act, the offender would have to avow that she does, despite having repented the act and having been forgiven for it. To be sure, under these conditions the matter is unlikely to arise. The truly repentant ought not dwell on the past misdeed, and the hypothetical interrogator's bringing up the nasty event would be deemed insensitive and obtuse. Still, the mere possibility of such an avowal seems to belie the claim that revisionary practices accomplish anything approaching the removal of the misdeed from the ambit of the wrongdoer's self. So even if the preceding arguments establish that revisions of the self's temporal boundary are conceivable and metaphysically possible, it may be felt that as long as the wrongdoer herself remembers the wrongful act, such revisions do not in fact occur.

One way to defuse this objection requires that we take a closer look at the facts. These, as I had the objector recount them, are complex. One fact, the one that gives the objection its bite, is the supposed avowal. But an equally salient fact is that the avowal is prompted by an inappropriate question likely to provoke indignation and disdain. If the misdeed were forever inscribed in the offender's past, as the objector implies, this aspect of the situation would be puzzling. Admittedly, an inquiry into the truth may sometimes be considered tactless, but why would it seem to be a serious transgression? How can dredging up the past strike us not just as uncouth but also as unfair? Obviously, important norms are here at play, colloquially rendered by expressions such as "let bygones be bygones," designed to discourage an appeal to the past by rendering such an appeal highly inappropriate. Barring a rude violation of these norms, the offense will not come up, and the various attitudes and other ramifications ordinarily associated with it will have been effectively extinguished. These are powerful facts that need to be accounted for no less than what happens when the norms are breached and the past is exhumed.

The proposed account offers a straightforward explanation for all these facts. A serious wrongdoing invariably casts a long shadow over the offender's life in the form of lasting negative attitudes and other consequences. When, due to the operation of the revisionary practices, the shadow disappears, we ought to conclude that its source in the wrongdoer's life has been removed. But this is only part of the story. The possibility, no matter how remote, that the past misdeed may still surface must be accounted for as well. The key is a point I made earlier concerning the indeterminacy of a border change. Various parties can draw a state's border in different ways without there being a single overriding authority to choose among them or a fact of the matter as to which is correct. A similar indeterminacy, the product of a plurality of competing versions, pertains to the temporal boundary as well. Revisionary practices give rise to a new version of the state, and correspondingly of the individual self, from which the wrongful act is excluded. When this version is enacted, it replaces the older one as superior or more authoritative. As long as this version is adhered to, as by and large it will be, the misdeed is indeed excluded and does not cast a shadow. But the new version does not obliterate the other one; it only supersedes it. So if one insists, cruelly or obtusely, on unearthing and scrutinizing the older version, one is not strictly speaking mistaken, but merely cruel or obtuse.

Still, this appeal to discursive norms may seem to be an evasion. Jogging the offender's memory in the hypothesized circumstances, though inappropriate, is possible. And this possibility is unsettling. Doesn't the offender's memory, even when dormant and merely dispositional, disprove the claim that the offensive act is no longer hers? Moreover, if recognizing a change in a temporal boundary requires that the wrongful action not be mentioned (as in "don't mention the war"), the practical result is akin to forgetting, since it makes the lessons garnered from the experience publicly unavailable for future use. If a change in temporal boundaries is to provide a viable model for escaping the past, such a change must be less precarious, and in particular less vulnerable to recollection.

To allay these worries we must identify their source. Suppose that Gertrude is charged with battery for hitting Kim. An eyewitness is found. Plainly, for the purpose of testimony, having observed the event is not enough; the witness must remember it. Memory thus serves as a crucial conduit that makes available the initial information acquired by watching the event. Notice, however, that though the testimony is highly relevant to the charge against Gertrude, it does not settle it. Witnesses don't allocate responsibility; they only provide information that bears on such allocations. The allocation of responsibility requires a judgment, and the authority to make it. Testimony regarding Gertrude's alleged attack is one thing; a decision concerning her responsibility, another. Now Gertrude's own memory can play a similar evidentiary role to the witness's. After all, she too was present at the scene of the alleged offense, and so can draw on her memory to provide a first-hand account. But if Gertrude's own memory is treated as equivalent to the witness's memory and as playing the same evidentiary role, it would not be able to settle the question of Gertrude's responsibility any more than the witness's. The objection we're considering (that an agent's remembering a wrongdoing inescapably saddles her with responsibility for it, thus disproving my account of revisionary practices) must assume that first-person memory is more than evidence relevant to responsibility: to remember performing an action is to reveal oneself as the author of that action. This view of the significance of biographical memory reflects a conception of memory as the key to personal identity and as the thread that links the disparate elements of a human life.

Although this relationship between memory and personal identity is highly contested, we can reduce the area of contestation, and canvass at least some of the issues involved, by focusing on a particularly prominent advocate of this view, John Locke, and by giving the objection under consideration a Lockean gloss. Locke's version is particularly congenial here, since he famously distinguishes the identity of a human being conceived as a biological organism ("an animal of such a certain form"[21]) from the identity of a "person" or "self," which is "a forensic term appropriating actions and their merit." Since Locke further maintains that "in this personal identity is founded all the right and justice of reward and punishment," we are at present interested exclusively in his views regarding *personal* identity, or (what amounts to the same thing) the identity of a self rather than that of a human being, biologically conceived.

Now at first sight (and according to much of the Lockean tradition, at second sight too), Locke would indeed be in agreement with our objector, who considers Gertrude's memory of the attack on Kim to be sufficient to settle the issue of her responsibility. According to Locke, personal identity is indeed constituted by first-personal memory—"whatever has the consciousness of present and past actions is the same person to whom they both belong"—and so is one's responsibility: "I being as much concerned and as justly accountable for any action was done a thousand years since, appropriated to me now by this self-consciousness, as I am for what I did the last moment." Call this the *sufficiency thesis*. In light of this thesis, the persistence of memory even after revisionary practices have run their course would indeed disprove my claim that these practices absolve the wrongdoer of responsibility by removing the offense from the ambit of her self. Is the sufficiency thesis sound?

In addressing this question, we should note that Locke goes beyond the sufficiency thesis, insisting that memory is also necessary for responsibility: just as Gertrude's remembering the attack would ground her responsibility, so her forgetting it would negate responsibility. This *necessity thesis*, however, is patently implausible. Consider a robber who sustains a concussion during a heist, and when he comes to, no longer remembers the entire affair. Would that amount to denying that he'd participated in the crime or absolve him of liability? A negative answer is, if anything, even clearer in a parallel case in which credit rather than blame is meted out. Think of an intrepid firefighter, who suffers a memory-erasing injury while performing a heroic act; would she be denied the laurels that would otherwise be her due? Locke recognizes that the law does not in fact conform to the necessity thesis, as it convicts defendants of crimes they do not recall, and tries to account for the disparity between his theory and the law by pointing to evidentiary exigencies faced by law. Memory, Locke argues, is subjective, and so forgetting easy to feign. Expediency thus mandates that the law dispense with memory as a condition of liability, despite the resulting injustice. However, Locke's attempt to reconcile legal practice with his own view is unconvincing, for two reasons. First, the evidentiary worry does not arise in the case of reward: no one is likely to feign forgetting in such a case. So Locke would have to acknowledge, counterintuitively, that by forgetting her heroic acts, the firefighter must forfeit all credit for them. Second, criminal liability routinely depends on establishing a defendant's intent or other state of mind; such subjective elements of crime do not present an insurmountable obstacle to law enforcement. Memory raises no special difficulties in this regard.

These considerations only show that memory is not necessary for responsibility, whereas the question before us is whether memory is sufficient. But though, in principle, the sufficiency thesis might be independent of the necessity thesis, that principle would not be the one actually espoused by Locke. That much is suggested by the very fact that Locke deems it necessary to defend not just the sufficiency thesis but the necessity thesis as well. When he insists in the face of pervasive legal practice that memory is necessary for responsibility, he bites a hard bullet indeed; and his appeal to expediency to explain this practice is ad hoc and patently unconvincing. Why doesn't Locke follow the more inviting road of allowing that memory is sufficient but not necessary for responsibility? A likely answer follows from Locke's main objective, which is to advocate a particular theory of personal identity. To understand why Locke insists that memory is necessary for responsibility, and not just sufficient, and why the two theses stand or fall together, we need turn to this broader objective.

In a thumbnail sketch, Locke's theory of personal identity consists in an alleged alignment between three key terms: memory, identity, and responsibility. I am responsible for the actions I remember since memory is what links me to them, what makes them mine. It is crucial to this theory that the three terms be coextensive, and Locke's defense of the necessity thesis is part of an attempted demonstration that they are. Conversely, rebutting the necessity thesis drives a wedge between memory and responsibility, thereby breaching this tripartite equation. This leaves two options: retaining the equation between memory and identity (by adhering to the view that memory is the criterion of personal identity) while cutting responsibility loose, or retaining the equation between identity and responsibility and cutting memory loose. In making the choice we need to bear in mind that as applied in the present context neither the notion of identity nor that of memory is a unitary one. Regarding identity, recall that Locke distinguishes the identity of a human being from that of a person or a self.

Remembering an action or experience does, plausibly enough, establish the continued existence of a human being, that is of the organism bearing the memory, between the time of the action or other experience and the present. But this is not the identity that concerns Locke. His main point in distinguishing *human being* from *person* or *self* is to mark off those aspects of the human condition that he designates as "forensic." Responsibility is a defining aspect or characteristic of the forensic, and so indispensable to Locke's concept of self. Since, as the rejection of the necessity thesis shows, memory cannot be convincingly seen as constituting responsibility or as coextensive with it, and the three-way equation (between memory, identity, and responsibility) cannot be maintained, we must conclude that the self's identity (unlike that of a human being) coincides with the self's field of responsibility, whether or not memory persists.

This conclusion is reinforced by the realization that memory isn't a unitary notion either. When we contemplate autobiographical memory, we tend to focus on a paradigm case. In such a case, memory is not just a matter of the path by which knowledge is acquired and retained. In addition, the bit of knowledge possessed by way of autobiographical memory is experienced as self-regarding or reflexive. In the typical case, such reflexivity has an affective side as well as a cognitive side. Specifically, to remember an action as one's own is to entertain toward it such self-regarding attitudes as pride, or satisfaction, or remorse. But though this is the paradigm case, not all instances of what we would ordinarily describe as memory fit this description. We often possess knowledge that in its modes of acquisition and retention accords with those of memory, while lacking the full-fledged phenomenology. Once we separate the purely cognitive aspect of memory from the affective aspect, memory is no longer univocal, and no longer appears convincingly as constitutive of responsibility. Just as forgetting an action does not by itself remove it from the ambit of the self and does not absolve the agent from responsibility for it, so remembering it in this attenuated sense does not encompass it within the self nor secure responsibility.

The possibility of affectless memory also casts light on the paradigm case, in which memory does involve self-regarding emotions. Emotions such as pride and shame are not brute stirrings in the heart. To entertain such emotions with respect to an action involves a judgment that the action is a suitable source of them. The relationship between the possession of first-personal knowledge of a past action and such emotions is accordingly a normative relationship. Since in the paradigm case the knowledge and the emotions are linked, the link may appear inexorable, inducing the impression that memory is constitutive of both identity and responsibility. But once the two factors that are conjoined in full-fledged memory are pried apart, it turns out that the factor that is constitutive of responsibility is not the possession of first-hand knowledge of the past affair, but rather the appropriateness of entertaining such attitudes as pride or shame with regard to it. And given Locke's forensic conception of the self, the same factor must be seen as defining the boundaries of the self and its identity even in cases of paradigmatic memory, in which the relevant attitudes are tied to the possession of first-hand, internal knowledge of the predicate actions. Moreover, given the complexity of what *memory* designates, its negation cannot be perspicuously rendered by the single term "forgetting"; this dichotomy between remembering an action and forgetting it turns out to be too restrictive. There is conceptual room for a stance toward performing a past action in which one retains the purely cognitive aspect of memory, but forgoes or overcomes the affective aspect. We can say about such a person that she unremembers the action without forgetting it. Revisionary practices can lead to this intermediate stance.

Memory and History: The Collective Case

Appeals to forgetting as a strategy of coping with a nasty past are not limited to individual disputes, but are made, even more commonly, in connection with collective ones, particularly states. But here too the choice between remembering and forgetting is not exhaustive. Rather, like in the individual's case, a change in a state's temporal boundary allows for the intermediate possibility of unremembering past events while retaining knowledge of them. This possibility is suggested by a distinction that has come to occupy center stage within scholarly fields dedicated to the study of the collective past. In the last quarter-century or so, this study has greatly diversified its interests and methodology. Part of this diversity came to be marked by a salient, if highly contested, opposition between *history* and *memory*, with scholars proclaiming themselves, sometimes vehemently, as studying the one or the other.[22] Juxtaposing history to memory as two modalities of knowing the past reveals in the collective case a logical space for an epistemological relationship to the past similar to the one we have just noted in the case of the individual self: retaining or losing historical knowledge is one thing; remembering or forgetting a past event is another. Like individuals, collectivities too can cease to remember an event while retaining knowledge of it. A change in their temporal boundaries allows them to occupy this middle ground.

The juxtaposition of memory to history in the study of the past centrally involves the idea of *collective memory*, the extension of the notion of memory to a collectivity's relationship to its past.[23] Talk of collective memory is part of an intellectual swell that effaces at least to some degree the distinction between individuals and collectivities by maintaining that individual identity is in part a matter of people's social roles and collective affiliations.[24] One way of capturing the gist of this view is by highlighting the correspondence between singular and the plural first-person pronouns. As was already discussed in Chapter 1, the reflexivity of both *I* and *we* serves to signify people's self-awareness. The two pronouns thus provide parallel modalities of people's self-conception. In this regard, the notion of collective memory does not break new ground; it is just an implication or extension of the more fundamental point regarding collective identities and their relationship to the individual self. Just as in the individual case memory licenses a conversion of a present-tense "I'm doing X" into a past-tense "I did X," so in the collective case, collective memory licenses a conversion of a present-tense "we're doing X" into "we did X." Consequently, those who urge the creation or the retention of some collective memories commonly do so as part of a constructive effort to forge or shape a collective identity by subsuming certain actions and events under people's use of *we*.

Consider in this light a historical event analogous to the imaginary conflict between Arcadia and Tasmania we discussed earlier—the British victory over France at Waterloo. Note what is not here at issue: the British victory itself. In exploring epistemological relations to a past event, we take the event itself as given. Specifically, we accept talk of "Britain" and of "winning" as permissible references to a collective subject and its action. As in the case of Arcadia's attack against Tasmania, when speaking about "Britain's victory," we ascribe to the collective subject a single intentional action that supervenes on the individual actions. Such an ascription of victory to Britain amounts to stating a historical fact. This historical fact can be validly stated by anyone, unlike the corresponding collective-memory statement, which in this case would naturally take the form "we won the battle of Waterloo," and which can only be made by some. How and by whom can a nineteenth-century war be remembered today? Who may permissibly use the *we* locution in reference to this past event, and what's the special significance that attaches to this usage when construed as an expression of collective memory?

To answer these questions we must revert to the initial ascription of victory to Britain. Here too the third-person statement assumes that some people were entitled to use the self-referential, present-tense statement, "we are winning this battle." Such a statement could have been appropriately made not just by Wellington, his generals, or any of the soldiers, but by any contemporaneous Brit. By virtue of what? Simply by virtue of being British—that is, being identified with the same collective subject to which the victory is ascribed. Moreover, the contemporaries' identification with Britain evinced by first-person-plural locutions underwrites the kind of self-regarding emotions I have mentioned, such as pride or shame. Now given that such identification makes appropriate the *we* statement in the first place, and so underlies the very ascription of a victory to Britain over France, no new puzzle arises regarding the possible use of a first-person locution by British people today. The longer temporal horizon need not undo the reflexivity involved. Britain persists over time, so identification with it would give a present-day Brit a basis for using a past-tense reflexive locution regarding the battle, similar to the basis that was available to the battle's British contemporaries for making the corresponding present-tense statement in the past. By the same token, the emotions that attend the present-day report made at the time of the battle can also be perpetuated by the reflexivity of collective memory, and conveyed by a present-day Brit via a "we" reference to the battle.[25]

This account of collective memory parallels the account of individual memory as illustrated by Gertrude's case. And here too, as in her case, a different option exists. Once more, the crucial reminder is that *Britain* is not a natural-kind term, and its persistence is not that of a material object. To speak of Britain as a unified subject is to take seriously some propositions regarding certain geographic regions and certain events. It is, for example, to accept that, say, Lake Windermere is *in Britain*. And, by the same token, it is to recognize certain goings-on in the nineteenth century as *Britain's doings*. And as I have argued in the previous section, such propositions are founded on a cluster of norms and attitudes that range over people, territories, and events. But precisely which people, territories, and events depends on the content of the norms and attitudes and is variable, indeterminate, and contested. Consequently, the Britain that plays a constitutive role in forming a present-day Brit's identity need not include the victory over Napoleon.[26] Just like in the individual case, in the collective case too there is a logical space between the polar options of knowing a past event on the one hand and forgetting it on the other. Since memory is *reflexive knowledge*, there are two ways of ridding oneself of it: by losing the knowledge, or by retaining the knowledge while losing its reflexivity. Like everyone else, contemporary Brits may retain the external historical knowledge of the Napoleonic wars without this knowledge being part of their collective memory—that is, without its being the kind of knowledge that is bound up with responsibility and with the affective attitudes and responses that go along with it. Although the British may share with everyone else a range of emotional attitudes toward the battle—perhaps admiration for the fighters' bravery or the generals' ingenuity, horror at the carnage, and the like—this range will not include emotions predicated on being a party to the battle, such as pride in the victory, or resentment against the French. A British person holding this intermediate position will best express it by her willingness to acknowledge that the British won at Waterloo, while being reluctant to avow that "we won." At bottom, the point is really quite simple and mundane, encapsulated in the colloquial expression that many former adversaries, now reconciled, are wont to use in reference to the source of their previous acrimony: "It is all just history now."[27]

But is this transposition of a past action from memory to history really tenable? It may be pointed out in opposition that when a contemporary British child reads in a history book that Britain won the battle of Waterloo, the child will reason, "I am British; hence, we won the battle. Why am I not allowed to use this expression? Why is this bit of knowledge not part of my collective identity, and hence collective memory, as a Brit?" In response, we could say something along the following lines: "Though Britain did win the battle, it does not follow that this victory is still constitutive of your British identity. Brits no longer appropriately derive shame or pride from it; they no longer enjoy the spoils nor owe amends to the French. The version of Britain as a victor has been superseded by a version in which that battle no longer plays a role. What you say is true as a matter of history, but not as a matter of memory, and your way of putting it misleadingly suggests the latter." This, after all, is my argument in a nutshell, and it ought to convince the child. One might reasonably object, however, that this reasoning will rather baffle the child, being too complicated or convoluted compared to the child's own straightforward, if simplistic, reasoning. This is indeed an important objection, but its import is somewhat different than might first appear. The teaching of history and the cultivation of collective memory are related but importantly different enterprises that can be easily confounded. One implication is that in the interest of reducing strife and acrimony, and cultivating reconciliation and peace, some history is better taught only to adults, lest it be inadvertently transformed into memory.[28]

IV. LIMITS OF REVISION

If revising the past along the lines just proposed is indeed possible, a further question arises about the limits of revision. The question is particularly acute with regard to forgiveness, since many believe that forgiveness has its limits. The reason they cite for the limitation is psychological: some acts are unforgivable in the sense that the enormity of evil defies our capacity to overcome resentment.[29] Without disputing this view, I note that it does not, nor does it purport to, provide any principled reasons against forgiving even the most egregious crimes; it only underscores people's inability to do so. Since forgiveness is generally thought to be a good thing, this inability would seem to be a regrettable external limitation. Moreover, this view opens up a gap between repentance and forgiveness. The psychological limitations on forgiveness need not have their counterpart in the case of repentance, and at any rate, the psychological limitations in both cases are unlikely to be the same. Consequently, cases may arise in which an offender truly repents an offense with no prospect of forgiveness. The tighter we take the link between forgiveness and repentance to be, the more unsettling we would find this state of affairs.[30] My proposed account contrasts with the standard one in both of these respects. First, rather than focusing on the victim's psychological limitations, the constraints on forgiveness my account implies reflect the normative significance of the wrongdoer's identity. Second, since the constraints focus on the wrongdoer, who is the common object of all the revisionary practices, they apply not only to forgiveness but also and to the same extent to repentance and pardon. The magnitude of evil plays a role here as well, but its significance is different from the standard account, and additional considerations come into play. In spelling out these limitations on redrawing temporal boundaries, and so on the scope of the revisionary practices, I focus on the individual case and consider only the self. But similar considerations apply in the collective case, and extending them to that case with suitable adjustments would be quite straightforward.

The constraints on revisionary practices can be best understood in light of an earlier observation. In discussing Arcadia's border change,

I have highlighted the balance between continuity and change that this case illustrates: to remove the pollutant from Arcadia's territory is to release Arcadia from responsibility while retaining its integrity as the object of these changes and as the beneficiary of the release. Since in my view revisionary practices redraw the temporal boundaries of the self, the redrawing cannot be so extensive as to effectively amount to a change of identity. The wrongdoer's identity conditions thus set the limits of revision. Considerations of identity preclude revision when the wrongdoing looms so large within the offender's self that removing the wrongdoing would not result in a viable or recognizable version of that self.[31]

Note that the severity of the wrong done retains its relevance within this account, though for reasons other than the victim's psychological resistance.[32] Doing major harm ordinarily requires greater effort and resolve than inflicting minor harm, and the features of mind and character on which such an act depends are likely to be pervasive and central. Furthermore, the scale of harm inflicted provides at least a rough measure of the action's significance within the perpetrator's life and its ties to various aspects of it. Both of these factors may stand in the way of effecting a neat excision of an egregious misdeed without destroying the offender's identity in the process.

My account also draws attention to constraining factors other than the magnitude of evil. Let me mention three. One concerns the way wrongfulness is to be measured. If the offender harmed many individuals, the standard view would tend to assess wrongfulness distributively, since people's capacity to overcome resentment is likely to be particularly sensitive to the wrong experienced by each of them. Consequently, victims may find it possible to forgive their individual injuries without regard to aggregate harm. On my approach, by contrast, the aggregate harm dominates. Since we're primarily interested in the overall significance of the wrongful behavior in the wrongdoer's life, the sum total of harmful actions is a more suitable measure. The second factor is the duration of the wrongful behavior within the offender's life. Revision is less likely to satisfy the identity conditions in the case of a lifelong hitman than in the case of someone who killed the same number of people in one shooting spree early in life. Even if the crimes are equally heinous, committing them as part of an enduring career makes them into a central source of meaning and a defining characteristic of the life story as a whole. The third factor (discussed in Chapter 1) concerns the distinction between personal activities on the one hand and impersonal ones, such as those done in an official capacity, on the other. Since the latter typically call for, and perhaps are defined by, a large measure of detachment and compartmentalization, they are relatively secluded within the offender's self. Other things being equal, it is easier to recreate a viable version of a self with impersonal wrongs removed than it is in the case of someone who commits wrongs in a personal capacity.

One final comment. I earlier noted that the limitations that are commonly thought to apply to forgiveness are for the most part a matter of the victims' psychology, specifically their finite capacity to overcome resentment. This appears as a brute fact and, given the value of forgiveness, an unfortunate one. Are the constraints imposed on revisionary practices by the offender's conditions of identity any different? Aren't they also regrettable constraints on what could be a gentler and more lenient world? This is a nagging thought, so it is important to underscore the fundamental difference between these two sets of limitations. Unlike the victim's psychology, the offender's identity is essentially implicated in the operation of revisionary practices from the start. To see this, recall that the reactive attitudes such as guilt and resentment play a decisive role in defining a person's responsibility and that by doing so they participate in the construction of a self. It makes sense to speak of revisionary practices only against the backdrop of such constructive practices and in relation to them. The revisionary practices also participate in the construction of selves by setting limits on the scope of the reactive attitudes and the constructive practices to which they belong. But the ability of revisionary practices to set such limits is in turn restricted by the identity-based constraints. The main point is this: constructing a self, like anything else, must accord with some general imperatives of construction.[33] Such imperatives aren't just constraints on the enterprise but are just as much its enabling conditions.

The identity-based constraints to which revisionary practices are subject form a part of a single set of imperatives that guide and enable the construction of selves. Reactive attitudes, limitations imposed on them by revisionary practices, and identity-based constraints on revisionary practices are all interlocking parts of one and the same enterprise, the enterprise of constructing a self, or, what comes down to the same thing, being one.

4
Regret, Luck, and Identity

In the previous chapter I examined our attitudes to past misdeeds in light of a meaning-oriented, constructive conception of self, and in terms of the revisionary practices that this conception helps explain. But though revising the past is often an option, it is not the only one. Whether or not the option of revision is open to them, people may cling to the past while disapproving of it. Regret marks such an attitude. Like some of the revisionary practices, most particularly repentance, regret involves a critical stance toward the past. But regret is not revisionary; it is more passive than that. Regret consists in a painful hopelessness in the face of one's past actions and their aftermath, and in this regard resembles despair. In contrast to revising the past, to regret is to dwell in the past's dark shadow. It may be of some comfort, therefore, to realize that not everything about one's past can be regretted. Regret is subject to identity-based limitations similar to those discussed at the end of the previous chapter in regard to revisions. The connection between identity and regret is of interest in its own right. But this connection also bears on another notion that has attracted considerable philosophical attention, moral luck. I argue that the same identity-based considerations that inhibit regret also delimit the role luck plays in our moral life. The key in both cases, of regret and of luck, lies in the same constructive conception of self that I've been discussing thus far. If who we are depends on what we do, some of our actions are immune to regret as well as to luck. The aim of this chapter is to explain why. In linking the notions of regret and luck I follow the lead of Professor Bernard Williams, whose well-known essay, entitled "Moral Luck," helped put this topic on the philosophical agenda. However, Williams's discussion raises some puzzles. Dealing with these puzzles will help navigate us toward an improved account.

Williams's essay is not only the eponymous essay in one of his books,[1] but it also inspired the book's fetching cover, a rather striking painting by Paul Gauguin[2]—appropriately, since the essay's central example is Gauguin's decision to start in remote Tahiti a new life, devoted to painting, in derogation of the pressing human claims made on him by his family and other people he left behind. According to Williams, our retrospective assessment of Gauguin's decision crucially depends on its outcome, on whether he succeeded or failed. Williams's main claim is that "in such a situation the only thing that will justify [Gauguin's] choice will be his success itself."[3] Since many fortuities bear on whether Gauguin's venture succeeds, the justification is a matter of luck. In the first section I examine Williams's treatment of the Gauguin example, and point out some difficulties that arise. In the following two sections I suggest an alternative account of Gauguin's case, an account that, I believe, better upholds Williams's main insights, specifically his central claim regarding the connection between Gauguin's success and the possibility of regret. In the final section I draw from my own account implications that depart from some of Williams's conclusions.

I. THE PROBLEM

The fact that Williams has put the notion of moral luck on the philosophical agenda creates a potentially distorting lens through which to see his paper. One is inclined to seek in the paper, in vain as it turns out, a defense or a demonstration of moral luck. Indeed, seen as a vehicle for demonstrating moral luck, the Gauguin example, around which Williams's argument revolves, would be a curious choice. Much more common examples abound of what would ordinarily strike one as the role of luck in moral judgment, such as the proverbial negligent drivers, only one of whom runs over a pedestrian who happens to cross the street at the critical moment. Why then focus on such a recherché example as Gauguin's?

Gauguin's case does in fact serve Williams's goals well, but to see this we must be clearer about what these goals are.[4] As I see it, they are both methodological and substantive. The methodological purpose served by the example concerns Williams's insistence on providing an argument for the role of luck, instead of resting his case on a direct appeal to our intuitions. The stock example of the two drivers that I have just mentioned is a case in point. The discussion of such cases often amounts or rather escalates to not much more than a contest of intuitions, with some writers affirming and others denying the relevance of fortuity to culpability. Unlike these cases, Gauguin's more complicated example provides Williams with the context for an argument designed to show why luck plays an indispensable role. The substantive point is that Williams is not primarily interested in the relevance of luck to *moral* judgments, but rather in a broader question regarding the role of luck in human life. He alludes at the start of the paper to "a strain of philosophical thought which identifies the end of life as happiness, happiness as reflective tranquility, and tranquility as the product of self-sufficiency," and to "certain doctrines of classical antiquity" that promised, at least to the sage, an immunity to luck.[5] According to Williams, Kant's moral theory is a modern variation on this ancient aspiration to extricate central aspects of ourselves and our lives from the vagaries of luck. The challenge that Kant's moral theory purports but fails to meet is accordingly twofold: not only to display *some* conception of morality as luck-free, but to do so with respect to a conception of morality that occupies a central or superior position within the self and within human life. Only such a conception of morality can satisfy the ancient yearning to eliminate luck from central, not just peripheral, aspects of ourselves. Gauguin is in this respect an apt example not because his is a particularly clear case of *moral* luck, but rather because luck seems to play such a decisive role in his life. This feature of Gauguin's case helps bring out the tension between the two desiderata that Kant's moral theory tries to meet. We must either view the justification afforded to Gauguin by his success as a *moral* justification, and thus acknowledge the existence of moral luck, or else we must accept that Gauguin is inescapably dominated by nonmoral factors that compete with morality and may displace or overcome it, thereby relegating morality, free of luck as it may be, to a more peripheral position than we ordinarily ascribe to it.

It is, however, easier to state Williams's goals than it is to fill in the steps he takes to meet them. In broad outline the argument is clear enough. Gauguin faces a dilemma as to whether or not to desert his family in order to pursue his artistic aspirations. As Williams depicts him, Gauguin is fully aware of the conflicting considerations as well as the uncertainty of the outcome. When Gauguin decides to go to Tahiti, he accordingly takes the risk that his painterly ambitions may fail. Williams is not primarily concerned with the decision itself, however, but rather with its retrospective evaluation by Gauguin. This perspective, according to Williams, naturally brings in the notion of regret. Ordinarily, a bad decision is a pro tanto ground for *agent-regret*. The appropriateness of regret can accordingly serve as a test of the badness of a decision. When we apply this test to Gauguin, we find that whereas failure "must leave him with the most basic regrets," regret would be incoherent in the case of success.[6] Whether Gauguin fails or succeeds, however, and hence whether or not he comes to regret his decision, is in part a matter of luck, and to that extent the retrospective justifiability of the decision is also a matter of luck.

As this summary makes clear, the crucial step in the argument is the appeal to regret and the claim that Gauguin's successful execution of his artistic project prevents it. But when we look closely at this claim, some troubling questions arise. One question concerns the very appeal to regret: using regret as a measure of the justifiability of the decision seems either perverse or otiose. In order to tell whether regret is appropriate it appears that we must first be able to assess the decision as *regrettable*— that is to say, as in some respect bad or undesirable. Trying to derive the existence or absence of justification from the appropriateness of subsequent regret seems to have things backward. An even more troubling question concerns the argument's central claim: why can't a successful Gauguin coherently regret his decision to become an artist? A seemingly obvious answer is that Gauguin values being an artist so highly that he cannot in good conscience wish that he had not become one; and for this reason he cannot regret the decision that led to this career either. But although some of the things that Williams says lend support to this simple answer, it is not really convincing, and stands at odds to other claims. Three difficulties in particular arise.

First, to say that Gauguin would not regret his decision simply because of the importance he attaches to his artistic success is to beg the question how his interest, even a dominant one, ought to compare and compete with those of others whom he has injured or wronged. Moreover, we know from the start that Gauguin was willing to sacrifice the interests of others even in the face of the mere possibility of success; why, then, should there be any expectation that he would come to regret the decision when success did strike? What could the impossibility of regret possibly teach us that we did not know already at the time of the decision? Indeed, Williams's main point is not that a successful Gauguin is unlikely or disinclined to regret his decision, but that he cannot *coherently* do so; the simple interpretation we're considering sheds no light on this stronger claim. The second difficulty is closely related. Williams insists that there is a discontinuity between the ex ante standpoint of decision and the ex post standpoint of evaluation, a discontinuity that makes it impossible for the deciding Gauguin to fully anticipate the position from which the assessment will be made. Since luck bears some of the responsibility for Gauguin's eventual success, it also must bear some of the responsibility for a genuine shift in the normative state of affairs. But no discontinuity between the two temporal standpoints and no shift in the normative situation seem to occur if success consists of nothing more than the realization of Gauguin's earlier hopes. When making the decision, Gauguin can anticipate the two scenarios of success and failure, as well as the great importance that artistic success would have in his life; all the factors that bear on the justifiability of the decision thus seem to be present at the time of the decision. Finally, on the simple interpretation, the distinguishing mark of Gauguin's decision is its great importance in his life: the value he assigns to it outweighs the harm to others he has caused. But importance is a matter of degree, whereas Williams insists that Gauguin's decision is qualitatively and not just quantitatively distinct from decisions we are able to regret. What precisely is the distinguishing mark of Gauguin's decision that sets it apart from ordinary ones?

These difficulties present a challenge. We need an account (1) that points out what is distinctive about Gauguin's decision, (2) so as to explain the gap between the prospective standpoint of decision and the retrospective standpoint of assessment, (3) as well as the special significance that attaches to the possibility of regret, (4) rendering regret in the case of success not just unlikely, but incoherent.

II. A SOLUTION

In attempting such an account, my point of departure is another query: what kind of luck is Gauguin claimed to have enjoyed? The backdrop to this query is a distinction Williams draws early in his paper between two types of luck, *constitutive* and *incidental*. Though he doesn't define the terms, his import is quite clear. The kinds of cases I've mentioned at the outset, illustrated by the two negligent drivers only one of whom happens to hit a pedestrian, or by two would-be killers, one of whom misses her target, belong to the latter category. But these are not the kinds of cases Williams has in mind. The theme of moral luck, Williams maintains, grows out of an older strain in Western philosophy that sought to free the good life from the "contingent enemies of tranquility." Such a life, however, was thought to be open only to the sage, and as Williams points out, "it was a matter of what may be called constitutive luck that one was a sage or capable of being one."[7]

But Williams is not quite interested in constitutive luck, as illustrated by the sage, either. As I've already mentioned, Williams associates a more modern outgrowth of this older theme with Kant, who offered a conception of morality as a distinct area from which all luck, even constitutive luck, is eradicated, since "the successful moral life ... is presented as a career open ... to a talent which all human beings necessarily possess to the same degree." Williams himself, however, believes that "the aim of making morality immune to luck is bound to be disappointed" because "the dispositions of morality, however far back they are placed in the direction of motive and intention, are as 'conditioned' as anything else." Though this leads Williams to conclude that "morality is subject, after all, to constitutive luck," this conclusion, he says, is not what he's going to discuss. Rather, against the backdrop of Kant's attempt to purge morality of luck, Williams wants to consider "the agent's reflective assessment of his own actions," specifically whether "at the ultimate and most important level" it can be a matter of luck "whether he was justified in doing what he did." As we have already seen, Gauguin's case is designed to provide an affirmative answer.

At first blush it does indeed appear that, as treated by Williams, Gauguin's story is not about constitutive luck. Constitutive luck, as this term is used by Williams and as it has come to be widely used by others since, would have come up had Williams probed the *ground* for Gauguin's decision, such as perhaps superior talent or great ambition. Others less talented or ambitious would not be as attracted to an artistic life or as lured by the prospect of glory and fame, and so would be less disposed to embark on a similar venture to their family's detriment. The distinctive course followed by Gauguin would on this account be a product of constitutive luck. But Williams focuses on the *consequences* of Gauguin's decision, specifically his painterly success, rather than on its origins. Given Williams's binary distinction between constitutive and incidental luck, this puts Gauguin's good fortune in the incidental category, and specifically, to use a further subdivision that has taken hold, it categorizes it as a case of *consequential* luck, similar to the stock examples of the unlucky driver (who kills) and the unlucky shooter (who misses) I've mentioned.[8] But, then, what does Gauguin's more complicated case add to these stock examples and what lesson does it teach us that they do not?

To answer these questions we need attend more closely to the binary distinction between incidental and constitutive luck. As commonly understood, constitutive luck concerns a person's enduring characteristics that precede and provide the ground for the actions that are under assessment. Since consequences are subsequent to the assessed action, they appear to be a matter of incidental luck. So understood, however, the classification misses the distinctive feature of Gauguin's case that makes it an apt example for Williams's purposes. My suggestion instead is that Gauguin's is a case of what is in effect *constitutive consequential* luck. The case is designed to show that a person's constitution can be related to an action or decision in two ways: not only as its ground, but also as its product. Just as being a sage is the constitutive ground for certain actions and decisions that are the manifestations of sagacity, so being a painter is the constitutive product of Gauguin's decision to leave for Tahiti. The common denominator is that being a painter stands to Gauguin in the same constitutive relation as being a sage stands to the sage. My suggestion accordingly is that what distinguishes Gauguin's decision to devote himself to painting from "the 'normal science', so to speak, of the moral life,"[9] is that Gauguin's is what I will call a *constitutive decision* that launched a *defining project*. As I will try to show, this best explains why a successful Gauguin cannot coherently have regrets.

What does it mean, though, to say that being a sage or a painter is *constitutive* of a person? What is a *defining project* and what does it define? To answer these questions I need to distinguish two broad conceptions of the relation between a person's identity and his or her life. On the first conception, personal identity is fixed antecedently to or independently of the course of one's life. Fixed by what? Perhaps by the spatiotemporal career of a particular biological organism or by a noumenal self or a pure ego. But the constructive view, which I have discussed in preceding chapters, suggests a different answer. The human subject is formed or constituted in the course of her life and by actual experiences and events, which forge a self seen as a more or less unified or integrated narrative or dramaturgical whole. Whatever the imagery, the answer to the question of who a person is cannot be entirely detached from the actual life she leads. The difference between these two conceptions can be helpfully drawn in terms of the kinds of counterfactuals it is possible to entertain regarding individual human beings. On the first view, which separates a person's identity from his or her life, it should be possible for the same individual to have lived a radically different life; all we need imagine to make this intelligible is that a particular organism (or noumenal self, or pure ego) has undergone a very different course of experiences. Not so on the constructive view. If people's identities are fixed in the course of their lives, the variations on the actual course of a person's life that we can intelligibly imagine while retaining the person's identity (i.e., the variations that would still count as variations on the life of the same person), are limited. If the imaginary departure exceeds a certain threshold, no sense can attach to the claim that we're still imagining the same person.

The notions of a constitutive decision and a defining project can now be understood in these terms. A decision is constitutive when it launches a defining project. A project is defining when it plays a sufficiently dominant role in the person's identity. What counts as sufficiently dominant seems to me inescapably vague, and amenable to conflicting intuitive judgments. But a rough test might be this: a project's role in a person's life is dominant when any (otherwise ordinary) life that includes this project would resemble that person's life more closely than would this person's actual life with the project imaginatively removed. This in turn means that a counterfactual in which this project is eliminated would be an identity-disrupting counterfactual—that is to say, it would no longer be a counterfactual about the same person as the one in whose life the project does play a defining role.*

Although Williams does not explicitly endorse the constructive view, some of the things he says, in the present essay and elsewhere, come pretty close. I'll mention two. One is his rejection of "[John Rawls's] model of rational deliberation as directed to a *life-plan* ... which is that of one's life as a rectangle, so to speak, presented all at once and to be optimally filled in." This model, Williams argues, is false since "it implicitly ignores the obvious fact ... that the standpoint of that retrospective judge who will be my later self will be the product of my earlier choices."[10] Even more instructive is the function that Williams assigns in other writings to people's projects. Williams maintains that having a project "is a condition

---

* Though to simplify matters I talk about identity in binary terms, as I argued in Chapter 1 (pp. 25–26), the constructive view is consistent with a scalar picture of the self.

of [a person] having any interest in being around" and that without any project "it is unclear why [we] should go on."¹¹ To see the present relevance of this view, contrast it with the view that our clinging to our lives is a matter of brute survival instinct, which we share with other animals. Though attachment to life is indeed likely to have some such biological origins, Williams's view is a reminder that here as elsewhere biological provenance is superseded by distinctly human phenomena, in this case the recognition that one's existence is optional and amenable to reflective assessment. For the ordinary affirmation of one's own existence to have such normative significance, it must have some evaluative grip. And what in turn provides the necessary traction is some *content* that we take to be our own and that we value as such.¹²

Apart from its conformity with some of Williams's positions, the constructive view provides answers to the questions that were posed at the end of the previous section. To begin with, seeing Gauguin's decision as constitutive and his project as defining elucidates some of Williams's comments about what distinguishes this decision from more ordinary ones. Williams notes that in the case of "many decisions which are part of the agent's ongoing activity, ... [o]neself and one's viewpoint are more basically identified with the dispositions of rational deliberation, applicable to an ongoing series of decisions, than they are with the particular projects which succeed or fail on those occasions."¹³ Not so in the kind of situation exemplified by Gauguin. Here, according to Williams, one identifies more fully and more fundamentally with the project on which one embarks than with the process of deliberation itself. Williams does not much elaborate what is involved in the two patterns of identification that he contrasts, but what he says echoes the approach that I have followed in previous chapters, and that is notably associated with the writings of Harry Frankfurt, according to which *identification* names a process of self-constitution by means of which the self is formed and its boundaries are drawn.¹⁴ One important result mentioned by Williams of Gauguin's identification with his artistic career is that this project provides him with his "standpoint of assessment": Gauguin's evaluative judgments are inescapably shaped by the fact that his life "derives an important part of its significance for him" from being a painter. In the same vein, Williams denies the existence of "some currency of satisfactions, in terms of which it is possible to compare quite neutrally the value of one set of preferences together with their fulfilments, as against a quite different set of preferences together with their fulfilments."[15] Instead, our satisfactions are a matter of having our preferences satisfied, and what those preferences are is determined by the kinds of projects illustrated by Gauguin's case.

We can also see now why Williams attaches special significance to the possibility of regret. Regret, or more accurately agent-regret, is first-personal and retrospective. Both of these features are essential to Williams's argument. Privileging the agent's own point of view is easy to understand when we recall Williams's well-known position that only internal reasons exist.[16] This position relates to a view of rationality as an agent's disposition to act on the balance of reasons that apply to her. Reasons can be said to apply to an agent, however, only if they are rooted in the system of her own values and desires. We accordingly cannot charge an agent with the irrationality of failing to abide by reasons, unless the putative reasons are internal to the agent in this sense. The insistence on the relative independence of the retrospective standpoint of assessment from the prospective standpoint of decision can be understood in these terms. Artistic success brings in its wake the domination of Gauguin's life by a system of values and considerations that would not otherwise be his. Since the shift in Gauguin's life brought about by his decision to go to Tahiti involves his identification with the artistic life as he conceives of it, it's a shift in what is internal to him, and therefore in what is available to him, from a first-person perspective, as a basis for evaluative judgments. There is, on this view, a fundamental difference between the hypothetical and for this reason merely external possibility of being an artist, on the one hand, and the internal reality of actually being one, on the other. It is not enough, accordingly, for deciding-Gauguin to anticipate the standpoint of artistic success, since he cannot as yet identify with that standpoint; it is not yet his. Or, to put this in reverse, he is not yet the person who will eventually come to occupy that standpoint if success does strike.

Though this explains the significance Williams attaches to the possibility of regret, the main question still remains: why is a successful Gauguin not only unlikely to regret his decision, but unable to coherently do so? Even if the considerations that bear on the retrospective assessment of his decision differ from those available to him at the time of making it, it is not clear how the later standpoint rules out regret. The constructive view offers an answer to this question. To see it clearly, we must first recall Williams's remarks about regret in general and about agent-regret in particular. This is what he says:

> The constitutive thought of regret in general is something like "how much better if it had been otherwise", and the feeling can in principle apply to anything of which one can form some conception of how it might have been otherwise, together with consciousness of how things would then have been better . . . But there is a particularly important species of regret, which I shall call "agent-regret", which a person can feel only towards his own past actions . . . In this case the supposed possible difference is that one might have acted otherwise, and the focus of the regret is on that possibility, the thought being formed in part by first-personal conceptions of how one might have acted otherwise . . . There can be cases of regret directed to one's own past actions which are not cases of agent-regret, because the past action is regarded purely externally, as one might regard anyone else's action.[17]

For Gauguin to regret the decision thus requires more than just having misgivings about his ill-gotten gains; he must wish that things were otherwise, that he had made a different decision. But in light of his identification with his artistic career and the defining role it came to occupy in his life, such regret cannot be coherently entertained for two related reasons. The first reason concerns the outcome of Gauguin's decision. Suppose that the alternative to going to Tahiti involved becoming a bank teller in France. For Gauguin to wish that he had pursued this option would be to opt for an impermissible, identity-disrupting counterfactual, which amounts to the incoherent wish that he were someone else. Given that Gauguin's identity came to be defined by his artistic career, it makes no more sense for him to have been a bank teller than for him to have been

Lloyd George. The second reason concerns the later Gauguin's relationship to the choice between the two options that he faced. For Gauguin to have agent-regret regarding his decision, he must relate to it internally rather than "purely externally, as one might regard anyone else's action." But this condition cannot be satisfied either. To take seriously the idea that the later Gauguin is constituted by his artistic career is to maintain that no internal relation can link him to a different decision, since following the other prong of the choice he faced would have given rise to an identity different from his. Wishing he had followed the other option is not to express agent-regret since it involves assuming an external perspective on the decision he faced and treating it as alien, as belonging to someone else.* [18]

III. SOME CLARIFICATIONS

Various objections to this account come to mind, and the following clarifications and elaborations are designed to address a few salient ones.

A. We must distinguish the limits imposed by a person's conditions of identity on permissible counterfactuals from the limits on change that these conditions may also impose. The claim concerning counterfactuals is that given Gauguin's artistic career, it makes no sense to think of the very same person as the one who would have stayed in France to become, say, a banker. This is not, however, to maintain that had the actual Gauguin gotten tired of painting and decided to work for a bank, we would have to think of the late-life banker as a different person from the early-life artist.† The distance between an artist's life and a banker's is not so great that it cannot be traversed within a single life. An artist, following perhaps a midlife crisis, might decide to "start a new life" by joining a bank.

---

* Although, following Williams, I focus here exclusively on regret, it is noteworthy that the constructive view imposes corresponding constraints on other attitudes, such as envy.
† Since Gauguin did not in fact make such a transition, this way of posing the hypothetical may be misleading; it's not a counterfactual about him!

Significantly, the colloquial expression in quotes indicates that the contemplated change is not trivial, and that it may indeed stretch the limits of identity. Even so, the change is tenable, all the more so due to the stipulated midlife crisis. If, following such a radical but identity-preserving life change, we were asked to spell out this hypothetical Gauguin's identity, to say who he was, we would have to mention both periods and both occupations. This Gauguin isn't just a painter, nor just a banker, but a painter-turned-banker. So understood, the aspiration to "start a new life" or "turn a new leaf" by changing the course of one's life is quite different from that expressed by the counterfactual thought "I'd like to have been someone else," which, if taken seriously, wears its incoherence on its sleeve.

B. Suppose now that prior to his departure for Tahiti Gauguin contemplated giving up painting and taking a job as a banker that had been offered to him. Even if, given Gauguin's actual choice, it makes sense to deny that he could have *been* a banker, it seems undeniable that he could have made the choice of *becoming* one. After all, choosing to go to Tahiti to be a painter rather than taking up employment with the bank is an event within Gauguin's life and a genuine choice he had made. My account may appear to deny this conclusion. "Can choose *X*" entails "can carry out (or attain) *X*." It would make no sense to say that one could have chosen filet mignon if the restaurant were out of it or if one could not afford it. So since on my view Gauguin could not have been a banker, it would seem to follow that he could not have chosen to be one either. The key to a different conclusion is, however, provided in Harry Frankfurt's view of the relation between the existence of alternate possibilities (and so the truth of determinism) and freedom of choice. In John Locke's well-known example (adapted by Frankfurt), the fact that unbeknownst to me the door to my room is locked does not vitiate my autonomy in willingly staying in the room. By the same token, Gauguin makes a genuine choice to forego a banking career and embark on a life as a painter, even though, as it turns out, pursuing the rejected path would not have been a real option for *him*.[19]

C. The suggestion that successful Gauguin (SG) is a different person from the hypothetical failed Gauguin (FG) raises a question of transitivity.

It might be pointed out that both SG and FG share the same youth, up to the point of decision. Call that common stretch young Gauguin (YG). Now clearly SG and YG are one and the same person; similarly, FG and YG are also one and the same. But if so, how can SG not be the same person as FG? There are two possible answers. One is to assimilate this situation to cases in which a form of life takes a branching form. The resulting conundrum is familiar, as are the various ways of responding to it, such as espousing a looser notion of identity that can accommodate this type of case. Alternatively, we can contest this picture of how life's temporal segments belong together. The objection assumes a straightforwardly additive picture: a life consists in the sequential accumulation of temporal segments. However, on the meaning-conception of self I've been pursuing, human life, like a text, is to be understood holistically: each segment is what it is, has the meaning or significance that it does, in virtue of its relationship to all other segments of the life to which it belongs, past and future. Just as the beginning of a story is not inert to what follows, so also the young-Gauguin cannot be simply detached from the subsequent life and considered as a common segment of both the successful and failed Gauguin. Rather, matters here are the other way around: given that SG is a different person from the hypothetical FG, we must conclude that they are different persons all the way back, and so deny that they share a common early identity.

D. Following Williams and common usage, I have been referring all along to Gauguin's failed alter ego by the same name as its actual bearer. Isn't this an admission that I do in fact consider the actual and the counterfactual figures as one as the same? The usage is indeed liable to mislead by creating the impression that the present discussion concerns the modal logic of proper names. My claim that, given that Gauguin was in fact a prominent painter, he could not have failed, may be construed in this vein as the claim that the name *Gauguin* necessarily refers to a successful painter, and so as subscribing to the so-called, and now mostly discarded, famous deeds conception of the reference of proper names. Though I doubt that the last word has been said about these issues, and in particular that this conception has been conclusively refuted, I need not in fact enter this fray.[20] The reason is that I don't consider the line of reasoning I am pursuing to be about the name *Gauguin* at all but about the person. That the name *Gauguin* successfully fixes the initial reference to a particular painter is not at issue here. Once this has been accomplished (in terms of whatever theory one favors as securing such reference), the questions regarding the status, relative to this person, of the counterfactual artistic failure no longer involve the use of the name since these questions are considered primarily from the first-person perspective. The thoughts whose coherence we're trying to assess, specifically those regarding regret, would be entertained by that person without recourse to a name, but rather by using the pronoun *I*. From his standpoint, the fact that the counterfactual figure would bear the same name as Gauguin's is no more relevant to his identity than, say, Golda Meir's is to mine.

E. Since successful-Gauguin is defined by his artistic success, he cannot regret his decision. What about his hypothetical alter ego, though? Regarding the unsuccessful Gauguin, Williams asserts that "his standpoint will be of one for whom the ground project of the decision has proved worthless, and this ... must leave him with the most basic regrets."[21] It might be objected, however, that my account effaces this contrast by rendering the two cases symmetrical. Just as success is constitutive of the actual Gauguin, so failure supposedly is of his counterpart. For the latter to regret his decision would accordingly be no less self-defeating or undermining than it would be for the actual Gauguin. This is not the case, however, since success and failure are not symmetrical in this regard. If successful-Gauguin had made a different decision, it would indeed have deprived him of his defining project. But making a different decision would not have had the same effect on failed-Gauguin. The reason for the asymmetry is that defining projects do not form complementary oppositional pairs. Specifically, while "painter" is a recognizable project, there is no corresponding project of "not painter," one that would play a defining role in most people's lives. To be sure, some people may turn failure into a vocation and a way of life. If failed-Gauguin were to wallow in his artistic failure and allow it to fester long enough, this could become his defining project. In that case the wish that he hadn't made the fateful decision would indeed become hollow.[22] But in the more likely scenario, realizing that being an artist is not in the cards, Gauguin would have turned to other pursuits, such as becoming a Parisian bank teller after all. Relative to such scenarios, the initial fateful decision to leave for Tahiti is eminently regrettable, seen as a source of gratuitous pain inflicted on family and friends.

F. Not many individuals are as clearly identified with a pervasive and all-consuming project as Gauguin, and even fewer make a move as dramatic and as consequential as his departure for Tahiti. The appeal of Gauguin's example lies precisely in providing a stark illustration of a constitutive decision that launches a defining project. But this appeal is also a limitation. How typical is Gauguin's case and how representative of the human condition as a whole? How valuable is the lesson it teaches us and how far does it generalize? The answer is that Gauguin amplifies important features present in other, more ordinary lives as well. First, even if one's life story is more diffuse, consisting of multiple themes and the product of numerous relatively inconsequential actions and decisions, it is a life *story* all the same. It might be easier to identify within such a story than in Gauguin's smaller projects and engagements, different relatively independent subplots as it were, that the agent might regret selectively and piecemeal. But the impossibility illustrated by Gauguin of wholesale regret, regret that in this case would purport to address a large concatenation of such fragments, remains. One cannot coherently wish away the life one has had in favor of another, regardless of the constituents and composition of one's life. Second, even piecemeal regret regarding relatively discrete junctures in one's life may be barred by similar considerations. Things are often intricately interconnected, and a seemingly inconsequential decision may turn out upon reflection to have led in fact to much of what has become of great significance to us. Our lives form a web, and by pulling in the spirit of regret on a marginal thread, the whole may unravel.

G. Though Gauguin's example thus amplifies a more general feature of human life, the fact that his is a decidedly simplified version raises another problem. In the absence of a dominant defining project, it becomes much more difficult to distinguish between identity-preserving and identity-disrupting counterfactuals, and correspondingly to devise a threshold of regret beyond which it loses its subject. Whatever the distinction and the threshold, we should not imagine them as clear-cut. The most we can do in this area is post some warning signs alerting people to a broad and ill-defined yet significant zone, in which certain attitudes that are perfectly intelligible outside of it lose their coherence.

IV. BEYOND LUCK AND REGRET

My account thus far supports Williams's main claim, asserting a connection between Gauguin's artistic success or failure and the possibility of regret. But since the grounds I have offered for this claim depart in certain ways from Williams's, some further implications of my account also differ from his. The difference concerns, in the first place, the issue of luck. I have argued earlier that Gauguin's case belongs to the category of constitutive luck, albeit of a consequential variety. Now, in designating an aspect or property of a person "constitutive," all one may mean is that this aspect or property is enduring and important. However, as used by Williams in regard to the sage, and as I have been using it in the present context, "constitutive" acquires a stronger sense. The term designates an aspect or property, or a cluster of aspects or properties, that forms a necessary component of the person's identity. It is doubtful that what is constitutive in this strong sense can be a matter of luck.

The reason for this doubt is simple. Luck is an evaluative term, pertaining to "the fortuitous happening of events favorable or unfavorable to the interests of a person."[23] So luck has to be ascribed to a subject, and implies an assessment, positive or negative, of an event relative to that subject and his or her interests. Accordingly, luck can be attributed only to a stable subject who retains his identity with and without the lucky event. But constitutive luck does not satisfy this condition. That one is who one is, is not a stroke of good luck or bad *for that person*; who else could one be? There is in this respect a close analogy between the logic of luck and of agent-regret. Similar considerations to the ones that tell against the possibility of agent-regret regarding a constitutive decision also weigh against viewing identity as a matter of luck.[24] Williams himself mentions the possibility that Gauguin presents a case of constitutive luck, adding that "it might be wondered whether that is *luck* at all."[25] Williams does not develop this thought, however, but goes on to point out that even if Gauguin's artistic accomplishments are due to constitutive luck, and so perhaps are not really a matter of luck, Gauguin is nevertheless the beneficiary of *epistemic luck*: the lucky circumstance of his having made a correct assessment of his artistic talent that made his project viable. My account removes this element of luck as well. On the constructive view, retrospectively, Gauguin's insight, determination, courage, as well as talent were all necessary for his artistic career, and so constitutive elements without which he would not have become the person that he was.

Why does it matter whether Gauguin's artistic career is to be seen as the product of luck? What is at stake? To answer this question, we need consider the denial that Gauguin is a beneficiary of luck in light of the substantive concerns that motivated Williams's exploration of luck in the first place. As was already mentioned, Williams associates the resistance to moral luck with Kant's effort to rid morality of luck, and then situates this effort within a broader context: an ancient aspiration to secure for people a measure of tranquility by keeping the vagaries of luck at bay. This is the sense in which the sage mentioned by Williams is a precursor of Kant's noumenal self. Now when the question of luck is posed in these terms, it turns out that the reasons that inhibit Gauguin's regret are, in respect of tranquility, equivalent to the denial of luck.

Many people, even those whose lives have gone reasonably well, can nonetheless recognize with hindsight numerous wrong turns and missed opportunities. Aware that this is the only life they have, they are unsettled by such recognitions, and by the ardent wish that things were otherwise, that they had taken a different turn. The line of thought I have suggested can serve as a palliative or antidote by reminding them (us) that these wishes and fantasies have their limit: they are constrained by the conditions of human identity. If the counterfactual reveries become extravagant and so exceed a certain threshold, they are no longer reveries about the agent himself and turn into the thought that someone else might have existed instead. The realization that one could not have been fundamentally different from what one has turned out to be is at the end of the day (and it is of importance that the thought is fully available only toward the end of the day) a source of a certain comfort and tranquility.

The measure of comfort and tranquility this realization can buy is limited, but then, relative to other contenders, it comes at a low price. Some strategies to remove luck so as to attain tranquility require radically narrowing the range of one's concerns by withdrawing into an austere and barren inner citadel; others involve a belief in some form of fatalism or predestination, which tends to induce a listless, resigned, "que sera, sera" mentality. By comparison, the identity-based, retrospective essentialism I have described provides its measure of tranquility, such as it is, on the cheap.[26] Prospectively, the future is open-ended and, up to a point, up to me. There is nothing in the constructive view to chill enthusiasm or ambition in the conduct of one's life and in the venture of self-constitution. Only in retrospect is the thought available that things could not have been radically different *for me*. To be sure, given that the thought awaits us toward the end of the road, we can anticipate it earlier on. But this, if anything, increases its value without the undesirable side effects. We still have every reason to make the best choices, knowing that they will determine how we live as well as who we are, but with some reduced anxiety: we also know that the forgone options will eventually lose their relevance to us, since they will one day merely be steps on someone else's hypothetical road. This anticipatory thought may accordingly allow us to borrow in advance against the fund of later-day, retrospective acceptance and tranquility and to some extent benefit from it without detriment to our choices and projects.

Whatever the degree of tranquility thus attained, however, tranquility is not the same as contentment or satisfaction, let alone happiness; its contrasting terms are agitation and turmoil rather than discontent, dissatisfaction, or unhappiness. This reminder is important not only to avoid false advertisement, but also because of its bearing on the matter of justification. As I've mentioned earlier, Williams treats Gauguin's inability to regret his decision as amounting to a measure of justification against the moral charges that can be brought against him. This justification proceeds from the agent's point of view, supposedly because this point of view provides a benchmark for a certain kind of criticism that is of special interest to Williams. By pointing out that a decision is defective in light of considerations that are available to the agent herself, so that she is in a good position to recognize the defect, we ascribe to the agent a failure of rationality of sorts; we are hoisting her by her own petard, so to speak. The inability to regret gives the agent a defense against this charge, since it negates the allegation that the decision falls short *by the agent's own lights*. Williams largely leaves open the specifically *moral* significance of this charge and this justification; neither does he give much guidance concerning the weight of this type of justification. Whatever his view on these issues might have been, it is worth pointing out that my proposed account further erodes the level of justification afforded by the inability to regret.

Gauguin's case is somewhat misleading in this regard. Since being a great artist is admirable, the constitutive considerations that prevent his regret coincide for him with a sense of satisfaction. But a defining project need not be laudable. We can imagine instead a lifelong swindler who in old age wakes up to the nastiness and wastefulness of his life. On the constructive view, he can regret his life no more than Gauguin could regret his. But this, one would think, does not give the swindler even the modicum of justification that Williams claims for Gauguin. The reason is that not wishing for an alternative to a state of affairs is not the same as approving of it. This obvious truth is sometimes obscured by a pervasive conception of choice as consisting in ranking the members of a choice-set in light of one's preferences, and then opting for the highest-ranking item. On this model all valuation is relative to the composition of the choice-set.[27] But this tends to efface a crucial experiential difference we all know firsthand between choosing from a set of good options and choosing from a set of bad ones. Though choosing the lesser evil is just as rational as choosing the greatest good, one's attitude to the outcome in the two choice situations is markedly different: a lesser evil is still an evil, and though one may be relieved that one is not burdened with an even worse situation, one should not be expected to like the result. When the swindler realizes that a life of probity he now values would not have been his, and concludes that the life he had is, broadly speaking, the only life he could have had (assuming that he is not so desperate as to prefer not to have existed at all),[28] he is not bound to approve of his life and judge it worthy. Inability to regret is one thing, approval, satisfaction, contentment, another. As we saw, regret involves a past-oriented wish for an alternative state of affairs to the actual one. And since the wish is unsatisfiable, one is unsettled by an enduring frustration that cannot be relieved. The line of thinking I have described extinguishes in the swindler's case any such wish and so removes the frustration and the agitation, leaving, however, room for a cooler and more somber disapproving stance.[29] This is true of Gauguin as well. As we can now see, the fact that he may not coherently regret his decision does not imply that he need approve of it. He too may realize that this decision was responsible for what he has become, and so not regret it, while also recognizing that his life, successful in some respects as it was, imposed on others unjustified costs.

Finally, the swindler brings us back to moral luck. The issue of moral luck typically arises when the fortuitous consequences of a decision are deemed relevant to its moral assessment by aggravating or mitigating the agent's blame. Such instances of (arguably) moral luck are ubiquitous so long as the decisions and the consequences have a relatively limited significance within the agent's life. The main interest in the swindler's and by analogy Gauguin's case is that they draw attention to a different kind of assessment in which constitutive elements of a person's life are put on the scales. Such a case presents us with a standpoint beyond regret and, for corresponding reasons, beyond luck, but one that is well within the scope of morality. Since a person's constitution or identity is not a matter of luck, when the target of moral assessment involves constitutive elements, luck drops out of the picture. This conclusion of course doesn't help us cope with the problem of moral luck when it does arise. But given the intractability of the problem,[30] it is welcome news that its scope is somewhat narrower than we may tend to think.

PART II

Value and Humanity

5

Individuals, Citizens, Persons

In discussing the interplay between norms and their subjects, individual and collective, my main emphasis thus far has been on the role of norms in the construction (and revision) of subjects. I now shift attention to the norms themselves by inquiring into what their involvement in the construction of their subjects can teach us not just about those subjects but also about the norms. In pursuit of this agenda, the present chapter casts a wide net. The aim is to draw from the meaning-conception of self that I have introduced earlier some implications for the general shape of the practical domain, a domain consisting of the totality of norms concerned with guiding our behavior and shaping our life. I call this all-inclusive field *ethics*. So understood, ethics comprises two prominent subfields, morality and law. It also includes a third: the less commonly recognized yet highly significant domain of prudence, which consists of norms guiding us toward the accomplishment of our individual aims. In discussing ethics, I begin by inquiring about law. Exploring law's claim on us, what I call its normative grip, reveals it to be intermediate, in a sense to be explained, between the two other clusters of ethical norms, moral and prudential. Recognizing in this way law's intermediate position offers in the first place a clue to the kind of authority law itself ordinarily claims. More importantly, situating law between prudence and morality suggests a picture of how all three branches of ethics relate to each other, as well as the way they all relate to their common subject, the human self. As is obvious, all this adds up to a rather tall order, and in this chapter I make in its pursuit only some preliminary and tentative comments.

I. THE POLITICAL QUESTION

It is commonly believed that countries, their governments, and their laws make at least a prima facie normative claim on citizens. To be sure, attitudes to one's country, its government, and its law may diverge, and each raises some distinctive philosophical issues of its own: under the heading of patriotism, philosophers explore the general, mostly affective attitude to the country; political philosophers tend to focus on the question of the government's authority; and legal philosophy is centrally concerned with the duty to obey the law. But though separable, these issues are closely related. Ordinarily, a vital aspect of allegiance to one's country is acknowledging its government's authority, and law is by far the most significant medium through which that authority is exercised. The divergent issues that arise in this area have a common core: we are expected to pay some heed to our country's interests by, in part, accepting its government's authority, an acceptance manifested in part in a disposition to obey the law. What grip, if any, does this composite claim have on us? Call this *the political question*.

In one form or another, the political question has occasioned over time mountains of writings. Under these mountains, however, is buried a simple if dispiriting truth: we are no closer to a satisfactory answer than we have been before. Philosophers who till these fields have their employment secure. In these circumstances, adding yet another molehill to the landscape may seem foolhardy or worse. However, my aim in engaging with this question is not to offer a better answer, since the aim is not to provide an answer at all. It is rather to use this question as the vantage point for an imaginative reconstruction, partial and simplified, of the normative terrain as a whole. The results are the rudiments of a theory, guided by an old insight that goes back at least as far as Plato: that social and political arrangements are refracted in, and are a refraction of, the structure of the human self; to study the one is to study the other.

Two preliminary points. First, the political question arises with particular acuity with respect to an unjust state. "My country, right or wrong" is a well-known, and for many, notorious, sentiment. But we must also query allegiance to a just state. Our obligations to our own political system are supposedly different from our obligations to other systems, no matter how just these other systems may be. The fact that any given country, government, or law is just does not by itself bind us to them in the way in which we are supposed to be bound to our own. Second, the political question is a quest for justification. Such a quest does not arise in a void. Justification usually proceeds as an attempt to silence some qualms or reply to putative or actual opponents. Allegiance to the state, political authority, and law's bindingness need to be justified. Why? A common answer fixes on the state's coerciveness, since coercion by itself is presumptively bad. But coercion is not my primary concern. In focusing on normativity, I mean to attend to an aspect of the state, its government, and law that is independent of coercion, and, if anything, is antithetical to it. The state's and so the law's normativity consist in an appeal to voluntary allegiance and compliance. The political question is an invitation to assess this appeal quite apart from the fact that the state is in a position to enforce it. What challenge other than coercion gives rise to the political question and guides the efforts to answer it?

It is instructive that there are in fact two prominent challenges, diametrically opposed: one associated with an individual, self-regarding standpoint, the other with a universal, other-regarding standpoint. Seen from the individual's standpoint the question is, why should I assume the burdens the state seeks to impose on me and accept the setback to my own interests it often demands? From the other standpoint the question is, why do my political community's claims get priority over similar claims of other people or humanity as a whole? Each of the two opposing perspectives is commonly tied to a normative orientation of its own: individual self-interest defines the domain of prudence, whereas the universal concerns are the turf of morality. The political question accordingly arises between the prudential and the moral, and is answerable to both.

That the challenges to the state's normative claims come from two opposing directions is sometimes obscured by the fact that the same idiom, of autonomy, is used to express both challenges: being subjected to the state's authority and deferring to its demands is allegedly inimical to one's autonomy. But here the polarity is hidden by an ambiguity in these claims between *personal* and *moral* autonomy. Roughly, personal autonomy concerns a person's ability to carry out her wishes and desires and so advance her interests. Moral autonomy, at least as interpreted by Kant, is a matter of acting on universally valid principles one endorses.[1] The charge that political authority and the law threaten autonomy can accordingly amount either to the claim that they restrict people's capacity to pursue their own goals, or that they displace the universal principles that as moral agents people otherwise endorse.

Given the two polar challenges, it is not surprising that answers to the political question should often consist in efforts to account for the state's normative claims in one of two opposite ways, arguing either that these claims arise out of self-regarding individual concerns and are congruent with them, or else that they are the implications of a universal morality and part of it. This is not the place to canvass the voluminous literature, other than to comment that the very volume and endurance of the two contrasting lines of thought raise some doubt that either is fully satisfactory. In any case, there is a prima facie phenomenological objection to both reductionist accounts, as unable to capture the experience of the political domain as a *distinctive* site of normative considerations, marked precisely by their failure to neatly align with the self-regarding/other-regarding divide. For example, some people pay their taxes resentfully, betraying a conflict between their self-regarding wish to keep the money and the state's demands. The same people may feel personally offended and outraged when their country's embassy is attacked or flag burned. The state's claims seem in this way to belong to a large and variegated category of what appear to be *intermediate* interests (values, attitudes) and their associated reasons and norms, which cannot be classified clearly and stably either as one's own or as those of others. Although a satisfactory answer to the political question would have to meet both the prudential and the moral challenges to the state's normative claims, the answer also needs to account for the perceived distinctiveness of these claims, rather than collapsing them into one pole or the other.

I have mentioned that the twin challenges to the state's normative claims are sometimes phrased in the idiom of autonomy, either moral or personal. Here, too, the apparently intermediate location of the political between the individual and the universal can be observed, confounding the binary division. Autonomy is self-government, and a state's sovereignty is the realization of a people governing itself. Who, however, is the referent of this reflexive expression? It may appear that I have already answered the question in the course of posing it by designating "the people" for that role. But the history of political philosophy is in part the record of pursuing two radically different interpretations of this answer and of coping, inconclusively, with the difficulties to which each of them leads. "The people" either labels an aggregate of individuals, or a single entity, existing over and above the group of individual members. Both answers, however, create a rift between the self-government of the state and the autonomy of its individual members: each individual is governed by a group of other individuals in the one case, or by an independent collective entity in the other. In neither case does the reflexive subject of self-government coincide with the individual self. But here too familiar facts appear to belie this picture. In the name of national self-determination, people often favor a more oppressive regime of their own over a more benign foreign rule. In doing so, they experience themselves as promoting their own autonomy rather than that of some third party, be it other individuals or an impersonally perceived collective entity.

It is possible, of course, to dismiss all such attitudes that people exhibit toward their country as deluded and wrongheaded. But even if this were one's verdict, it would make better sense to reach it on substantive rather than conceptual grounds. We should be hesitant to diagnose large segments of human history as displaying a *conceptual* error. The reluctance stems in part from the explanatory paucity of such an account. Given how pervasive the attitudes in question are, an adequate account, even if it does not justify these attitudes, should tell us something about what prompts and sustains them. Ascribing to people a conceptual error that renders their attitudes senseless or incoherent is unlikely to meet this goal. It would be more fruitful to try to maintain conceptual room for political autonomy, seen as a genuine and distinct possibility, even if we denounce on substantive grounds its supposed realizations.

II. THE MORAL QUESTION

When the political question is raised, and the state's normative claims are brought before the court of morality, this court's jurisdiction is for the most part taken for granted. That the political question arises between two contrasting poles—of prudence and morality—reminds us, however, of the challenge that the self-interested individual poses not just to the state and its law but to morality as well. For this individual, keen to advance her interests and satisfy her desires, morality presumes to stand in the way. Why would the individual care about its demands? How are we to understand morality's grip in possible derogation of our own interests and desires? In Kant's well-known formulation, how is morality possible? Call this *the moral question*. Clearly, our answer to the political question must be linked to our answer to the moral question.

Adding the moral question to the political question, while compounding difficulties, also provides a clue. Both questions must respond to the same challenge, posed by the self-regarding individual. Given the similarity between the two questions and the common challenge they face, strategies for coping with the moral question may be employed in coping with the political question too. One response to the moral question, of which Kant's own moral theory is a prime example, resorts to abstraction. Since morality purports to speak in a single voice to or on behalf of individuals whose interests and desires potentially conflict, it presumably requires a unitary standpoint, occupied by every human being. Abstraction paves the way. By abstracting from actual, concrete individuals, their interests and desires, we efface differences and construct a single platform on which they all stand. In Kant's case this feat is accomplished by means of the noumenal self, characterized exclusively by the possession of a rational will, and by the uplifting image of a Kingdom of Ends, a forum in which abstractly conceived noumenal selves spell out the practical implications of their shared humanity.[2]

It is instructive to note that the most influential recent engagement with the political question, that of John Rawls, purports to follow Kant in this regard. Since Rawls considers justice to be the primary virtue of political institutions, his response to the political question takes the form of a procedure for constructing a society's constitution, laws, and institutions that embody sound principles of justice. Rawls explicitly models his procedure on Kant's approach to the moral question.[3] The participants in the original position, a forum analogous to the Kingdom of Ends, are abstracted from actual human beings by means of the veil of ignorance, and so reach principles of justice in their shared capacity as citizens, oblivious to distinguishing characteristics and conflicting ends that keep them apart.

On a closer look, however, Rawls's use of abstraction turns out to be at once too timorous and excessive in ways that help reveal some of the broader issues involved. To appreciate the first weakness, we need to compare Rawls's theory to Kant's. Despite their surface similarity, the approaches are fundamentally different, exposing a crucial ambiguity in the notion of abstraction and its relationship to the self. In employing abstraction, Kant is making a metaphysical claim. His moral theory is grounded in a bifurcated metaphysics that distinguishes between the world of appearances—that is, the world as it appears to creatures with the particular perceptual and cognitive capacities that human beings happen to possess—and the world as it exists apart from humans' perception of it, the world of things-in-themselves. People belong to both domains. As phenomenal selves they belong to the world of appearances, in which psychological *inclinations* participate in the same system of perceptual and cognitive capacities by means of which all of human reality is constructed. Qua noumenal selves, however, they are things-in-themselves, to which ex hypothesi they have no experiential access. We can, however, use our philosophical imagination to project on this blank screen the aspects of our moral condition that the phenomenal self cannot by itself accommodate. Specifically, we can view moral reasons as applying to us as noumenal selves and motivating us in this capacity.[4]

Post-Kantian philosophy, however, is generally averse to this bifurcated metaphysics, and at any rate Rawls abjures it. Cut off from such metaphysical moorings, Rawls's abstraction differs fundamentally from Kant's. Unlike the Kingdom of Ends and its noumenal inhabitants, the original position is a *hypothetical* meeting of *imaginary* representatives, whose characteristics purport to be nothing more than theoretical stipulation. The original position and its abstract inhabitants accordingly play a much more attenuated role in answering the political question than the Kingdom of Ends and the noumenal self play in answering the moral. The normative force of the principles of justice and of the laws and institutions they generate comes from outside the theoretical devices Rawls employs. He appeals from the start to people who are assumed to possess a sense of justice; the original position serves only as a heuristic device designed to instruct them about what justice, to which they are independently committed, requires.[5] But appealing in this way to a sense of justice is unsatisfactory. If we are puzzled about the source of our alleged commitment even toward a just state, positing a sense of justice that accommodates such a commitment from the start is too ad hoc, and does little to solve the puzzle.

Rawls's abstraction is also excessive for the task he undertakes. Depriving the participants in the original position of all individuating characteristics is designed to replicate Kant's subject of morality, the noumenal self. But what would stop such an abstract self from assuming a universal perspective? Why would its interest in justice and the scope of the principles it adopts be confined to domestic institutions and apply only to citizens of a single state? This indeed is the gist of the critique that communitarians launch against Rawls. On the communitarian view, only a "situated" self, thickly constituted by communal norms and practices, can sustain the burdens of communal life and exhibit the other-regarding concerns that justice mandates.[6]

But this communitarian critique of Rawls's position, and the alternative it presents to liberalism's abstract strain, raise difficulties of their own. First, by privileging the community and its norms, the communitarian position militates against a universal morality, and weighs instead in favor of moral relativism that many, including some communitarians, find unappealing. Second, when the communitarian trains her critique on Kantian abstraction, she tends to downplay the individualist challenge to which the political question must also respond. After all, the communitarian's situated self isn't quite the concrete, prudential self either. The integration of the individual into the community denoted by the "situated" conception of self risks displacing not only the universal standpoint of morality but also the unique standpoint of the individual and its normative significance. I consider these next.

III. THE PRUDENTIAL QUESTION

In contemplating both the moral and the political question, the self-regarding individual provides the natural, taken-for-granted point of departure, posing a seemingly obvious challenge with which morality and law must contend. The claims of morality and of law are commonly perceived as *demands* made on the individual, and so her responding to them is deemed in need of explanation in a way that her pursuing her own interests is not. Removing your hand from a burning stove is easily explained in terms that don't seem to apply to your pulling someone else's hand from harm's way. Nothing corresponding to the heavy machinery of morality or law that comes into play in the latter case seems to be involved in the former. Your own sharp pain does all the motivating as well as explanatory work.

But even this simple example reveals a difficulty in the notion of the self-interested individual and in the normative challenge it is taken to present. To act in a self-interested manner is not the same as to act on impulse, instinct, or whim. Much as you're inclined to escape an occurrent pain, prudence might require that you endure it, say, for medical reasons. Removing one's hand from the fire is explained by the fact that the fire hurts. But when you refrain from doing so on account of prospects of greater future pain, we need an altogether different account, since unlike occurrent pain, future pain does not hurt. Why would you resist present desires or assume burdens on behalf of a future self?[7] Call this *the prudential question*.

This question too can be posed in the idiom of autonomy. I have earlier mentioned the distinction between personal and moral autonomy, and suggested that political autonomy represents a distinctive category intermediate between the two. But what does personal autonomy amount to, and what does it have in common with moral autonomy? A possible answer invokes Kant's distinction between psychological inclinations and rationality. Just as moral autonomy is a matter of subjecting psychological promptings to the discipline and oversight of a universal standpoint that encompasses humanity as a whole, personal autonomy requires subjecting those same promptings to similar control from a standpoint representing one's life as a whole. Juxtaposing the alleviation of one's own occurrent pain to that of someone else's conflates two different issues: the contrast between the self-regarding and the other-regarding with the contrast between inclination and rationality. To exhibit personal autonomy requires that one submit one's psychological inclinations, even when self-regarding, to a regime of prudence that resembles in this respect the regime that governs other-regarding concerns as well. The addict, for example, has cravings for narcotic drugs, and yet to be autonomous he must comply with prudential considerations that mandate that these cravings be resisted. How are we to understand this regime and the autonomy it enables?

Not only are these serious puzzles, but they resemble the ones raised by law and morality. When considering the political question and the moral question, we saw how abstraction can provide the requisite unitary perspective, universal in one case, communal in the other. Abstraction from what? The natural answer presumes a concrete individual, whose properties are fully determinate and given. But reflection on the problem of prudence discloses that no such individual exists. A temporally unified individual must be *constructed* in light of some template, idea, or plan. Here too unity must be *imposed* on an endless experiential manifold and an equally unruly menu of potential responses and acts. And here, too, abstraction is the route to the unity we seek. As we have just seen, prudence can be every bit as demanding and cumbersome as morality and law. The difference is that when, as in our example, prudence requires that I sustain some occurrent pain, it points to my self-interest (say, in a medical procedure) and so it speaks on behalf of my own future self. But as we have also noted, this future self is an abstraction, and to give its claims priority over the present suffering self I must espouse a position of spatiotemporal neutrality between the two; I must subsume the occurrent experience and the immediate urge to withdraw from the pain within the same abstraction that includes the future promise of health or other enjoyment or relief. In short, no less than the other branches of ethics—morality and law—prudence too depends on abstraction; it requires, if you like, a veil of ignorance of its own.

We can draw two lessons from these remarks. One concerns the crucial role that abstraction plays even at the level of the individual and indeed in constituting one. The second is that the abstraction in the case of prudence is not the same abstraction employed in the case of either morality or law. Prudence would seem to require that we introduce yet another abstract conception of the self, a conception that would now be in competition with both the universal abstraction of the noumenal self and the communal abstraction of the situated self.

IV. THE ABSTRACT SELF

We have started our discussion by attending to the political question: why should we obey the law or recognize the authority of the state is a familiar and persistent challenge. As it turns out, however, an adequate answer to the political question must do more than assess the claims of the state in moral and prudential terms, since these two domains pull in opposite directions, and are themselves under a similar shadow of doubt. An answer to the political question must be part of a more general account that encompasses morality and prudence as well. We have also considered attempts to account for each of the three normative domains we've distinguished in terms of a corresponding abstract conception of self. But some formidable difficulties arise, of which three are particularly salient.

The first concerns the relationship among these conceptions. To align each of the various normative standpoints (universal, communal, individual) and their correlative normative orientations (morality, law, prudence) with a suitable conception of self is to replay the tension among the normative domains as a conflict among conceptions of self, and so does not bring us any closer to a unified account. The second difficulty concerns each of the accounts that an appeal to abstraction is expected to provide for its respective domain. It is natural to speak in this connection about an abstract conception of self. But this locution conjures up a certain imagery in which the abstraction is a mere *representation* of something else. This imagery comes into play, since the notion of an abstract conception of self is naturally construed in light of the broader idea of "an abstract conception of X," in which X is implicitly taken to be some concrete material object, such as an elephant or a chair. And obviously, only representations of such objects can be more or less abstract, not the objects themselves. A drawing or description of an elephant may render it in various degrees of resolution and detail, and so be more or less abstract. But it makes no sense to talk about a more or less abstract version of Jumbo itself. Now if abstraction relates to human beings as to elephants, then human beings cannot be any more abstract than Jumbo can. On this view, and as our discussion of Rawls illustrates, abstraction can yield only hypothetical representations of human beings, thereby creating a gap between the unitary normative standpoint that abstraction is expected to create, and the concrete individuals that are supposed to occupy this standpoint. Unless we suppose in each case that people are already disposed from the start to act prudentially, or legally, or morally, in what way does an abstract representation help account for the normative grip that each of these domains is supposed to exert? Why should any of us care for one or another *representation* of ourselves? Finally, the third challenge that a unified account of ethics faces results from the exclusivity or comprehensiveness that each of the domains appears to claim. Morality, law, and prudence, each claims authority over human life as a whole, at least in the sense of being in charge of defining over which issues each has a final say. This suggests an apparently inescapable conflict that a unified account would be hard put to resolve.

The key to the response I propose requires that we reconceive the relationship of abstraction to self. Instead of a competition among variously abstract representations of self, we need to think of a single conception of self *as abstract*. On this conception, abstraction pertains to the actual self, rather than being a property of its representations, so that different levels of abstraction can be all internal to the self. This conception of self is implicit in the meaning-oriented, constructivist approach to the self we've discussed in previous chapters, and in the traditions of thought on which we have already drawn: it is the view of the self as an ordered configuration of meanings, for which the literary and dramaturgical imageries provide some familiar templates. Such literary and dramaturgical analogies alter our understanding of the way abstraction relates to human beings. In the case of physical objects there is a clear distinction between the object and its representation, for example, Jumbo and a drawing or description of it. In the case of literary objects, this distinction is effaced. The point can be made succinctly in terms of the two different uses of the verb "tell," intransitive and transitive. In telling me *about* a physical object, an elephant or a car, you provide a description of the object or an account of it. The description or the account is external to the object: in describing the car, you don't give me the car or any part of it. But when it comes to literary objects, *tell* can be used transitively. To tell a story or a joke is not to describe but to *transcribe* it; it is to convey to the listener the very story or joke that is the subject matter of the telling. Telling a story, transcribing it, can be performed at various levels of abstraction or detail. Suppose that I ask you to tell me the story of *Macbeth*, and you oblige with a synopsis. This may be fully responsive to my request. Whether the level of abstraction of your narration is adequate will depend on such contextual considerations as the degree of my curiosity or whether I am in a rush, and such considerations may call for greater abstraction as much as for more detail. Just as interpretation can add detail to a story without changing it, a synopsis gives us a shortened version of it. Different renditions of a story that vary in level of abstraction are equally *versions* of the story itself.

In addition to such "vertical" differences among versions in level of abstraction, versions can also diverge "horizontally," when they differ in some of their detail, for example, the story of *Faust* as rendered by Marlowe, Goethe, Lessing, Heine, and Mamet. In what sense are they all, despite their differences, versions of a single story? Here too the answer lies in abstraction. Since increased abstraction effaces differences among the versions, at a higher level of abstraction the different versions merge into a single story, whereas at lower levels of abstraction (or higher levels of resolution) the differences among the versions appear. By the same token, when we think of the self as abstract, the content or meaning constitutive of the self can also range over various levels of abstraction. Distinguishing characteristics that appear at lower levels of abstraction are effaced at higher levels, and so interpersonal commonalities and unities appear.

This point can also be made in terms of the dramaturgical imagery. Many of the roles constitutive of our identities are nested: a cardiologist and a dermatologist are both physicians. In what sense do they occupy different roles and in what sense one and the same? As in the case of the different versions of the same story, roles too can diverge at lower levels of abstraction and converge at a higher level. Now as we further ascend the ladder of abstraction, we reach the idea of a *person* understood in terms of the convergent abstract content of all human lives. When, moving in the opposite direction, we descend the ladder of abstraction, and increase resolution, individuals come into view. As we have seen earlier, to be an individual also involves abstraction, though the level of resolution is much greater (or, conversely, the level of abstraction lower) than that pertaining to being a person. Individuals enact or realize at a high level of specificity, and therefore in vastly ramified and divergent ways, a singular meaning or content that pertains to all persons as such.

Person and *individual* thus label the two polar extremes on a spectrum of abstraction over which the self ranges. This spectrum contains innumerable intermediate levels, such as those occupied by the role of cardiologist and physician just mentioned. But here we need draw a further distinction. Both *person* and *individual* are comprehensive terms, in that at their respective levels of abstraction they each pertain to a human being as a whole, whereas *cardiologist* and *physician* are partial, pertaining to some aspects of their bearer's identity but not to others. In addition to such terms referring to partial roles, however, there is logical room for a comprehensive term that applies to a human being as a whole, but at an intermediate level of abstraction. *Citizen* is such a term.[8] To be French, for example, is to be constituted by a concatenation of meanings that at a suitable level of abstraction defines a common identity of being French. These three terms—individual, citizen, person—accordingly designate the same human being conceived at different levels of abstraction: *individual* alludes to a cluster of meanings unique to her, *citizen* to meanings she shares with the other members of a political community, and *person* to the more abstract content shared by every human being as such.

V. ANSWERING THE QUESTIONS

We can now combine this conception of self as abstract with the tripartite division of ethics discussed earlier. On the resulting picture, the three subdivisions of ethics—prudence, law, and morality—relate to us in the same kind of way: morality defines in part what a person is, thereby helping constitute the common identity of all human beings; law defines in part what a citizen is, thereby helping constitute the common identity of, say, the Brazilians or the French; and prudence defines in part what each individual is, thereby helping constitute each individual's unique identity. Since the three branches of ethics correspond to different levels of abstraction of the self, they represent points on a continuum rather than standing for a disjunction or an opposition. Even so, they can each be loosely associated with a different value or goal. Applying to people at the highest level of abstraction, morality upholds dignity, the value all persons have qua human beings. Law spells out the more specific requirements of justice among the members of a political community. Prudence, operating at an even greater level of specificity, at which each individual's particular experiences come into view and take pride of place, is oriented toward the individual's happiness. Acting in one's capacities as an individual, a citizen, and a person, one acts, respectively, prudently, legally, and morally, and so one pursues happiness, realizes justice, and respects dignity.

This picture suggests straightforward answers to the questions regarding the practical domain we have raised. First, to see morality, law, and prudence as operating at various levels of abstraction explains how each of them can apply to one's life as a whole, without being in necessary conflict with the others. Since they are each other's abstractions, or in reverse order, each other's elaborations, each of these normative systems can claim exclusive dominion over the self's corresponding level of abstraction, consistent with recognizing the others' exclusivity at other levels. This picture also relieves the pressure to divide all interests, reasons, attitudes, and the like into self-regarding and other-regarding. This binary division is replaced by a continuum of increasing abstraction and correspondingly greater convergence of content, a continuum of which the unique individual and humanity as a whole are the two extreme poles. Political reasons (attitudes, etc.) pertain to intermediate levels of abstraction, which create smaller clusters of partial convergences of content, and hence more limited pockets of solidarity than the entire human race. Finally, the tripartite division of autonomy into personal, political, and moral also finds its place. Autonomy at all three levels involves subjecting impulse to norm. The norm must be internal, though, rather than externally imposed. But to be internal it need not be, indeed it cannot be, invented by the agent or pulled out of thin air. Rather, a norm is internal insofar as it fits, at a suitable level of abstraction, within the structure of meanings that defines the agent as an individual, a citizen, or a person, or, to put the same point differently, insofar as the agent identifies with it, or endorses it, as an element within the overall structure of meanings she enacts. Within this picture, the subject of the self-government exercised by the state, and hence of political autonomy, is not an aggregate of individuals, nor is it an impersonal collective entity, but rather each citizen, abstractly conceived.

VI. IDEAL AND REALITY

As I indicated at the outset, this sketch is preliminary and raises more questions than it answers. But I find it generally appealing, and thus, the questions it raises worth pursuing, both for the unitary conception it offers of what otherwise are often treated as disparate phenomena, and for the link to what seems to me an independently attractive conception of self. These gains, if such they are, were yielded to a large degree by the starting point: conceiving of law (and the political) as intermediate between morality and prudence, and correlatively, conceiving of citizenship as intermediate between (universal) personhood and individuality. But this starting point, despite its appealing theoretical yield, is troublesome. I conclude this chapter by airing some doubts in this respect.

The preceding account of citizenship, and relatedly of law and the state, is highly idealized, in two senses. The first is in the Weberian sense of an ideal type. By highlighting certain salient features of a segment of our experience, we get a schematic representation that exhibits what is arguably an inner logic that connects various aspects of that experience. Such a model can serve as a methodological baseline or template in light of which the relevant range of real-life phenomena can be studied and assessed. But the proposed account also presents an ideal in a more substantive sense, as something attractive and appealing. It does so in two related ways. One is by showing that some conflicts and tradeoffs we experience among various normative claims made on us are not necessary; in an ideal world, we might eat some cakes and have them too. The other is by holding out a vision of a harmony within the self in the form of a narrative unity among various levels of abstraction that merges the demands of humanity, community, and individuality into a coherent whole.

Such ruminations, however, are too utopian to guide our aspirations, and are better seen as reminders of how far we fall short. Clarifying an ideal, and so increasing awareness of how remote it is, may rather serve as a caveat against delusion and as a bulwark against wishful thinking. Given the human propensity to mix reality with fantasy, we should remain ever vigilant in drawing the line between the two. One way of doing so is to retain a robust grasp on reality, but another is to spell out the fantasy. In either way we improve our capacity to tell which is which. In this concluding section I accordingly indicate some of the idealizations the previous account indulges, and the ways they affect where we stand relative to this account.

To begin with, in posing the political question I have followed a common usage by associating it with talk of a political community. But such talk is not innocuous. As indicated in Chapter 1, the term *community*, no matter how broadly and loosely used, does not designate the entire array of social formations, and contrasts with other collective terms such as *bureaucracy* and *organization*.[9] Formulating the political question in the idiom of community accordingly loads the dice from the start in favor of certain values and ideas—concerning bonds of culture, tradition, history, and language among citizens—that do not apply in the case of many states. It is in light of such "thick" bonds that citizenship can plausibly designate a *comprehensive* identity. When such factors are missing or fractured, citizenship is no longer a sufficiently significant source of meaning to unify the citizens and secure their solidarity. But even relatively homogenous countries do not entirely fit the image of community. We often encounter the state as a vast bureaucracy or, perhaps more accurately, as a conglomerate of bureaucracies—formal, impersonal, and instrumental. Such social formations exhibit a mechanical, functional unity that is a far cry from the enactment of shared communal meanings. Even when governmental organizations are harnessed in the service of communal goals, they have well-documented tendencies to depart from those goals, develop their own interests, and become self-aggrandizing and self-perpetuating. They create a very different environment, and call for a different set of attitudes, than those suggested by the idiom of community.

These aspects of states bear directly on another cardinal idealization in the account I have proposed. It concerns our supposed identification with our role as citizens. Identification labels the integration of the role within the self, and so is crucial to the location of the norms governing the role as internal to us and so as constituents of our autonomy. But as we have noted earlier (in Chapter 1), not all social roles are integrated in this way. Some are enacted in a detached, impersonal, and strategic manner; we engage in them only due to some external inducement, a threat or a reward, but otherwise maintain them outside the scope of our identifications and on the periphery of the self. When citizenship is conceived in the context of the state's bureaucratic persona, it becomes such a detached role; we enact it in interaction with alien, impersonal forces, and we respond in kind.

This finally brings us to the most radical idealization in my account. I have formulated the political question as an inquiry into the state's normativity, leaving coercion aside. The state's normativity consists in part in an appeal to its citizens that they obey its laws. Some believe that this appeal must always be resisted; autonomy requires no less.[10] I have tried to show that under some conditions, allegiance to the state and a disposition to obey its laws may be an expression of political autonomy, on a par with one's personal and moral autonomy. But the state is a quintessentially coercive agency. Its normative appeal is backed by sanctions. This fact too militates against identification with the citizen role, and introduces a rift between obedience and autonomy. The real enemy of autonomy is not the state's demand for loyalty, nor the law's demand for obedience, but the enforcement of these demands by coercive means.[11]

Two aspects of coercive enforcement are of critical importance here, its logic and its scope. The logic of coercion is somewhat disguised by the fact that enforcement is never fully effective, and so leaves room for people's discretionary behavior. But this state of affairs counts as an imperfection and a failure, or else the product of various exogenous constraints on the exercise of coercion, such as the retributive considerations that ordinarily limit the permissible severity of criminal sanctions. The logic of coercion does not by itself allow for such leeway. By using coercive threats, government does not merely seek to provide its subjects with an additional reason for compliance. To be coercive, the avowed purpose of the threat must be to bring about the commanded behavior independently of the agent's own values and desires. The scope of coercion may also mislead, by appearing more limited than it is: after all, are not only those who violate the law actually put in jail? But this impression also misses the point. The main strategy of legal enforcement is deterrence, that is, coercive threats. And these are not selective; they address everyone, the good and the bad, with the same invidious message: obey, or else.

These features of coercion bear directly on the nature of citizenship. Inviting someone's voluntary obedience, as the normative face of law purportedly does, only to back up this invitation with coercive threats designed to secure compliance irrespective, renders the initial appeal disingenuous. Relatedly, the state's pretense to respect its citizens' autonomy is to this extent a sham. By supplying a wholesale, decisive, external motivation for carrying out citizenship's obligations, a motivation that bypasses or overrides the agent's own will (informed as her will may be by this very same role's script), coercion acts as an alienating factor, disrupts identification, and casts the citizen's role as pro tanto distant and detached. The result is to sunder full identification with the citizen role, and render a certain ideal of citizenship and its location within the self practically unattainable.

This is for the most part a negative conclusion; but we can also glimpse its more positive, if somewhat paradoxical, complement. When state coercion crosses a certain threshold and registers as oppression, it may provoke the subversive display of a community spirit, a common enactment of a suitably abstract self, guided by what is sometimes referred to as "higher law." Such public reaction is designed to drain the existing government's pronouncements of their putative authority, and instead expose or perhaps rather constitute them as mere "positive law" exclusively sustained by brute force. Counterpoised to the detached citizenship of ordinary times, we find at such moments the realization of a kind of citizenship that comes closer to unifying loyalty to the political community with loyalty to oneself, and gives fuller expression to an ideal of political autonomy than is otherwise the case. This is possibly one reason why despite great individual hardships, such times of upheaval can present their protagonists with some of their finer moments.

Two further conclusions follow. One is to somewhat chill enthusiasm toward an idea, favored by some, of world citizenship supposedly tied to a global government. Since such a government is bound to be both bureaucratic and coercive, the previous considerations alert us to the danger that it would tend to fracture our humanity and alienate us from it, and so from morality. A similar conclusion applies to the other end of the spectrum of abstraction where individuality is at stake. At issue are paternalistic laws, such as those seeking to regiment people's dietary or sexual practices for, say, health-related reasons. These laws amount to the enforcement of prudence, and so pose the corresponding danger of fracturing our individuality and distancing or alienating us from segments of it as well.

6

Dignity and Self-Creation

The previous chapter examined the general shape of the practical domain, suggesting a division of ethics into three branches—morality, law, and prudence—each corresponding to a different level of abstraction of the self, designated respectively as *person, citizen,* and *individual.* In this chapter I focus on one part of this picture, morality, and relatedly on the notion of person, which signifies the most abstract, and so the universal, aspect of human identity. As already indicated, linking morality to such an abstract self is one of Kant's central ideas, as is his related conception of human dignity as the core or foundational value for a universal morality. But human dignity is of course not an exclusively Kantian notion, and though I engage mostly with Kant's views, I link them to some other sources, in the interest of exploring the relationship between a dignity-based morality and the constructive, meaning-oriented conception of self I introduced in earlier chapters.

I. WHY DIGNITY

The notion of human dignity has a long history, much of which precedes the writings of Kant, and some of which I mention later on. But Kant's writings are by far the most influential attempt to formulate a moral theory grounded in this notion. Kant's influence on liberal moral philosophy has to be seen against the backdrop of the dominance of utilitarianism and as an antidote to it. Part of the critique of utilitarianism targets its welfarism and juxtaposes it to a Kantian view that valorizes individual autonomy. But even a casual reader of the legal and the philosophical literature will have noticed a significant shift from autonomy-talk to dignity-talk that has been taking shape in recent years on the deontological side of the normative divide, with an increasing emphasis on respect for persons as the preeminent concern. Seen in this context, the merits of a dignity-based morality are to be assessed not only as against those of a welfare-based utilitarian approach but also as against those of an autonomy-based Kantian approach. I do not conduct a full-scale inquiry to establish the superiority of the dignity-based view in these regards, but discuss one example, that of slavery, to illustrate some of the difficulties that a focus on either welfare or autonomy as the foundational moral value encounters. This invites, even if it doesn't quite mandate, a consideration of dignity as an appealing foundational value on the basis of which a moral theory can be constructed.

The institution of slavery has long served in the liberal literature as a stock anti-utilitarian example and as a demonstration of the merits of a deontological approach. The challenge that slavery poses to any moral theory comes from a pretheoretical conviction that slavery is a paradigm of injustice, and that the opposition to it is categorical rather than contextual and contingent. It has been often maintained that utilitarian moral theory fails this test. One way in which slavery serves as a counterexample to utilitarianism is by targeting its aggregative aspect: as long as enough people are sufficiently benefited by slavery, the institution is justified on utilitarian grounds, no matter how wretched the slaves' lives turn out to be. Utilitarianism is here castigated for its willingness to sacrifice some people in order to benefit others.[1] But slavery presents the utilitarian with an additional embarrassment, more pertinent to our present discussion, in the form of the specter of the happy slave. Here we focus on a particular slave who, we are asked to imagine, is quite happy with his lot. The difficulty of raising any objection to his enslavement on utilitarian grounds highlights the utilitarian's impoverished conception of value, and draws attention to the independent value of autonomy (or its cognates) in our ordinary moral scheme.

But upon reflection, the appeal to autonomy does not straightforwardly underwrite a categorical opposition to slavery. To see this we must inquire more closely into how precisely slavery relates to autonomy. Two different moments should be distinguished. The first concerns the circumstances of enslavement. We ordinarily assume that enslavement itself is involuntary, foisted on the slave through brute force. But what about voluntary enslavement?[2] To avoid the presumably unwelcome conclusion that voluntary enslavement is acceptable, it must be maintained that through this exercise of one's autonomy one sacrifices more autonomy than one gains. I am not sure how convincing this argument is in its own terms. After all, promises and contracts involve some restriction on freedom of choice, and yet, since the restriction is self-imposed, promises and contracts are generally perceived as expressing autonomy and promoting it. Should each promise or contract be made vulnerable to an assessment of its overall effects on the parties' autonomy? Be this as it may, the entire onus of this response to the problem of voluntary enslavement rests on the second moment in the relation of autonomy to slavery: whether or not the slave agreed to the enslavement, the ongoing regime under which he lives is assumed to consist in a severe limitation of his freedom of choice. But here too we must tread carefully. Is it really necessary that to be a slave one's choices must be severely curtailed? Everyone's options are limited, so the slave's situation would be distinctive in this regard only if his options were more restricted than those of non-slaves. But that need not be the case. Imagine a slave whose master, out of benevolence or enlightened self-interest, gives him considerable free rein. It may perhaps seem that the slave's predicament will still turn out to involve limitations on choice if we attend to the reliability of the slave's choice opportunities and not just to their number: the non-slave's options appear precarious since they can be withdrawn at any time at the master's whim. However, the slave's options need not in fact be less secure than the non-slave's. We can posit a master whose firm, perhaps obsessive character makes it all but impossible for her to depart from her benevolent policy toward her slaves, rendering the range of choices afforded to them no less secure than that available to their free counterparts. In short, de facto curtailment of autonomy is not essential to slavery. What distinguishes the slave from his free counterpart is a matter of legal status: someone who enjoys de facto freedom of choice may yet be enslaved de jure. But if a slave does in fact enjoy the same level of welfare and exercises the same degree of choice as some free people, wherein does the evil of his enslavement lie? Why is de jure slavery odious even in this case?

It is open to the reader to deny the premise of these questions, and maintain, along broadly rule-utilitarian lines, that what makes slavery in general a heinous institution is precisely the fact that real-world slaves are deprived of both welfare and autonomy to a shocking degree. Stipulate away these incidents, and you have removed those features that make slavery the paradigm of injustice. Such readers would get off board the argument at this point. My own belief is that not many will, accepting instead the judgment that to describe someone as a slave is to pronounce him a victim of injustice, rather than to invite an investigation into the actual circumstances of his life. And it is this judgment that ushers in the idea of human dignity and the related notion of respect. What remains evil about slavery even in the case of the slave who is de facto relatively free and content is the affront to human dignity. Slavery is the paradigm of injustice because it denies people's equal moral worth and thus treats them with disrespect.

But why ascribe to all human beings an equal moral worth and treat them with respect? What does such ascription and treatment amount to or require? And in what sense can an action offend against dignity without otherwise affecting the victim negatively, such as by derogating from his welfare or autonomy? Questions such as these have of course long troubled moral philosophers, eliciting from some a skepticism toward the very idea of dignity and its location at the foundation of morality. At any rate, these questions pose a double challenge: to demonstrate that the notion of dignity can do some useful work in a moral theory, and to offer an account of dignity that shows it to be a substantial and attractive ideal in its own right. Various exponents and advocates of dignity, most notably Kant, have done much over the centuries to meet these challenges and put at least some cardinal doubts to rest. But the recently renewed interest in dignity inevitably awakens opponents as well. My aim accordingly is to draw from the tradition, and again, mostly from Kant, a few threads and weave them into a safety net of sorts that will provide dignity's friends with some reassurance and some support.

II. WHAT DIGNITY IS

As I have already noted, the term *dignity* has acquired great prominence in recent years, both in public discourse and in the philosophical literature. And where there is prominence there is often also notoriety. Dignity has many ardent devotees as well as some vocal detractors. But though all sides use the same term, it is not clear that they always address the same topic or have in mind the same concept. Dignity has come to mean different things to different people.

Take, for example, a recent article, provocatively entitled *The Stupidity of Dignity*, in which Stephen Pinker laments the ascendance of dignity in public discourse. As it turns out, however, Pinker is talking about what he describes as a *psychological* concept of dignity:

> Dignity is a phenomenon of human perception . . . [C]ertain features in another human being trigger ascriptions of worth. These features include signs of composure, cleanliness, maturity, attractiveness, and control of the body. The perception of dignity in turn elicits a response in the perceiver. Just as the smell of baking bread triggers a desire to eat it, and the sight of a baby's face triggers a desire to protect it, the appearance of dignity triggers a desire to esteem and respect the dignified person.[3]

Pinker juxtaposes this psychological notion of dignity with the distinctly moral ideal of respect for persons. However, it is precisely the latter notion that many others identify with the concept of dignity. To assume that there is just one concept here, and then call it stupid or wise, is a trap we should be careful to avoid. There appear to be a number of concepts of dignity in circulation, too dissimilar even to be thought of as different conceptions of one concept.[4] In seeking an account of dignity, it is accordingly prudent to replace the definite article with the indefinite article and speak about *a* concept of dignity. Dignity, as I'll use the term, stands for an affirmation of the equal, or perhaps rather unique, and supreme moral worth of every human being, an affirmation designed to play a foundational role in morality and by extension in law as well.

Sources

The concept of dignity on which I focus has two main sources, theological and philosophical. The former is the biblical idea of *imago Dei* (in the original Hebrew, *b'tzelem Elohim*), claiming that human beings were created in the image of God; the latter source is for the most part in the writings of Immanuel Kant. However, tracing the concept of dignity to these two sources raises serious difficulties. One concerns the relationship between the sources. Kant himself does not couch his discussion of human dignity in the ancient imago Dei idiom. Though Kant professes religious beliefs, his moral theory is resolutely secular. The two sources thus seem to be in tension rather than complementary. Each source also raises problems of its own. As to imago Dei, many of those who pledge allegiance to human dignity do so within a secular liberal worldview; what possible interest can they take in Man's alleged resemblance to God? Kant's appeal to children of the Enlightenment is clearer, but here we face the problem that, as I've previously mentioned, Kant's own moral theory is grounded in the metaphysics of the thing-in-itself, and relatedly of the noumenal self, that few contemporary normative Kantians espouse. So it appears not only that the sources of dignity we inherited, the religious and the metaphysical, are at odds but that neither is particularly appealing to many of us today. I will argue to the contrary that despite religious misgivings and metaphysical doubts, the two sources remain viable. Contemplating Kant's concept of dignity against the background of the imago Dei idea makes sense and reveals a common ground that is hospitable to any nonbelieving humanist, eager to uphold humanity's moral worth without the support of a divine warrant, while also staying away from the more esoteric aspects of a Kantian metaphysics.

I start by considering the imago Dei idea. To see its relevance to a secular sensibility, we should distinguish in it two different claims or moments. One, call it the *creation thesis*, is the belief that the world in general, and human beings in particular, are God's creation. The second, the *resemblance thesis*, holds that humanity resembles God. The first thesis does not distinguish humanity from the rest of creation; rather, it is the latter claim that gives rise to human dignity. The resemblance can be interpreted in different ways, but one attractive theme sees it in terms of the knowledge of good and evil. It is in this respect in particular that humankind's resemblance to God is said to imply humanity's divine stature and so its special worth. Obviously, the creation thesis cannot be accepted by the secular mind. Even so, my suggestion is that the resemblance thesis can. But how? If man was not created by God, whence the resemblance? And what is the resemblance a resemblance to?

Possible answers to these questions are provided by a tradition of thought, most famously associated with the German philosopher Ludwig Feuerbach,[5] that reverses the creation thesis. Rather than being God's creation, people have created God, and indeed created Him in their own image, by projecting an idealized vision of themselves. We can appeal to this view to reinterpret the imago Dei idea. The cardinal difference between the religious standpoint and its secular reinterpretation is that humanity, which from the religious standpoint is the image, turns out to be the original, reflected in a mirror of its own creation. On this reinterpretation, the resemblance to God is there all right; only the direction of fit is different. The idea of God thus bespeaks a human devotion to an ideal of perfection and a commitment to strive for the realization of its implications for one's life. To recognize that the source of the ideal lies in the believers and that they are the ultimate authority for the imperatives by which they live is to ascribe to them an uncontestable worth, commensurate with the value that they themselves ascribe to the being they conceive.

In contemplating this reversal of the imago Dei idea we should note that the atheist does not fault the believer for ascribing to God the value that she does. If He existed, He would be worthy of the reverence the believer displays. Nor need the atheist deny that resemblance to God—that is to say, the partial possession of His attributes—would entitle the possessor to a pro tanto measure of the same attitude. The difference of opinion concerns God's existence, not the counterfactual constituents of His sublimity. But in this dispute the atheist should, if anything, invest the imago Dei idea with greater, not lesser, significance, since, unlike the believer, she is better situated to trace the divine attributes to their origin in the human mind and heart. For the believer, reverence is the proper attitude toward God conceived as an absolute authority. But short of revelation, which is not, after all, an essential aspect of all religious faith, the way this authority is brought to bear requires that the believer form her own conception of the divine will. Her resemblance to God offers her a measure of hope. As seen by the atheist, the religious person's striving to decipher and follow God's will makes entirely good sense, with one crucial difference: God's role in this story is that of a placeholder or a regulative idea, potentially useful but dispensable. And this difference, far from denigrating the believer's striving to live up to God's demands, elevates this striving and its subject even further, since it credits the believer not just with the will to approximate perfection but also with the ability to conceive of perfection and give it content and shape. This suggests why, insofar as the value of humanity is concerned, there is not much gained in dressing up the idea of human dignity in a religious garb. If anything, the opposite is the case, since tracing the ideals that the believer associates with God to their human origins serves to elevate humanity and augment its importance. Even so, religious traces in the discourse of dignity need not be erased within a secular frame. Instead, they can be fruitfully transposed into a system of thought that explicitly casts human beings as the origin of all value.[6]

Such a view can be found in Kant's moral theory and specifically in his conception of human dignity. But before turning to Kant, let me refer to another beacon of the idea of dignity, in between the Bible and

Kant: Giovanni Pico della Mirandola and his famous fifteenth-century *Oration on the Dignity of Man*.[7] As we have already noted (in Chapter 1), Pico proclaims the theme of human self-creation. This is what distinguishes humanity from the rest of creation and indeed gives it its special, elevated worth. In speaking of human self-creation, Pico is, of course, not suggesting that human beings create their own organism. Our essence or identity, the answer to the question of what we are, is a matter of our pursuing projects, goals, and, in the broadest sense, values. But why is self-creation a source of elevated worth? An appealing approach to this question is to give Pico's view a Kantian gloss. We can link the notion of self-creation, as well as the (reversed) imago Dei idea, to an interpretation of Kant's conception of dignity, while avoiding the metaphysics of the noumenal self.

The Value of Valuation

The key to a Kantian morality of dignity is no doubt the Humanity formulation of the Categorical Imperative, probably the most often cited statement in all of Kant's work: "Act in such a way that you always treat humanity, whether in your own person or in the person of any other, never simply as a means, but always at the same time as an end."[8] But in order to successfully turn this key, we must relate it to what Kant says directly about human dignity. This is brief and merits quoting in full.

> Now I say that man, and in general every rational being, exists as an end in himself, not merely as a means for arbitrary use by this or that will . . . In the kingdom of ends everything has either a price or a dignity. If it has a price, something else can be put in its place as an equivalent; if it is exalted above all price and so admits of no equivalent, then it has a dignity . . . Now morality is the only condition under which a rational being can be an end in himself; for only through this is it possible to be a law-making member in a kingdom of ends. Therefore morality, and humanity so far as it is capable of morality, is the only thing which has dignity . . .

> For nothing can have a value other than that determined for it by the law. But the law-making which determines all value must for this reason have a dignity—that is, an unconditioned and incomparable worth—for the appreciation of which, as necessarily given by a rational being, the word "reverence" is the only becoming expression.[9]

We can distinguish in these quotations three points: the equivalence between dignity and being an end; the view of people as ends and hence the ascription of dignity to them; and the claim that ascribing this value to people is the core of morality. To elucidate Kant's concept of dignity requires that we understand these three points and their interrelation. Different accounts have been proposed, in part because there may have been more than one strand in Kant's own mind. I sketch a variant of one of these strands that I find attractive.[10] I call it *the value of valuation*.

The first step is Kant's insistence on human intelligibility.[11] In Kant's own hands this idea is bound up with his metaphysics. However, purged of the metaphysical groundings, and in the sense relevant to the practical domain, this amounts to holding that all human action makes sense, has a point; it is, to use another idiom, meaningful. What makes action intelligible, what gives it meaning, is that it is done for the sake of something or other. That for the sake of which an action is done is its end. Now the same idea can also be expressed in the vocabulary of value. To act intelligibly requires that the end for which one acts be deemed worth pursuing, and so valuable. In this sense all action consists in the attempted realization of purported values. One goal of a theory of the practical domain is accordingly to account for the values we pursue. What Kant can be seen as offering in this regard is a theory of value centered around a binary division between two types of value: *price* and *dignity*. Roughly, price expresses the value of things for us, that is *for* persons, whereas dignity expresses our own value; it is the value *of* persons.

But this is too rough. This classification, as well as the distinction between our own value and the value things have for us, on which this classification depends, must be clarified and refined. Starting with the classification of values, *price* is not a unitary value: Kant further distinguishes between *market price* and *fancy price*. Though he does not elaborate much on this subdivision, commentators tend to associate the latter with esthetic value.[12] Kant accordingly distinguishes three kinds of value: pragmatic, esthetic, and moral. Building a house or a table is the realization of pragmatic value; listening to music, visiting a museum, taking a trip to the Grand Canyon, and playing basketball or soccer are realizations of esthetic value; keeping a promise, helping a blind person cross the street, and visiting with a sick friend are realizations of moral value.

It is also evident that all three kinds of value make a claim on us, have a certain force, though the nature of the claim or the force varies, forming a hierarchy. And this requires a clarification of what it means for something to have value *for us*. The italicized expression is ambiguous between (1) serves our interests and satisfies our desires, and (2) is deemed valuable by us. Now some of the things we value, those that possess what Kant labels *market price*, are valuable for us in the first sense. But others are not. We enjoy or admire the Mona Lisa or the Grand Canyon because of the value they possess; they are not valuable because of the satisfaction they provide. And this is true, even more emphatically, of moral values. We perceive them as having, in Kant's idiom, a *categorical* force, which is independent of our contingent needs, desires, and goals. Nevertheless, everything for the sake of which our actions are performed or toward which they are oriented, and so everything that is valuable, is valuable *for us* in the second sense: all the values we pursue, all the ends that make our actions, and more broadly our lives, meaningful, originate in us.

To view the values that guide our actions and our lives as originating in us is also to view ourselves as self-governing, and thus as autonomous. And this interpretation of our autonomy as a matter of being the authors of our lives naturally leads to a further idea, of being our own authority: we implicitly view ourselves as validating our values.[13] To recapitulate: to be intelligible we must pursue ends, and this is the same as projecting and realizing values. Since we deem these values worth pursuing, we must endorse them. This is the sense in which, in pursuing any value at all, we must recognize ourselves as the ultimate authority. Now the key to the authority relationship is the notion of *deference*: to recognize an authority is to defer to it as a source of valid guidelines and demands. Since each person must recognize herself as a definitive authority, she defers to herself; she enacts an attitude of self-respect.

But as we have noted in Chapter 2, even if each person is the ultimate authority for the ends she pursues and so for the values she endorses, the resulting deference and the dignity it implies would seem to be distributive: I implicitly assert my own dignity; you, yours. Morality, however, is mostly concerned with respect for others' dignity rather than merely for one's own. To see why respect extends to humanity as a whole, we need to attend more closely to the notion of intelligibility. If to encounter a human being is to encounter an intelligible being, then it is to encounter a being with whom communication and, hence, mutual interpretation and understanding are in principle possible.[14] For this to be the case, I must be able to see another's values, no matter how different from mine, as *values*, that is as ends capable of making sense of her actions and more broadly of her life in the same way that my values make sense of mine. And this involves a further aspect of intelligibility: its dependence upon abstraction.

When David puts on a suit and tie, he knows what he is up to: he is going to *the opera*, to see *Fidelio*. The italics draw attention to two possible descriptions of David's end at different levels of abstraction. But though other formulations are possible, notice that some such abstraction is necessary in order to account for David's dressing up. If instead of referring to "the opera" David were to conceive of a highly detailed, step-by-step depiction of the route that leads from his home to the opera house, and of a brick-by-brick description of this end point, while omitting the designation of his destination as the opera, then despite the abundant detail, or rather because of it, he would be at a total loss to know what to wear. The situation is similar when making sense of another person's conduct. David observes Ruth wearing a t-shirt and jeans. Why? She explains that she is on her way to a soccer game. But suppose David has never heard of soccer. At this point, the more abstract idea of a ball game, or failing that, just a game, may help him make sense of Ruth's attire. If this is not sufficient, the explanation of Ruth's behavior may have to appeal to even more abstract notions, such as entertainment or edification, which David associates with his own venture. Why does Ruth put on this casual dress? Because like David she is "dressing appropriately for the occasion." What is this occasion? Like in David's case, it is a form of entertainment or edification, or, like him, she is going to have a good time. Variation in dress style at the more concrete level is rendered intelligible by appeal to such notions as "dress code," "appropriate," and "occasion" at the abstract. In order for David and Ruth to be intelligible to themselves and so potentially to each other, they must in principle be able to see what they are each up to. And so they must be able to ascribe to each other ends, and thus values, that can be construed *as* ends and values, that is as pertaining to endeavors appropriate for a human life and making sense of it. This amounts to their viewing themselves as respectively articulating at a relatively high level of detail a cluster of highly abstract meanings that they both associate with the very idea of a human being and thus have in common. Whereas the interpretation of "human being" implicit in David's life will differ in innumerable ways from the one implicit in Ruth's, each of them is capable of pursuing and enacting their disparate interpretations only when conceived as *interpretations*, designed to manifest at a higher level of resolution content that at a high level of abstraction belongs to the category of humanity as such. Stated in reverse, in fixing their individual identities, both David and Ruth are enacting and articulating a more abstract identity, their identity as persons, which they share with everyone else.

When Kant speaks about respecting the humanity in oneself, he can be understood as appealing to that shared abstract meaning. But this also suggests that respecting myself (in the relevant sense) while disparaging others is not an option: my attitude toward others would amount to disparaging the very same cluster of meanings that, when abstracted from my own pursuits, I must hold in high regard. This allows us to identify a sense of respect that cannot be selective along individual lines. When the attitude one has toward any individual human being addresses that individual qua intelligible being, and so as a site of meaning, this attitude must extend to everyone else. And since leading my life requires that I defer to myself and so assert my own superior worth, this attitude of mine extends to humanity as a whole, and so to each of its individual manifestations.

As I said, more than one road leads to this conclusion, though probably none that is completely clear of potholes and bumps. Whatever the precise route leading to it, the conclusion is remarkable. One of Kant's great insights is the idea that moral content can be derived from purely formal considerations. The very fact that we pursue any ends at all, and so have any values at all, quite apart from their content, attests to our own value, and so provides a foothold for a system of moral values designed to acknowledge this value and give substance to this acknowledgment. This account gives morality a particularly secure position that other systems of value lack. All other values are in principle contestable. But as long as we contest them, we are committed to the validity of *some* value. And as long as we are committed to the existence of any value, we are committed to the supreme value of ourselves, as the origin of that value and the authority for it.*

III. DIGNITY, HONOR, AND WORTH

Not all advocates of dignity, let alone its detractors, subscribe to a Kantian interpretation of this idea. It will help clarify the view I have just outlined if we compare it with a different conception of dignity, one that abjures Kantian origins. This will be easier to do if we provisionally

---

* Since on this line of reasoning dignity is established by backward derivation from the human endeavor of projecting and pursuing values, it is of the utmost importance what those values are: to take our dignity, and so ourselves, seriously, requires taking seriously our various projects and the values implicated in them. And within the picture I discuss, these projects and values are to be seen at different levels of abstraction, from the individual to the universal human scale. This is where our attitudes to animals and the environment come into the picture and assume the greatest importance, not just in their own right but from the standpoint of our dignity as well. Kant himself recognizes duties with regard to nonhuman beings, though his way of accommodating them within his overall theory is not always satisfactory. For an illuminating discussion see Allen Wood, "Kant on Duties Regarding Nonrational Nature," *Aristotelian Society, Supplementary Volume* 72 (1998): 189–210. But these issues fall outside my present topic.

diversify our terminology, and use not just the term *dignity*, but also two other quasicognates that play a role in this discussion: some use *dignity* as a synonym for or an extension of *honor*, whereas others consider *dignity* as equivalent to *worth*. The two terms are not quite symmetrical, however. *Honor* is an ordinary term, and its philosophical use is for the most part in keeping with its common usage. *Worth* is a more specialized term, deriving its meaning along such lines as I have just sketched primarily from Kant's moral theory. This difference in provenance of the two terms signals a more substantive difference in the conception of dignity they each designate. By employing *honor* and *worth* to designate two contrasting poles, we can distinguish a range of senses with which *dignity* is used.

Honor and worth can be fruitfully contrasted along four dimensions: origin, scope, distribution, and grip. Honor is of social origin: it derives from and reflects one's social position and the norms and attitudes that define it, whereas worth, at least as used by Kant, has metaphysical origins: the alleged radical autonomy of the noumenal self. Consequently, honor is in principle limited in scope, capable of privileging only those who occupy certain positions while excluding others who occupy different ones; whereas worth has a universal scope, applying to every human being as such. Relatedly, the distribution of honor is typically uneven and hierarchical, reflecting and indeed in part constituting social stratification; worth is evenly distributed over humanity as a whole. Finally, the grip that worth has on its possessors (or, conversely, the grip they have on it) is much stronger than the grip of honor. Honor is contingent, in the sense that it must be earned or granted, and so can be forfeited or withdrawn; whereas worth is categorical, attaching to all its possessors by virtue of their being human, no matter what. These contrasting clusters of attributes go hand in hand with a familiar claim, to the effect that the ascendance of dignity talk marks a trajectory from honor to worth. Since Kant, and with increasing momentum in the past few decades or so, honor has been superseded by worth as the favored interpretation of dignity.

But at least one prominent author, Professor Jeremy Waldron, has been swimming against this current. He advocates a conception of dignity as universalized high social rank, which amounts to tying dignity back to honor rather than to worth.[15] To be sure, Waldron's dignity-as-rank is not the same as honor itself. Waldron most emphatically does not advocate a return to a hierarchical social system of valuation in which people's dignity varies with their social status, let alone to a state of affairs in which the dignity of some is built on the degradation of others. His conception of dignity is every bit as universal in scope and as egalitarian in distribution as that of the most devout Kantian. Waldron wholeheartedly endorses the universalization and equalization of dignity in the modern age. The question he raises and the challenge he poses concern only which notion, honor or worth, offers a sounder interpretive framework for these achievements. Since there is general agreement that the scope of dignity ought to be universal and its distribution egalitarian, the focus is on the two other dimensions of comparison, origin and grip. Waldron's preference for tying dignity to the tradition of honor rather than to the philosophy of worth is first and foremost a view that universal and equal dignity is better anchored in evolving social practice than in Kantian philosophy.

One specific way Waldron proposes for ensuring a universal extension of a socially grounded conception of dignity links dignity to social roles. The stepping stones toward this universalization of dignity are the more distinctive and circumscribed *dignities* associated with certain elevated roles:

> One might speak of the dignity of a judge, in regard to his judicial appointment . . . Or one might speak of the dignity of a clergyman, such as a bishop, in terms of his responsibility for the administration of a diocese, or even the dignity of a rector, in terms of his elementary right to administer the sacraments or direct their administration in a particular parish.[16]

The connection between these discreet dignities and the ideal of universal dignity is forged by a notion of *responsibility rights* introduced by Waldron. He argues that many roles, such as those of parents, consist in part in rights assigned to their bearers, rights that are at the same time allocations of responsibility. Waldron sees a natural fit "between the idea of role-based dignity and the idea of responsibility-rights." And so he proposes to explore "how far we can extend the responsibility analysis, moving step by step from specific roles like parenthood in the direction of certain responsibilities that people in general might be thought to have in relation to their human rights as such." Along this trajectory, Waldron moves from the dignity he associates with the role of parents to that of citizenship. Proceeding even further, if somewhat hesitantly, he finally proposes to extend the same approach to encompass the dignity of humanity in support of universal human rights.

Waldron's view of dignity as universalized high social rank is linked to another theme: privileging law over morality as the primary habitat and dominant source of dignity. Though the alignment need not be perfect, we generally tend to view law as a social phenomenon. Tracking dignity to its legal provenance is an astute step that leaves open difficult conundrums of moral philosophy, while allowing us to make progress on the main practical issues associated with the concept of dignity today. And as Waldron demonstrates, by leveling up and expanding a notion of honor, dignity-as-rank is capable of underwriting an equal dignity for all.

But all these ways of grounding and expanding dignity-as-rank come at a price in the dimension of grip. As conceived by Waldron, the social origins of dignity cannot offer the grip that the Kantian position does. Expanding the scope of dignity and leveling it up are doubtlessly great social and legal achievements, but this is also their vulnerability: what is socially and legally granted can be socially and legally withdrawn. The worry is not about the fragility of dignity-as-rank in the face of changing winds of politics or brute force. Nothing is sturdy enough to withstand these kinds of adversities. The fragility in question is an argumentative one; it takes place in the space of reasons and justifications, not in the space of struggle and mayhem. It is here that a difference exists between, on the one hand, celebrating and cheering on the morphing of local and hierarchical honor into universal equal dignity, and, on the other hand, providing an argument in favor of this development that would give it some normative grounding. The challenge Waldron poses is accordingly quite formidable: can we retain the social origins of dignity while securing its categorical grip?

The approach I've outlined can be now seen as responding to this challenge, not by muting but by amplifying the social factor Waldron highlights. The theme of human self-creation takes us beyond the social origins of people's status or value, which Waldron explores, to the social origins of people themselves. If the bearer of dignity is not a noumenal self, ensconced in an ethereal Kingdom of Ends located in a nether region of things-in-themselves, but a socially constructed self, the distance between dignity-as-rank and dignity-as-worth shrinks, and the two conceptions tend to converge. Interpreted along these lines, a socially grounded conception of dignity turns out to be universal, equal, and secured by categorical grip. How?

We can start from the end, the categorical grip. The problem we noted with a socially based conception of dignity is its apparent contingency: society may fail to confer equal dignity on all. This possibility does not arise under the constructive view. If the source of dignity is in human self-creation, the process by which dignity is conferred is the very same one by which the human person is constituted, and so there can be no slippage between the two. Since self-creation is an attribute of humanity, dignity associated with self-creation is also universal in scope: it is coextensive with humanity as a whole. Finally, dignity acquired through self-creation is equal, since it accrues to us qua subjects of construction rather than as its products, and so irrespective of the content and variability of what is being produced.

The reassurance that the contours of dignity encompass the entire human race raises, however, an apparent discrepancy with the social orientation of Waldron's approach. As I have already argued (in Chapters 1 and 5), human self-creation can be given a collective interpretation, as involving humanity as a whole, or a distributive interpretation, according to which each individual forges her own identity. The social construction of the self, which fixes on society as the arena of human self-creation, is intermediate between these poles. Now since Waldron dwells particularly on the social (and relatedly legal) origins of dignity, to bring the self-creation theme into alignment with his approach would seem to require that we adopt this third interpretation. But as I have also argued earlier, a choice between the universal, the social, and the individual as the site of self-creation is not necessary, or indeed possible, since each of these interpretations implies the others as well. To see the point, recall the picture introduced in the previous chapter of the social as intermediate between the individual and the universal. Intermediate in what dimension? One answer would be numerical, as *many* is intermediate between *one* and *all*. But the view of self-creation as manifesting human intelligibility and as occurring in the medium of meaning supports a different answer. Meanings are abstract, and so the difference can be conceived as a matter of levels of abstraction: the social is more abstract than the individual, and the universal, yet more abstract. Or stated in reverse, social meanings are a more concrete elaboration of universal meaning, and individual meanings a further and yet more concrete elaboration of social ones. Seen in these terms, "humanity" labels at a high level of abstraction the meaning that individual human beings express or enact in endlessly ramified and divergent ways. Within the same picture, the social designates a concatenation of meanings at an intermediate level of abstraction, between the individual and the universal. Focusing on it and privileging it, the way Waldron does, does not threaten to displace the universal or the individual standpoints. It only amounts to the view that the social is a particularly fecund source of meanings, and so is especially vital to the process of human self-creation and its study.

Similar comments apply to the link Waldron draws between human rights and social roles. Here the alternative, worth-based conception of dignity I favor is not so much in the form of an alternate route to the same destination as a suggestion that we reverse the direction of travel. As we have seen, Waldron's procedure is to start with concrete roles, each vested with a certain dignity, and build his way up, through increasing abstraction, to the universal standpoint of humanity as a whole, where human rights come into view. On this approach, the dignity of a human being is modeled on, or derived from, that of parents or citizens. In a more Kantian picture, by contrast, the primary bearer of dignity is the person, abstractly conceived: Kantian dignity resides in the first place in our shared humanity. Relatedly, the order of derivation regarding the dignity attached to more specific roles is reversed. No dignity attaches to the roles as such; to speak of the dignity of an office or a role would be a category mistake.[17] Rather, an elevated value accrues to a role because of its integration within a person's life. The dignity of a parent, for example, is not to be understood as a worth that resides in the parental role, and which the parents themselves have in part by virtue of assuming this role. It is the other way around: performing the parental role is a site of dignity and calls for respect because of the way it fits into the parents' life and identity. The person's dignity comes first; that of the role is derivative or secondary.

What difference does it make, though, whether the role borrows its value from the value of its holder or instead bestows that value on her? As a practical matter, do these two not come down to the same thing? After all, roles do not exist separately from people who occupy them, and so cannot realize whatever value we associate with them other than in conjunction with the role-holder, on whom in Waldron's view they bestow dignity. And vice versa: people's identity, or as I put it earlier, meaning, derives at least in part from the roles they hold, and so their worth must be realized and recognized in connection with their performance of these roles. Even so, the order in which we proceed, upward or downward, matters. Though the two pictures, Waldron's and the Kantian, broadly overlap, there are some significant differences nonetheless. I will mention three. The first concerns the universality of dignity. As I have already noted, Waldron acknowledges a "strain" in extending the role-based conception of dignity to the universal standpoint of humanity. For those, like Waldron himself, who care much about human rights, and who, like him, link them to the notion of dignity, the strain should be a worry: it makes universal human rights seem rather precarious. This worry is allayed when dignity is vested in humanity from the start: being human is all it takes to have an elevated moral worth.

But ascribing dignity to humanity may seem to raise a corresponding worry, associated with another possible strain: how do we move from the alleged moral worth of the species to that of each of its individual members? Isn't ascribing dignity to abstract humanity bound to eclipse the value of individual lives and their concrete engagement with the kinds of specific roles that form Waldron's starting point? However, this worry too is the product of thinking of human beings in biological terms, and so envisaging the relationship of *Homo sapiens* to individual human beings as akin to that between, say, *Loxodonta africana* and individual elephants. But when we think of the human self, along the lines I have been following, as intelligible and constituted by meaning, the value of abstract humanity and of the concrete individual is the same value, since it is the value of one and the same subject conceived at different levels of abstraction. And so to talk about someone's dignity as an individual, as a parent, and as a person is to designate at different levels of abstraction the same subject's moral worth.

Finally, insisting that the only proper subject of dignity is the human person also draws our attention to the possibility that not all roles, no matter how important, are sites of dignity. To be such a site, a role must be integrated into our lives: only when a role falls within the boundaries of the self does its performance become an occasion for the exercise of autonomy and a basis for personal responsibility. But not all roles are enacted in this way. As I have observed earlier, some are enacted in a detached, impersonal, and strategic manner. We engage in them only due to some external inducement, a threat or a reward, but otherwise maintain them outside the scope of our identifications and on the periphery of the self.[18] The performance of such roles falls outside the scope of the person's dignity as well. These variations in how different roles relate to their bearers apply to all roles, and so in particular to what I have earlier (in Chapter 1) called *affiliations*, that is roles (or aspects of roles) that tie the bearer to one collectivity or another. The implications just mentioned of variations in role-distance on the dignitary significance of a role accordingly raise a further question regarding the collective reach of dignity, which I consider in Chapter 8.

IV. SOME PITFALLS

The increasing prominence of dignity-talk is often identified with or seen as part of what has come to be called the *rights discourse*. Under the interpretation I have outlined, however, it is more accurate to see the rise of dignity as having a different focal point and so as inviting a moral discourse more concerned with values. As a centerpiece of such a discourse, the concept of dignity offers a platform on which both secular and religious humanism can meet to conduct a mutually beneficial dialogue. But although it is possible to embrace the ideal of human dignity without the support of a religious warrant or Kantian metaphysics, those sources may not be easy to escape. A central cluster of issues to which I would like to draw attention concerns the nature of the person whose dignity we assert and so links up with our discussion of boundaries of self in previous chapters. Dignity is the supreme worth of every human being, but what does that include? The scope of dignity must track the boundaries of the self, but where do these boundaries lie? When dignity mandates respect for persons, what is the precise target of this respect? The idea of human dignity inevitably raises such pressing questions of human ontology. Extricating the concept of dignity from its religious and metaphysical origins, however, excludes the answers to these questions proffered by religious doctrine and by Kantian metaphysics and so leaves them open. But unless we are careful, the very same religious and metaphysical ghosts we hope to exorcise may surreptitiously come to haunt us through this opening. Three specific pitfalls illustrate this wider theme. I label them, tendentiously, *religious cooptation, choice worship*, and *body fetishism*. I will briefly indicate each.

Religious Cooptation

By religious cooptation, I refer to the possibility that religious doctrines be inadvertently and uncritically incorporated into what is supposed to be secular public discourse. Consider the Vatican's recent missive on the implications of human dignity, entitled *Instruction Dignitas Personae on Certain Bioethical Questions*.[19] Much of value can be garnered from this document, but not surprisingly the document is rife with distinctly Catholic doctrine unrelated to the idea of dignity. The danger is that this doctrine gets mixed up with the discussion of dignity, thus borrowing the latter concept's prestige and rhetorical force to support policies that from a secular standpoint turn out to be inimical to human dignity. For example, the document's opening statement, to the effect that "[t]he dignity of a person must be recognized in every human being from conception to natural death,"[20] runs together the affirmation of human dignity with a controversial ontological doctrine, namely that the human person begins at conception. In a similar vein, the document prohibits, again in terms of a concern for human dignity, any fertility techniques seen as violating the distinctly religious doctrine that marital sex is the only permissible form of procreation. The present caveat is reinforced by another recent document: a report entitled *Human Dignity and Bioethics*, issued by the President's Council on Bioethics.[21] This document is the main target of Stephen Pinker's attack on dignity that I mentioned at the outset.[22] Though the report is hardly the last word on the concept of dignity and a poor reason to berate the value of dignity as such, the similarity in tone as well as in substance of the Council's report to the Vatican's missive is indeed disconcerting.[23]

Choice Worship

The second pitfall, choice worship, relates to a central theme in neo-Kantian liberal thinking. Kant is enlisted to the liberal cause mostly through the centrality to his moral theory of the idea of a free will. A liberal sensibility that celebrates individual choice can easily assimilate Kantian ideas by embracing autonomy as its fundamental value. The result is a tendency to identify autonomy with choice and to see choice as the seat of dignity as well. On this line of thought, to respect persons is to respect their choices. But whatever the attractions of this bit of liberal

Dignity and Self-Creation

dogma, it cannot be sustained on Kantian grounds. The Kantian support for the valorization of autonomy is linked to a rather specialized conception of autonomy. A wide gulf separates this system of ideas from the liberal celebration of individual choice.

Doubts that choice as such, as the expression of the individual's will, is of moral value arise when we consider that to value choice is to give at least some positive valence and pay some respect to the will's determination to kill, rape, or steal. A choice-liberal need not, of course, condone such choices: these choices violate other people's rights, rights that themselves can be seen as expressing or protecting these people's autonomy. But invoking such countervailing considerations is an unsatisfactory response, in that it implies that the nefarious choices have *some* moral value, whereas they have none. The choice-liberal is committed to saying that qua a determination of a person's will, *any* choice is pro tanto valuable. But our moral and legal judgments go the other way: the fact that an act of homicide, rape, or theft represents the agent's considered choice and reflects a genuine determination of his will serves to aggravate the moral and legal severity of the action rather than mitigate it.[24]

It will be said in response that the Kantian liberal I describe is a straw man. The more likely position held by liberals, Kantian or otherwise, is more qualified. They do not simply value any choice or, for that matter, all displays of autonomy. Rather, they deem choice or autonomy valuable only subject to a limiting generalizing proviso—that is, when it is consistent with equal choice or equal autonomy for all. Under this formulation, choices that strip others of their autonomy lack moral value from the start. But as an interpretation of the moral injunction to respect people, this restatement of the liberal position is unsatisfactory for two reasons. First, the valorization of the will must be *content independent*:[25] to defer to people's wills is to assign to them at least some prima facie value as they are, no matter what their content. And, as it turns out, the actual content of the will does not always abide by the strictures imposed by the generalizing proviso. To insist that only choices respectful of others' autonomy have any value at all is to subject the will to an external evaluative standard, one that is patently at odds with ascribing to the will intrinsic value of its own. Second, the generalizing proviso does not apply to self-regarding choices, which are left unfettered. But, at least within a Kantian framework, not all self-regarding choices are morally permissible. Kant maintains that one ought to respect not just others' humanity but one's own humanity as well. This gives rise to duties toward oneself, such as, in Kant's view, a prohibition against suicide. Since these self-regarding duties may impose constraints on the actual content of the will, they manifest a conflict between dignity and choice, a conflict that the generalizing proviso is unable to remove.

Body Fetishism

One way in which we, as actual persons, differ from noumenal selves is that we are embodied. So, one natural step toward a more comprehensive conception of the person that does not focus exclusively on the will involves recognizing the body as an aspect of persons that is pertinent to their dignity. But here too we are on slippery ontological grounds. A narrow but important line separates the idea of respect for embodied persons from mere body fetishism. Talk, both religious and secular, of the body's sanctity and inviolability often crosses this line.[26] There is a crucial difference between, on the one hand, exploring the implications of people's embodiment for permissible and impermissible ways of treating *them*, and investing the body itself with moral value as a site of dignity and as worthy of respect, on the other.

To be sure, we often do attach value to bodies and their parts: since I am right-handed, my right hand is of greater value than my left. But notice that such practical valuations measure the body's value *for us*, in contrast to the kind of valuation the idea of dignity signifies, our own value. The suggestion that the body has dignity thus involves a category mistake. The grammar of dignity and of respect is concerned with what is done to the person rather than to the body. What is done to the body attains moral significance derivatively and can be fully revealed only in a language that pertains to persons rather than to bodies and their parts. Of

Dignity and Self-Creation

course, the value that the body has for us does have a bearing on how our own value ought to be protected and expressed. But the two—the body's value and our own—remain separate ideas that should not be confused.

It would help to avoid the confusion if we attend to the difference between our ordinary body-talk and our person-talk: not everything done to the body is also done under the same description to the person whose body it is. This is masked by cases in which the same verb describes both: to kick John's leg is to kick John. The same applies to *touching* and *injuring*. However, to break John's leg is not to break John, and to pierce his ear is not to pierce him. These are trivial examples, and the disparity they reveal between talk of the body and of the person is easily overcome. We are inclined to say that what was done to John in these cases is simply that his leg was broken or his ear pierced. But in other cases this gap between bodily predicates and personal predicates is wider and not so readily bridged. Touching the genitals may be *molesting* the person; pouring water on someone's head, *baptizing* him; tweaking someone's nose, *insulting* him. In these cases, we can attain to the normative significance of the respective actions only by replacing the bodily descriptions with such verbs as molesting, baptizing, or insulting, which pertain essentially and exclusively to persons, rather than to bodies.

Conflating body-talk with person-talk can have far-reaching and unwelcome implications. Here are two examples. First, consider Mary, who cuts open John's chest and mutilates his body in countless other ways. Yet if Mary is a surgeon, and what she does is surgery, then all of this bodily devastation amounts to *curing* John.* By failing to distinguish between the bodily and the personal, dominant legal doctrine would lead to the absurdity that every medical operation is a prima facie case of battery, to which the surgeon need plead a lesser-evil defense. The second example

---

* It may be objected that the example does not reveal the gap I claim, since it can be said that what Mary does, though in some ways injurious to the body, is designed to heal John's body, and so does not require a shift from body-talk to person-talk. I do not find this objection persuasive in this case; talk of healing the body is to use "body" as a metonym for the person. But if you are troubled by the example, think of electrical shocks, psychoactive drugs, and brain dissection, where interferences with the body are designed to heal the mind.

concerns a cluster of practices, most prominently the sale of human organs, that allegedly exhibit offensive "commodification."[27] I do not mean to advocate a market in body parts, but only to warn against a facile and overly confident judgment that such markets violate human dignity. Only if, say, kidneys themselves had a value beyond price would their sale be necessarily offensive. Since dignity resides in the person, to determine whether selling organs violates human dignity requires that we ascertain the meaning of such a practice and the message it conveys regarding the value of the persons whose organs are on sale.

Being alert to these and other pitfalls is important, but avoiding pitfalls does not yet give us a sense of direction and guidance in this difficult terrain. It would be nice to end this chapter on a more affirmative note, by at least gesturing in the direction of an ontology of persons that can serve as a firm foundation for the concept of dignity and determine the contours of respect. But to view ourselves as the authors of our values and as self-creating is to maintain that no such foundation exists. What we ultimately appeal to when we make a judgment about such questions as what a body-affecting action amounts to by way of affecting the person whose body it is, is the meaning of that action, which is the meaning we give it. And as Pico helped us see, to mark the ontological void in which we operate and that we must fill is not to lament a handicap that vitiates the idea of dignity but is rather to identify the source of this idea and its habitat.

7

A Morality of Crime and Punishment

I. MORALIZING CRIMINAL LAW

In this chapter I draw some implications from the morality of dignity just discussed for a theory of criminal law, focusing on the two central questions such a theory addresses: what to punish and why punish. A conception of criminal law that hinges on a morality of dignity runs counter to a trend that has characterized the evolution of liberal criminal law under the guidance of the harm principle. The trend has been to demoralize criminal law (the pun is intended), both in regard to the idea of crime and to the idea of punishment.[1] In light of the outrages perpetrated over the centuries in the name of this or that purported morality, an aspiration toward a morally neutral conception of criminal law is altogether understandable. Even so, such a conception is not viable. A morally neutral conception of crime separates a criminal offense from its corresponding moral prohibition; for example, the legal prohibition against murder is one thing; the moral prohibition, another. The separation is strained, especially in light of the role that blameworthiness plays in criminal law: if not from morality, from where does blameworthiness come? The obvious alternative to the immorality of the offense itself is supposedly the wrongfulness of breaking the law. But this alternative runs into two difficulties. One is the doubt whether a duty to obey the law exists. Whatever the correct answer to this doubt, it is hard to believe that the blameworthiness of a murderer would depend on it. In any case, the pretense of the harm principle to moral neutrality is specious. Historically, the principle is the outgrowth of a utilitarian moral theory, and the substantive connection between the principle and its utilitarian origins is hard to sever. It is not surprising, then, that the harm principle inherits and displays some of the problems associated with its supporting moral theory. A critique of the harm principle can therefore draw in part on a broader critique of utilitarianism as well.

Whether we consider harm to be morally neutral or view it as part of a utilitarian morality, a theory that considers criminal law to be an engine for harm prevention is unsatisfactory in yet another way. One of the main objectives of a theory in this area is to reveal a certain unity in criminal law and help distinguish it from neighboring phenomena. But a harm-based theory fails to circumscribe the criminal law and set it apart from other types of governmental use of power. The boundaries of criminal liability that the harm principle is designed to draw turn out to be vague, elastic, and porous. Generally speaking, boundaries can be seen as performing a dual function. First, they delimit what they enclose and keep it from spreading and blending into the vicinity; they are thus designed to prevent what we may call *spillover*. Second, they hold back the surroundings and keep them from infiltrating what is enclosed, thereby securing the integrity of the enclosure against its *colonization* by the outside. Now, in defining the scope of criminal law through the harm principle, the dominant concern has traditionally been spillover: keeping criminal liability from expanding too far. And as others have remarked, given the vagueness of harm and its ubiquity, the harm principle offers at best a weak bulwark against the expansion of criminality.[2] At the same time it may bear some of the responsibility for the widely discussed phenomenon of overcriminalization:[3] the tendency of criminal liability to spread into increasingly large areas of our lives, to wherever a whiff of harm can be detected. Here the harm principle may have had a paradoxical effect: introduced as a limitation on the reach of criminal law, it has turned into an engine that propels its ever-increasing expansion. To be sure, harm is seldom considered as a sufficient condition of criminality, only a necessary one. Even so, once the idea takes hold that harm is the gist of criminality, every infliction of harm becomes a candidate for criminalization.

Awareness of boundaries' dual role alerts us also to the opposite worry, that of safeguarding the integrity of criminal law and certain values that are embodied in it from being colonized by external practices and attitudes. One such worry is about the effects that the wide expansion of criminal liability may have on our attitudes to the core offenses. The equation we create between a tax evasion or a building code violation on the one hand and murder or rape on the other can be read in both directions. By flattening the normative landscape, the message is conveyed that the same attitude is in principle appropriate to all of the state's injunctions, irrespective of whether they track morality's demands. If the difference between a parking violation and assault is just a matter of degree, measured in the metric of harmfulness, the decision whether to engage in either ought to follow the same logic.[4] What logic is that? Here, a revealing locution is *paying the price*. When crime draws its meaning from its location in the felicific matrix and as part of the totalizing economy of pain and pleasure, it is subsumed, like all else, under a regime of "incentives" and carries a price tag. Whether the price set is low or high, it presents individuals with a single consideration: is it worth paying?

Though the issues regarding the borders of criminality I have so far discussed are pending and troubling, they are age-old and familiar. But criminal law in this country and elsewhere faces a newer challenge as well. The struggle against terror confounds established categories and blurs the distinction between crime and war. Extending traditional criminal law to coping with acts of terror domestically or abroad is often driven by the desire to extend the restrictions imposed on the use of state power within the criminal law, and so reduce carnage. But as the rhetoric of *the war on drugs*, and, more broadly, *the war on crime*, ominously reminds us, the equation between war and crime can also be reversed. The vision of the criminal law as just one outpost among many in the defense of society's interests may encourage a militant attitude that is impatient with what it takes to be lawyers' excessive fussiness in the face of harsh realities and the imperatives of effectively combating them.

The juxtaposition of the two common locutions I have quoted, "paying the price" and "the war on crime," is not adventitious. Markets and wars are two pervasive and powerful regimes, each valorizing a different set of values and attitudes: the relentless pursuit of material self-interest guided by a selfish maximizing rationality in the one case, and the use of collective brutality to advance social ends in the other. Both are antagonistic to the criminal law and threaten to colonize it from different directions. A conception of criminal law that accentuates its distinctive moral mission, thus clearly marking and fortifying its boundary, would accordingly serve a double purpose: to prevent the undue expansion of criminal law and its incursions into neighboring territories, and to protect the criminal law itself from being colonized by the logic of a morally neutral harm-prevention agenda in the dimension of crime, and by the logic of military force in the dimension of punishment. Does criminal law serve a valuable purpose that sets it apart?

In seeking an answer, it is natural to turn to Kant and to the morality of dignity discussed in the previous chapter. This can be done in a resolute spirit, of rejecting utilitarianism in favor of a Kantian morality seen as providing the exclusive basis for assessing legal institutions; or in a more compromising spirit, echoing an accommodation between the utilitarian and the Kantian views that has become prominent in recent years. The latter, composite view allows for utilitarian considerations to drive public policy and set its goals, subject to deontological side-constraints that override attainable gains in aggregate welfare. These constraints can be best understood in terms of a Kantian morality, which gives primacy to certain principles that guide and restrict the permissible treatment of individual human beings by government as well as by each other.[5] Seen in either way, resolute or compromising, my suggestion, elaborated in the next section, is that criminal law's core prohibitions are not primarily designed to further a utilitarian agenda but rather to uphold dignity-based moral principles. In the following section I extend the dignity-based approach to account for punishment.

The upshot can be briefly summarized. The distinguishing characteristic of criminal offenses is not the harmful end result, but the fact that the result is brought about through intentional human agency, since only such agency can convey a proper, respectful, or improper, disrespectful, attitude to people and is therefore the appropriate object of moral concerns. When it comes to human life, for example, criminal law's primary purpose is very different from that of, say, hospitals and fire departments, since criminal law is not designed to save lives but to prevent homicides. Correspondingly, punishment is centrally concerned with upholding the victim's dignity as well as affirming the wrongdoer's. Since on this interpretation of criminal law, crime is radically discontinuous with other sources of harm and punishment is radically discontinuous with other uses of state power, we get a criminal law that is both more secure and less threatening within more narrowly and more visibly drawn boundaries.

II. CRIMINAL OFFENSES

Cases of what appear to be harmless wrongdoing raise a well-known difficulty for the harm-oriented, utilitarian conception of crime. But though the difficulty is broadly recognized, it usually arises in the gray areas at the periphery of criminal liability; when it comes to core crimes, such as homicide, battery, or rape, it seems that harm plays a decisive role. But this is not always the case. One category of felonies, rape by deception, provides a conspicuous example. Consider *State v. Minkowski*,[6] in which the defendant, a gynecologist, was accused of raping during medical examinations a number of his female patients, who on recurrent visits had not realized what was going on. Most would agree that these women were indeed raped even before discovering the violations, despite the fact that at that stage it would have been difficult to find either physical or psychological harm. It is easy, of course, to condemn the defendant's conduct and justify criminal conviction on obvious rule-utilitarian grounds. But doing so would miss the target. Minkowski's actions are reprehensible acts of rape all by themselves, and they should be treated as such out of concern for the unsuspecting victims, quite apart from any broader welfare-related ramifications of condoning Minkowski's conduct.

Minkowski wronged his victims even if he did not harm them. How? It is natural to answer this question by appeal to the value of autonomy. Even in the absence of harm, the familiar story goes, the women were wronged because they were subjected to nonconsensual sex, in derogation of their autonomy. But this account runs up against another familiar conundrum: the limited role that victims' consent plays in assessing criminal liability. In *State v. Brown*,[7] for example, the defendant habitually beat his wife when she drank alcohol, allegedly as part of an agreement to help her overcome her alcoholism. In convicting Brown, the court rejected a defense of consent. How are we to assess this decision? Once again, it is easy to marshal public-policy arguments, this time oriented toward the protection of autonomy. There is, for example, good reason to be suspicious in general of agreements such as the one alleged. But here, too, as in *Minkowski*, we face the gap between the generic offense to which such considerations pertain, and the specific token, to which they may not. Even when we consider this case in isolation and assume that in this particular instance the wife did consent, we might still conclude that the beating is wrong.[8]

If neither the notion of harm, and relatedly human welfare, nor the notion of consent, and relatedly individual autonomy, by themselves provide a satisfactory account for these cases, what does? An account of criminal offenses based on the notion of human dignity can close the gap. The puzzle presented by *Brown* can be solved by recalling the discussion of slavery in the previous chapter. I have argued that slavery is an affront to dignity even when it does not adversely affect a particular slave in other ways: the meaning of slavery denies the slave's equal moral worth. How does this meaning accrue? One answer is that a meaning attaches to an action or a practice by virtue of certain empirical characteristics and consequences it *typically* has. After all, it is not a mere coincidence that slaves' lives are usually wretched and their autonomy is trampled. Exploiting a person by disregarding his own needs, interests, and desires is a paradigm of disrespect. But though the meaning of slavery has an empirical basis,

A Morality of Crime and Punishment

the meaning that attaches to slavery as an insult to dignity is retained even in the situation we imagined, in which the typical derogatory effects on the slave's welfare and autonomy are stipulated away. A similar account applies to the *Brown* case. The fact that physical violence ordinarily hinders both welfare and autonomy is reason enough to render it a blatant manifestation of disrespect. But here, too, the meaning of violence can outrun the reasons for ascribing that meaning to it. Although for the most part their significance is not attached to actions arbitrarily or at random, the connection between the reasons for ascribing to an action-type its significance as expressing disrespect and the tokens of that action need not be tight. Once an action-type has acquired a significance by reason of the disrespect it typically displays, all tokens of that action will possess the same significance and communicate disrespect even if that reason does not apply to them.

These observations buttress our judgment that the beating inflicted in *Brown* involves an affront to the wife's dignity despite her consent: when it comes to the meaning of these actions, the typical case of violence casts its shadow over the exceptional, thus amounting to an affront to the victim's dignity. But this explanation raises a further query: how widely is that shadow cast? Two kinds of examples will serve to illustrate the problem and help complete the account: medical treatment and contact sports. In both areas, the level of permissible violence far exceeds the level, if any, that would be tolerable in a *Brown*-type scenario. Why does the nasty record of the typical case of violence define the meaning of the beating in *Brown*, but not that of surgery or a boxing match?

Recall the case of Mary, discussed in the previous chapter, who cuts open John's chest and mutilates his body in countless other ways, resulting, let us now suppose, in John's death.[9] A grisly homicide? Far from it; just an ordinary, if unsuccessful, open-heart surgery. No district attorney is ordinarily alerted to such a case or would take notice of it. But why? Isn't Mary's action a prima facie case of assault, and given the results, of homicide as well? The prima facie case would not, of course, end the DA's inquiry, only trigger it. But once the inquiry is started, applying to this case the requisite criminal law doctrines is incongruous, and the results are uncertain. Given the initial charge, Mary must be able to raise some defense, and two seem to be available to her: consent and justification. But as *Brown* reminds us, consent does not in general exonerate when serious assault or homicide is involved. She may fare not much better under a justification defense. Depending on its precise formulation, the lesser-evil standard may not be met in this case, since as things turned out, the operation ended up shortening the patient's life rather than prolonging it as hoped. Though doctrinal waters in this area are too muddied to allow for any general and definitive statements, it is at least possible to view this ex post circumstance as marking the line between a genuine case of justification, and one in which the justification is only partial or shifts the burden of proof. These considerations are unsettling. Bringing to bear on medical treatment the doctrinal machinery of the criminal law would result in doctors routinely scrambling for cover. But as we have already noted, in practice, the first step that would lead us down this treacherous doctrinal road is not in fact likely to be taken: we ordinarily refrain from subjecting medical treatment to the categories of the criminal law. But how can such a gruesome affair as I've described fail to at least induce an initial criminal investigation? Part of the answer is linguistic. Surgeons don't use knives but scalpels; they don't slash or rip their patients' organs, but perform incisions instead; and so on. These linguistic markers together with other factors, such as the surgeons' green drab, invoke a comprehensive system of images, attitudes, and norms that constitute medical practice, thereby erecting a barrier, at once conceptual and psychological, that separates the goings-on within the practice from what happens outside. Consequently, the meaning of what Mary does in performing surgery is radically discontinuous with the beating administered in *Brown*, and the nasty connotations of violence do not ordinarily apply.*

Boxing (and other contact sports) can be distinguished from *Brown* along similar lines. A case of consensual wife-beating is still a case of

---

* This is not to deny, of course, that the theater of operation can sometimes serve as a stage of crime. A murderer can dress up as a surgeon, and kill her victim; a surgeon may deliberately fumble the operation, etc. But these departures from ordinary practice should be seen for

wife-beating, and it draws its offensive meaning from the typical cases in which there is no consent. But that meaning does not carry over to a practice we recognize and label as "boxing." Moreover, since within boxing violence is not demeaning to the participants, no disrespect will be conveyed by a boxer's punches even if the individual boxer holds the opponent below contempt and harbors the most disparaging emotions toward him.

III. PUNISHMENT

As in the discussion of offenses, I begin by observing some of the gaps left open by a welfare-oriented, utilitarian account of punishment, and then suggest how a dignity-based Kantian account can fill those gaps. Philosophical discussions of punishment commonly address the question of justification: what makes punishment legitimate? Dealing with this question assumes that punishment requires some form of justification. Why? Bentham's answer point to the similarity between punishment and crime. What makes punishment a presumptive evil is that like crime it diminishes utility by inflicting pain. This also points to the form a justification of punishment must supposedly take: punishment is justified inasmuch as it generates greater aggregate welfare by preventing crime, mostly through deterrence. A well-known difficulty with this justification is that it does not convincingly limit punishment to those guilty of crime: we can imagine extraordinary situations in which punishment would serve this purpose when imposed on someone who is innocent of any wrongdoing, as long as people believe in the defendant's guilt. Yet "punishing" the innocent even in those situations would be a moral outrage. A utilitarian may bite this bullet by denying the outrage, but others will find the bullet too hard to bite.

---

what they are: as *departures*. Neither the imposter nor the actual but murderous surgeon exemplifies in these situations medical practice. Seen in light of the nefarious scheme, the usual terms used to describe medical practice assume an ominous, borrowed quality; they appear, as it were, in scare quotes.

Even if a utilitarian account were successful in limiting punishment to the guilty in principle, other problems arise. Every system of punishment is fallible, and so involves instances of punishing the innocent. We take such lapses to be particularly alarming, and so subject the imposition of punishment to an unusually stringent system of substantive, procedural, and evidentiary restrictions. But what's so alarming about occasionally punishing the innocent? After all, government routinely disadvantages people for the sake of the greater good through taxation, civil damages, military conscription, fiscal policy, and the like. And yet none of these practices is as morally fraught as the practice of punishment, nor hedged by as strict a system of restrictions.

It is natural to focus in this connection on the severity of the deprivations punishment involves and view this as its distinguishing mark. But although punishment is often quite harsh, at least when understood along straightforward utilitarian lines, such a simple account of the distinctness of punishment does not hold up. First, the perception of the harshness of punishment does not depend on its aggregate but rather on its distributive effects. For example, the fact that the number of people who actually die by execution is, statistically speaking, quite small does not diminish our concern with capital punishment, since we deem it the most severe deprivation imposed on a particular individual. This stands in sharp contrast to the way other forms of governmental deprivation are evaluated— for example, the increase in road fatalities when, say, the speed limit is raised. Second, even in the individual case, the sheer level of hardship suffered through punishment does not quite make it stand out. For example, the hardships and dangers a conscript faces during training, let alone at combat, may far exceed what inmates face in jail. And yet we don't think of military service as raising the same moral issues as punishment or of the barracks as equivalent to jail. Finally, while going to extraordinary lengths to ensure that the defendant is indeed guilty of the crime charged, the law accepts with near equanimity the severe impact punishment often has on innocent parties such as the defendant's family.

Our practices and attitudes regarding punishment suggest that we view it as having moral significance that goes beyond the setback to welfare it involves. The similarity between punishment and crime that Bentham highlights is significant and morally consequential, but the preceding comments suggest that it has a more complicated shape. Like crime, punishment raises moral concerns, the intensity and shape of which are not adequately explained by the setbacks to welfare it involves. We need to adapt Bentham's insight to our earlier depiction of criminal offenses as strikes against human dignity. As we have seen in the previous section, when a criminal offense involves the infliction of harm, its moral badness is not exhausted by the badness of the harm. Rather, the evil of the crime is a matter of the significance with regard to the victim's moral worth of *inflicting* harm, when certain additional conditions obtain. As an example, consider first-degree murder. Its heinousness is based in the first place on the judgment that it involves the infliction of a most grievous deprivation. This judgment looks exclusively at the effects on the victim. In placing murder above, say, robbery, and at the top of the severity list, we do not investigate which crime is more socially harmful in the aggregate; we compare only the two felonies' distributive effects. Furthermore, it is significant that the murderer targets an individual victim, whose death must be the offender's conscious objective rather than just a foreseeable side effect of her action; and the action must be the product of "premeditation and deliberation," which marks it as more reprehensible than, say, reckless killing. This combination of factors—call it *mistreatment*—amounts to an especially egregious expression of disrespect: by deliberately inflicting a severe deprivation on a particular individual one enacts a conception of the victim as a mere means, someone whose own rights and interests can be trampled at will.[10]

It is easy to see that unlike other deprivations wrought by government action, criminal punishment is similar in these respects to crime, and so, unless justified, would present an unambiguous case of mistreatment. The deleterious effects of a fiscal policy on employment, for example, can be accidental and unforeseen, whereas the deprivation involved in punishment is always deliberate. Unlike taxation, which usually affects anonymous individuals in an impersonal way, punishment focuses on a particular defendant. Unlike quarantine, which may in principle be conducted in a five-star hotel, some form of deprivation is the acknowledged purpose of punishment, not just a regrettable side effect. Finally, criminal punishment involves harsh deprivations, with the harshness measured in terms of effects on the particular defendant rather than in aggregate societal terms. Being a form of mistreatment, criminal sanctions pose a greater threat to human dignity than other deprivations, and the person whose dignity is at stake is the defendant on whom the sanction is visited, rather than any others, like the family, who may be indirectly affected. The battery of restrictions created by criminal law is designed to mitigate this threat to the defendant's dignity by ensuring, as much as possible, that the defendant is justly treated rather than being the victim of the equivalent of a crime.[11]

This conclusion of course assumes that punishing the guilty, unlike inflicting sanctions on the innocent, is indeed just. This assumption can be interpreted in two ways, corresponding, respectively, to weak and strong retributivism: that punishing the guilty is *licensed* by justice or that it is *required* by it. On the former view, unlike inflicting sanctions on the innocent, punishing the guilty is respectful of their autonomy, and so is morally acceptable. But on this view a complete justification of punishment must include some affirmative reason, a reason that is commonly understood in crime-prevention, consequentialist terms.[12] Since we can imagine cases in which punishing the guilty would not advance such consequentialist concerns, the result is that at least in principle punishing some offenders would not be justified. Kant famously holds the stronger view. He speaks of the duty to punish a convicted murderer even as the final act taken by an island community that is about to disband. Though this scenario blocks an appeal to any future-oriented justifying aims of punishment, Kant maintains that the offender must be punished,

> so that everyone will duly receive what his actions are worth and so that the bloodguilt thereof will not be fixed on the people because they failed to insist on carrying out the punishment; for if they fail to do so, they may be regarded as accomplices in this public violation of legal justice.[13]

What do these dark words mean?

The example and the retributive view it conveys have spawned a broad range of interpretations, in part because what Kant says is unclear. So, for example, in a rightly celebrated paper, Herbert Morris argues along Kantian lines for a seemingly paradoxical right to be punished, seen as an aspect of an inalienable right to be treated as a person.[14] Morris draws on the connections between punishment and responsibility, between responsibility and autonomy, and between autonomy and respect. The failure to punish is a failure to hold the perpetrator responsible, which impugns her autonomy, and so treats her with disrespect. I will not comment on this and related lines of thought other than to note that they propose an offender-oriented theory of retribution. My suggestion, though, is that close attention to the quoted paragraph reveals an additional strand in Kant's view that amounts to a victim-oriented retributive approach, maintaining that in punishing the offender, or withholding punishment, the victim's dignity is at stake.

The first reason Kant gives for his retributive view does indeed focus on the offender ("so that everyone will duly receive what his actions are worth"). But then he makes two puzzling claims. The first is that failure to punish will result in the "bloodguilt" of the killing attaching to the community itself. But how does the killer's bloodguilt spread to the community, which after all had not shed the blood, just by virtue of its failure to punish? The second is the vague talk of the people becoming accomplices. Accomplices in what? The "public violation of legal justice" of which they supposedly stand accused just consists in the failure to punish, which is entirely the people's own failure; whose accomplices are they in this regard? We can make some headway if we see these two claims as connected. By failing to punish, the people share the killer's guilt because in this way they are implicated in the crime, and so become accomplices to it. But how can an ex post failure to punish implicate the community in a crime that had been already committed? And in what sense does punishing the offender take the community off the moral hook?

The answer I propose connects to my argument that criminal law's primary concern is not the victim's life, but the fact that the life was taken by another person, and that this, in turn, exhibits a concern for the victim's dignity. For if the life of the victim were all that mattered, it would make no sense to saddle the community with responsibility for the death when it fails to punish the perpetrator: ex post punishment would not have prevented the victim's death or restored him back to life. But if the victim's dignity is the central concern, the situation changes dramatically. Although the victim cannot be revived, his dignity can still be vindicated. So if the moral significance of homicide lies in trampling the victim's moral worth, there is still something posthumous the community can do about it: through punishment, that moral worth is reasserted. Hence, failure on the part of the community to punish the perpetrator is a failure to rectify, at least partially, the derogation of the victim's dignity, and so amounts to participating in the evil of the initial act.*

But why is punishment the appropriate medium for vindicating the victim's dignity? Can't the community rectify the offense to dignity in some other, gentler way? A radically different and gentler world is imaginable, and we should not write it off. But the burden of the argument is not to establish that punishment is the only appropriate reaction to crime in all possible worlds. A sensible objective is to examine our actual world, in which punishment exists and has roughly the shape and significance it does, and try to assess it in light of some broader moral considerations. Let me return in this vein to the initial claim that the mission of criminal law is to uphold dignity. In further elaborating this mission, we can distinguish between two ways of upholding dignity: by defending it and by vindicating it. Now, broadly speaking, a system of punishment is required in order to defend dignity by helping prevent dignity-offending criminal acts. Punishment does not always advance this goal, however; in particular, it does not advance it in Kant's imagined community that is about to disband. So the following question arises: why is the same practice that ordinarily serves to defend dignity appropriate for its vindication as well? The answer echoes the point I made in discussing criminal offenses. It concerns the meaning that accrues to a practice and characterizes instances

---

* This victim-oriented ground for punishment is cumulative with the offender-oriented considerations that either license punishment (on the weak retributive view) or mandate it (on the strong view).

falling under it even when the underlying reasons for that meaning do not apply in the specific case. Once punishment becomes the dominant medium for responding to offenses against human dignity for preventive reasons, it acquires a meaning that persists in cases in which prevention is not served. Failure to punish under these circumstances (unless some special considerations apply) has the offensive meaning of a failure to uphold, by vindicating, the victim's moral worth.

PART III

Collective Subjects

8

Collective Personhoods

Within a dignity-based morality and a dignity-oriented law, discussed in the preceding two chapters, the question of who has dignity is obviously of cardinal importance. Specifically, does dignity attach not just to individuals but to collectivities as well? This part of the book explores some legal ramifications of this question, discussing corporate criminal liability in the next chapter and collective freedom of speech in the last. The present chapter provides a background by touching on some general considerations that bear on extending dignity to collectivities, primarily to the business corporation, the collectivity that has come to occupy center stage in contemporary life. The discussion in this Part is cast within the by now familiar bifurcated normative universe consisting of two sets of norms: consequentialist norms associated with the pursuit of social utility, and deontological norms associated with the values of autonomy and dignity construed along Kantian lines. This division is bound up with a particular, "anti-utilitarian," conception of rights, according to which rights express and safeguard the proper respect due to their bearers by constraining the pursuit of aggregate welfare at the right-bearers' expense. The question of a collectivity's normative status thus splits into two, and calls for an examination not only of whether considerations of dignity apply to it but also of how it fares within the utility-oriented part of this terrain.

Although my main interest in this chapter is in the first of the two questions just distinguished, it will be helpful to first consider briefly the second: are collectivities suitable subjects of *consequentialist norms*? This question can be conveniently divided into two. The first, prompted by the *consequentialist* term in the italicized expression, asks whether it makes sense to attribute to collectivities causal efficacy and treat them as the point of origin of some objects and events. The second is prompted by *norms*; it asks whether collectivities are responsive to norms addressed to the collectivity as a whole and to incentives designed to back up or enforce those norms. These are foundational questions of social ontology, and writers have given different answers with regard to different collectivities. But at least when it comes to the large business corporation, an affirmative answer to both questions, an answer that ascribes to it what I will call *practical personhood*, crosses metaphysical lines and enjoys broad support. Though this is not the place to canvass this extensive literature, its gist as it bears on the issue at hand can be briefly indicated.

The main division is between "holistic" views—which affirm the existence of the corporation "over and above," as the saying goes, the aggregate of its individual members and their actions—and "reductionist" or "individualist" views, insisting that an adequate account of corporations (and other collectivities) should ultimately appeal exclusively to individuals and their interactions. The holistic views differ in the level of "robustness" of the existence they claim for corporations, or put differently, in the size or nature of the gap they posit between the aggregate of individual members on the one side and the corporation as a distinct and unified entity on the other. But they all share two abstract and general philosophical tenets. One is the distinction between constitution and identity, most commonly illustrated by the difference between a clay statue and the lump of clay of which it is made: for example, the statue can be destroyed without the lump of clay being destroyed.[1] For present purposes, this tenet implies that whereas a corporation is constituted by a bunch of individuals, it is not identical with them. Where does the difference come from? Here, the notion that comes into play is that of *emergent properties*. The world is after all full of composites with global properties quite different from the properties of their components; for example, water is wet whereas H_2O molecules are not. The same holds of human composites as well. In this vein, organization theory, broadly conceived, can be seen as carrying out a program of spelling out the various structural factors that mediate between what are seen as individual inputs on the one hand, and some global features or outcomes attributable only to the organization as whole, on the other. So, for example, when organization theorists characterize formal organizations by the presence of a decision-making process, they impute the requisite information-related functions to the organization, rather than to specific individuals, because what information is gathered, to whom it is disseminated, how it is decoded, and how it is combined and brought to bear on the final outcome critically depend on the structure of the organization, on the presence or absence of particular units or positions in it, and on the relevant standard operating procedures.[2] Similarly, speaking of organizational decisions presupposes the existence of some organizational *interests* and *preferences*, which lend a certain unity and intelligibility to the pattern of events we think of as corporate behavior. Portraying organizations as "intentional systems"[3] possessed of "organizational intelligence"[4] is a cogent way of expressing the view that organizations make decisions infused with cognitive content, that are the product of widely dispersed informational sources and diffuse individual interests and attitudes, all mediated by structures, processes, and chance, in ways that defy tracing the organizational decision to individual contributions.

Reductionists take a different ontological approach to collectivities, but their conclusions regarding the corporation's practical personhood converge for the most part with the holists'. The most prevalent brand of reductionism, methodological individualism, insists that an account of collective phenomena in terms of individual actors is in principle possible and desirable. But the proviso "in principle" is crucial, since it is consistent with conceding the epistemological and other practical obstacles to actually performing the reduction so as to eliminate the corporation as a unitary factor independent of its individual constituents.

The conception of organizations I presented in Chapter 1 similarly converges on the same outcome. On this view, the organization is constituted by an interlocking constellation of roles, interrelated by an orientation toward some mission or goal. To be sure, these roles are occupied by individuals, each of whom is also the occupant of numerous other roles. But at least in a well-functioning organization, the individuals' participation is dominated by their organizational roles, which thus secure a level of unity and coherence. There is room in this picture for normative control: to be constituted by roles is to be a normative subject, guided by a script and susceptible to changes in it. Orientation toward a unifying mission or goal also makes organizations appropriate objects of rewards and deprivations, similar to the kinds of positive and negative incentives by which individual conduct is often directed. Again, these rewards and deprivations have the traction that they do by virtue of the organizational goals that are embedded in the various roles constitutive of the organization.

These conclusions pave the way for the main question we raised at the outset, whether considerations of dignity apply to collectivities as well. By pursuing this question we tap into a conversation that is not for the most part conducted in these terms. Inquiries into the normative status of various collectivities are not commonly pursued by posing explicitly the question of their dignity; it is more common to raise the question in terms of the entity's moral personhood or its rights. But the questions are equivalent. Within a dignity-based morality, to possess dignity is among other things to qualify as a primary subject of morality, and so to be the bearer of what we think of as fundamental rights. So even if no one explicitly defends ascribing dignity to corporations,[5] some writers come close. They maintain that the kinds of properties I associate with practical personality—such as a capacity for unified action and for decision making—constitute people's moral personality as well. Once it is realized that corporations display these capacities, they too must be recognized as moral persons and be endowed with the appropriate rights.[6]

In order to assess this conclusion we need take a closer look at the relationship between practical and moral personality. Does the one entail the other? The negative answer I urge tackles what may appear as the most innocuous link in the chain of reasoning just outlined. It is an assumption not primarily about the ascription of moral personality to corporations, but more basically about the moral personality of human beings, to whom corporations are in turn assimilated or compared. On this view, in order to provide human dignity with the supposedly requisite foundation, we must start by composing a list of traits that would provide rational support for attributing dignity to their bearers, and then inquire which entities possess these morally significant traits. We can gain some perspective on this approach by relating the corporate personhood debate to a parallel discussion about the treatment of animals. The common concern is whether nonhuman entities possess traits of moral personhood that entitle them to moral consideration on the same basis as that extended to humans.[7] And in both cases, of corporations and animals, the investigation is prompted by a similar worry: to attach distinctive moral significance to humanity is to display a prejudice, "in favor of biological persons"[8] when corporations are at issue, and in favor of the species Homo sapiens when animals are.[9] The concept of a person that is detached from that of a human being and endowed with primary moral significance is designed to counter the alleged prejudice. The question of who is a person is supposedly open to objective, even-handed inquiry. Self-serving human favoritism is ruled out.

Relating the corporate personhood debate to that of animal rights is instructive, since the claims and the rhetoric in regard to animals tend to be more extreme, and so help highlight some dangers that lurk in the case of corporations as well. In both cases, humanity is put on the defensive, with some troubling results. One is the pressure to extend to these nonhumans the full panoply of human rights.* Most of those who write in this vein balk at this conclusion and try to resist the pressure. But once the notion of personhood is detached from that of humanity, much footwork is required to avoid this slide, and the pressure occasionally prevails. A second danger is the flipside of the first. Resistance to the idea that corporations and animals should be granted certain rights, coupled with insistence that a "neutral" concept of personhood is required to secure

---

* This is of course not to imply that our values do not extend to the welfare of animals and indeed to the inanimate environment as well; but these values belong to different normative departments, which are not my present concern. See note on p. 151.

an even-handed approach, creates pressure in the opposite direction, for it can also entail curtailing some human rights to bring them into alignment with those of nonhumans. Finally, and most alarmingly, once detached descriptive criteria replace the concept of a human being, it turns out that human beings satisfy these criteria to varying degrees, and some do not even make the moral cut at all.

To call these implications "dangers" is of course to appeal to a set of pretheoretical judgments or intuitions that not everyone shares. But those who do find these implications unappealing face a serious challenge. If certain traits and capacities I observe in Sarah credit her with dignity, and if subsequently I observe that General Motors exhibits equivalent traits and capacities, am I not bound, on simple grounds of consistency, to extend dignity to General Motors as well? The doubt I'd like to raise focuses on the antecedent of the conditional just stated. For the practical personality we ascribe to GM is indeed established by observation and study, even if what is being observed and studied is at bottom a cluster of human practices, discursive or otherwise. But ascribing to people an unconditional and inviolable worth is an altogether different idea, reached in a very different way.

To begin with, the train of thought that results in my ascribing dignity to Sarah does not start with her, but with myself, and is not driven by observation. Rather, we arrive at the idea of human dignity, our own and that of other human beings, by contemplating, in Kant's famous idiom, the conditions of possibility of our moral experience.[10] Such contemplation can only be conducted by someone who is aware of having this experience, and who wonders what might account for it. This inquiry essentially involves the inquirer's "I," as it is carried out in the first person and "from within." It consists not in registering any observations one makes, but in spelling out what the "I" conducting this inquiry might designate, so as to make the moral experience intelligible and credible. The conclusions of this inquiry apply, in the first place, only to whoever conducts it. But extending them to others does not involve observation either, nor is it a matter of parity of reasoning, but rather of continuing and expanding the initial, self-regarding thought. As we have seen earlier (in Chapter 6), contemplating what I take at the outset to be the content of my inner life turns out upon reflection to imply a public space. What gives my own life definition and meaning is at a high level of abstraction what gives definition and meaning to your life as well. Since the meaning constitutive of other human lives, abstractly conceived, is the very same meaning constitutive of my own life, more concretely conceived, I relate to other human lives in the same kind of way in which I relate to my own—that is, from within. And so if what I come up with in contemplating my own self grounds to my satisfaction my own moral worth, it turns out that I have also arrived by the same train of thought at another destination: that of accounting for humanity's special moral worth. The space of meaning revealed to me in the first-personal reflection and within which my own identity is defined, encompasses humanity as a whole, leading to the conclusion that my own dignity and the dignity of humanity are one and the same.

It may seem possible to uphold the approach against which I inveigh in Kant's own name. Doesn't he hold that moral personality, and so dignity, issue from a capacity for autonomy, and isn't this capacity an empirical trait that some creatures display and others lack? We are, of course, not bound to follow Kant every step of the way, but it is important to raise a red flag against the aberrations that result in this case from following him only part of it. In holding that autonomy grounds dignity, we should be careful to distinguish autonomy in Kant's own transcendental sense, from an empirical sense in which autonomy designates some observable human psychological capabilities, which though supposedly more advanced and sophisticated, are nonetheless of the same kind as those displayed by many other creatures, be they computers or giraffes.[11] After all, one of the main points of the idiom of dignity as used by Kant is to deny that people's value can be placed in the same metric as the value of anything else. And this relates to the further point that the role of human beings in the Kantian axiology I've presented earlier (in Chapter 6) is not in the first place as the objects of valuation but as its subjects, as the creators and origins of value: humanity creates a system of meanings within which facts become intelligible and evaluative judgments possible. People's own supreme worth is not itself the product of the resulting values but their precondition: a necessary presupposition of the validity or objectivity that we claim for the normative orders in which we dwell.

To be sure, human beings do generally display the kinds of traits I've associated with the notion of practical personality. Once a system of categories, concepts, values, and the like is in place, it makes room for, among many other things, human beings conceived as empirical objects of observation. And as the observation of human beings reveals, they do generally display the kinds of traits we commonly associate with one or another notion of personhood. But a crucial difference between their practical and moral personality remains. Practical personality is variable and contingent, whereas dignity is unitary and categorical. People differ in their level of rationality and agency, and some display such capacities only marginally or not at all. Similar variation occurs intrapersonally as well; the capacities in question fluctuate and are occasionally extinguished, as during sleep or a coma. But none of this affects dignity and the respect it mandates. Granted, the apposite manifestation of respect is sensitive to a human being's state and capacities. Though respect ordinarily requires some deference to self-regarding choices, for instance, this requirement is moot in the case of someone who can't make any. But whatever the requisite manifestation of respect, the underlying value, dignity, is possessed by all human beings fully, equally, and uninterruptedly.

But even if the approach to the derivation of human dignity I advocate is accepted, a question regarding the scope of dignity remains. To expand by abstraction along the lines I've charted my own use of "I" would indeed encompass within the resulting universal "we" all other I-sayers. But this would still appear to leave out some human beings, incapable of an "I"-, or any other corresponding, thought. The contours of "I" and so of "we" do not entirely coincide with those of the human species. In contemplating this point, it should be first noted how limited the issue raised by this observation is. The observation pertains only to such (fortunately rare) cases as the congenitally and permanently comatose.[12] Even so, this observation does present any humanist approach with a challenge, and despite many attempts to meet it, the issue persists.[13] Still, three points in mitigation can be made. The first is to note that this observation does not directly conflict with the denial that nonhumans are bearers of dignity: belonging to the human species may still be a necessary condition for the possession of dignity even if it is not sufficient. Second, there is no contradiction between associating human dignity with the meaning-conception of self and the idea of human self-creation on the one hand and a biological conception of Homo sapiens as a natural kind. In making this connection I have earlier referred to Pico della Mirandola's *Oration*,[14] and here too we can follow in his footsteps. Pico's *Oration* is a spin on the story of creation, and so he treats humanity as one biological species among others. The thesis of human self-creation is on this view grounded in a system of classification in which the extension of Homo sapiens is as naturally fixed as is the extension of Loxodonta africana. Who is a human being is a given; what she is, is not.* To be sure, the capacity for self-creation requires that the conception of humanity as a biological species be overlaid with another order of signification in which the organism is endowed with meaning and thus is thought of and treated in respect of its intelligibility. But attending to the meanings that distinguish humanity from other species does not undo the biological extension of the term. Think by analogy of the relationship in the case of books between the physical volume and, say, the novel it contains. Irrelevant complications aside, the extension of *book* in some library would be the same irrespective of whether one were to attend to the volumes or to the novels. For example, one can confidently count the books even if, illiterate, one could not tell apart *Anna Karenina* from *The Old Man and the Sea*.

And third, our responses to the marginal and exceptional conditions corroborate the view that counting their subjects as human beings dominates the way we assess their worth consistently with the conception of dignity I have presented. For consider again those who fall below the threshold of personhood due to a permanent vegetative state. Unlike a cabbage or a cucumber to which these people are implicitly and unkindly compared, the permanently comatose being fills us with horror and dread.

---

* Though the two questions can become entangled, such as in respect to determinations regarding the beginning and end of life.

Why? The question is not trivial, since in the absence of sensations, one common reason for such reactions to human predicaments, empathy for suffering, does not seem to apply. A possible answer has two parts. First, it is not a misfortune for a vegetable to be in a vegetative state, whereas it is a great misfortune for John or Mary to be in this state. Failure to satisfy the conditions of personhood (whatever they are) is for a human being to fall short. But this is only half the answer, since vegetables too may come up short in terms of desirable traits that apply to them, and yet fail to elicit in us a similar response. So the second reason for our dread in the face of the comatose human being is that we recognize in her a horrible version of ourselves. Not only because we may suffer a similar fate: depending on the details of the case, the likelihood of this may be quite remote. Rather, our reaction can be better explained by the fact that the comatose human exhibits a radically degraded version of the meaning of human life, which at a higher level of abstraction is the meaning of our lives as well.

The conclusion that we cannot ascribe dignity to collectivities on the basis of their practical personhood does not, however, bring the inquiry into collective dignity to an end. There may be other roads leading to ascribing dignity to collectivities. Indeed, the conception of dignity I have presented implies such an alternative road. I have earlier argued that the respect due to an individual, call her Kim, and the respect for humanity as a whole is the same attitude conceived at the polar ends of a single scale of abstraction, and that the same respectful attitude pertains to all the intermediate levels of abstraction that define Kim's identity as well. Just as at a high level of resolution Kim is to be respected as an individual, and at a high level of abstraction, as a person, she must also be respected as an architect, or a plumber, or a nurse. But in addition to such roles as these, Kim's identity, and so dignity, may be bound up with some collective affiliations. And this requires that we take seriously those clusters of meaning on which she herself draws when appropriately using the plural pronoun *we* to convey these collective aspects of her identity. To see the point, consider such invidious attitudes as racism, sexism, and anti-Semitism. Even when addressed to a specific individual, we treat an expression of these attitudes as an affront to all members of the target community, since these attitudes address their specific individual victims precisely in their capacity as bearers of an identity shared by others, and so implicate all of them as well. As a Jew, I am affected by an expression of anti-Semitism aimed at other Jewish people, since I correctly conclude that *we* are offended by it. This reaction can be plausibly seen as implicitly asserting the dignity of the Jewish people, which is, however, indistinguishable from my own dignity as, among other things, a Jew.[15] Put more generally, we can sensibly ascribe dignity to a collectivity when affiliation with that collectivity plays a constitutive role in the members' identity, thus underwriting their use of a nondistributive, collective *we*.

But though some collective affiliations are identity-shaping, and so come within the range of the members' dignity, others are not. In particular, the question arises whether this way of ascribing dignity to a collectivity is available with regard to the business corporation. It is not. The reason is that no individuals stand to the corporation in a relationship that would underwrite a credible use of the *we* locution so as to efface the distinction between things done to or by the corporation and things done to or by those individuals. For who would these individuals be? Of the corporation's various stakeholders, only two groups, employees and shareholders, are plausible candidates. The connection to the corporation of other groups, such as customers and suppliers, is too transitory and narrow to present an even prima facie case. But even when it comes to the two candidate groups, the affiliation with the business corporation is distant and impersonal. This follows in both cases from a conception of the corporation as the instrumental entity par excellence. The defining ethos of the business corporation, an ethos that provides the avowed basis for the corporation's structure, legitimacy, and normative claims, consists, in a nutshell, in four interrelated tenets: the business corporation is a specialized structure designed to perform a limited range of functions (producing some commodities or providing some services); by doing so it serves as a vehicle for increasing aggregate welfare and prosperity; the best way for it to attain these goals is by maximizing its profits within a competitive market, subject to some legal constraints; and this in turn is best accomplished by a primary commitment to increasing stockholders' returns, either in the form of dividends, or more commonly, by increasing the value of their shares.

How does this instrumental conception of the corporation affect the position of the employees? To answer this question, we must distinguish a notion of the *instrumental* from the related yet importantly distinct notion of the *functional*. As I use these terms here, *functional* denotes "having a special activity, purpose, or task," whereas *instrumental* denotes "serving as a means."[16] To speak of human beings in functional terms is to point to a pervasive and innocuous phenomenon. Pursuing various tasks provides people with meaningful projects and gives content to people's lives. Such a functional relationship to a task characterizes many primary roles within the corporation as well; for example, an engineer working for a corporation may reasonably draw part of her life's meaning from designing the widgets the corporation manufactures. But her affiliation with the corporation is a different matter. An instrumental conception of the corporation according to which the corporation "serves as a means" determines the nature of the corporation's relation with its employees, independently of their position or rank: they are its resource, or, in a common and suitable metaphor, they are cogs in the machine, and so means rather than ends. Role-distance is the countermeasure. Conceiving of the employees' corporate affiliation as a distant one, and so dampening their identification with the corporation diffuses the affront to dignity that would otherwise be involved.* It is, of course, in the corporation's interest to encourage identification and so enlist the employees' loyalty. But theirs is the mercenary's loyalty for hire, and their use of the collective *we* an acknowledged contrivance or else a massive display of bad faith.[17]

The situation regarding stockholders, the corporation's official owners, is different, and may appear reversed: rather than the stockholders being the instruments of the corporation, the corporation would seem to be their instrument. And this in turn might have weighty implications for

---

* That does not mean that there cannot be informal communal relationships *within* the corporation, but these are not relationships *with* the corporation.

identification: as a human being, I should never become part of an instrument, but an instrument may become part of me (as when a hammer is incorporated into a carpenter's physical extension or a brush of a painter's).[18] So a stockholder might be able to allude by a use of *we* to the corporation as included within her extended self. But though such a relation between stockholders and corporations is conceivable, it does not in fact obtain. Due to the separation of ownership from control, stockholders can be said to own the corporation only in a peculiar and truncated sense. This is not just a contingent or adventitious matter resulting from the dispersion of stock among numerous shareholders. Rather, the separation is rooted in the same ethos I've outlined that provides the interpretive backdrop for the corporate phenomenon as a whole. Lack of direct control over business decisions is a device designed to ensure that the corporation's long-term profitability take precedence over whatever any shareholder's actual preferences may happen to be. This has a crucial bearing on our conception of the stockholders themselves as mere placeholders for a narrow, artificially contrived "profit motive," over which, in their capacity as stockholders, they are not in charge. A stockholder is not at liberty to abjure the motive ascribed to her, or to integrate it with other values and desires that may prove antagonistic to the corporate interest. Far from being able to expand her self by means of her ownership of the corporation, the stockholder's corporate affiliation would project a truncated and pale shadow of that self—unless, of course, what is thus projected is not the stockholder's self at all, but a detached role that is appropriately wielded and manipulated by the stockholder at arm's length. The view of stockholding as a distant role that does not engage the stockholder's identity, and so does not involve her dignity either, is emphatically confirmed by the idea of limited liability, perhaps the single most important device in the mode of operation characteristic of the corporate economy: the structure of responsibility associated with the stockholder's role signifies a strict divide between the stockholder's corporate affiliation and her self.*

---

* This view of shareholding also implies that if by democracy we mean self-rule and so a realization of human autonomy, the expression "shareholder democracy" is a misnomer.

In summary, these comments are designed to support the following conclusions, positive and negative. Collectivities can be both consequentialist and deontological subjects. They are consequentialist subjects when treating them as unified agents and patients is pragmatically warranted by the kinds of organizational factors I have pointed out. But this does not make them into deontological subjects. Collectivities are deontological subjects when affiliation with them is bound up with the members' identity so as to implicate the members' dignity. Business corporations in particular have practical personality, and so are consequentialist subjects, but are not deontological subjects: the identities of their members do not merge with them and hence the members' dignity does not affect them. As stated here, these conclusions form at most the bare bones of a theory concerning the normative status of various collectivities.[19] The next two chapters are intended to put some more flesh on these bones.

9

Sanctioning Corporations

I. REFORMULATING THE QUESTION

In Chapter 7 I have considered the substantive reach of the criminal law in light of a dignity-centered Kantian morality. I now turn to examine some implications of the same approach to criminal law on its personal reach, specifically with regard to the much-debated question of whether corporations should be criminally punished.* For ease of reference I label this *the Question*. The Question arises in the intersection between two sets of issues that occupied us in other parts of the book, ontological and normative: we need a conception of what collective entities, in particular corporations, are, and of what is just or appropriate punishment. There is no agreement on either of these foundational matters, with the result that the Question remains highly contested. But though the Question receives conflicting answers, there is one point of tacit agreement: that the Question is properly posed. The very disagreement as to whether corporations (and other collectivities) should be criminally punished attests to a shared premise that this question sets the correct scholarly agenda, and that a positive or

---

* Though this question arises about collective entities in general, like many others, I focus on the large business corporation. This designation combines the strictly legal notion of incorporation with the sociological notion of an *organization*, which connotes structure and a certain level of complexity. My comments can be extended, with caution and necessary adjustments, to various other collectivities.

negative answer is the desired goal. My starting point in this chapter is to question the Question. By presenting us with a binary option the Question forces upon us a false dilemma that distorts the debate and induces unwarranted, sometimes paradoxical consequences. Refusing the Question is the first step toward escaping the dilemma and rectifying the terms of the debate to which it gives rise.

Two tacit assumptions regarding criminal liability underlie the Question: that criminal liability is, first, a unitary category that, second, derives its meaning from a paradigm case involving individual offenders. The first assumption is implicit in the single label used to designate the practice under consideration. The second assumption is implicit in the challenge that corporations supposedly present in this regard: punishing corporations is perceived as *extending* a practice whose natural domain is populated by individuals. It is easy to see how these assumptions shape the debate. The first defines its conceptual contours. The question whether to hold corporations criminally liable is presented as a package deal; we are asked to cast a yes-or-no vote, as it were, on a single option, that of subjecting corporations to an existing regime of criminal justice. The second assumption dictates the normative tenor of the discussion: in order to be punishable, corporations must be assimilated in one way or another to the paradigmatic individual offenders, and so the normative considerations and concerns that bear on punishing corporations turn out to be those that bear on punishing individuals. In light of these two assumptions, the dilemma to which I alluded is clear: punishing corporations requires forcing them, conceptually as well as normatively, into a preexisting procrustean bed designed to accommodate a different type of occupant; yet to refrain from punishing them is to exempt some powerful agents, capable of great social harm, from a significant instrument of social control. However, when made explicit, both assumptions look shaky, and ways of loosening their grip appear.

Consider the first assumption. *Criminal liability* designates a variegated cluster of ideas and a complex institutional structure. It is not made of whole cloth. Nevertheless, treating it, with the aid of a single label, as an undifferentiated unit, has considerable practical as well as intellectual merit. Thinking, no less than practice, hinges on such composites whose unity is for the most part taken for granted. Yet depending on the goals we pursue or the nature of the investigation we conduct, it is sometimes advisable to disaggregate a given composite and refine the analysis by attending more closely to the composite's components. The legal treatment of corporations is a sufficiently important matter to call for such an approach. Once we look at criminal liability through even the feeblest magnifying glass and subject it to the dullest scalpel, many disparate elements spring into view and can be pried apart. Criminal liability is a form of centralized social control that employs coercion, is initiated by the state, is rule-bound, is judicially administered, and so forth. Each of these elements can be in turn further unpacked: there is no algorithm for delimiting in advance the level of detail that would best serve in a thorough investigation of the kind the Question calls for; judgment is required to decide how fine-grained our approach ought to be. The Question, however, avoids such a judgment by hiding the multiplicity of issues and options that arise in this area under the terminological rug it blithely throws over them. However, when we peer under the rug or remove it entirely, we are in a better position to pick and choose among various elements in an effort to best adapt the practice of punishment as designed for individual offenders to the properties of the collectivities concerned.

Adjusting criminal punishment to a corporate context is also hampered by the second assumption underlying the Question. Conceiving of individuals as the paradigmatic criminal offenders implies a criterion, call it the criterion of individuality, in light of which the Question must be answered: corporations are punishable if and only if punishing them would amount to or be the equivalent of punishing individual human beings. There are two ways in which this criterion can be satisfied in principle, and they correspond to the two main schools of thought regarding the nature of collectivities that were discussed in the previous chapter: *holistic* and *reductionist*. As I pointed out, holists affirm the existence of collective entities over and above their individual members, whereas reductionists maintain that to talk about collective entities is to use a shorthand or indulge in a fiction, and in either case is to designate nothing but the multitude of individual agents and their interactions. Though the holistic and the reductionist approaches to collectivities are, ontologically speaking, polar opposites, their implications for the issue at hand can, perhaps somewhat surprisingly, converge. Whether the corporation is envisaged by the holist as an individual-like entity or by the reductionist as an aggregate of individuals, its legal treatment can be assimilated to the treatment appropriate for individual human actors. But in neither case is the fit comfortable and the conclusion happy. Consequently, deciding the Question in light of the criterion of individuality loads the dice in favor of a negative answer. For the holists, advocating corporate punishment requires that they identify in the corporation relevant human properties that permit analogizing it to an individual; such theorists risk committing the notorious anthropomorphic fallacy.[1] Reductionist advocates of corporate punishment find themselves on an equally treacherous path: they in effect favor the imposition of a form of collective punishment on a heterogeneous group of people many of whom do not satisfy the requirements of blameworthiness ordinarily required by criminal law. Attenuating these requirements in the present context seems both dangerous and ad hoc.

In light of these difficulties, it is no surprise that many theorists opt for the negative horn of the dilemma created by the Question by rejecting corporate criminal liability, much as this position collides with a pretheoretical reluctance to let corporations off the criminal hook.[2] Others resist this conclusion, contriving instead an affirmative answer.[3] However, these theorists too have been led astray by the Question and fallen into what may be a less visible but no less perilous trap. By resolving the dilemma in favor of corporate punishment, these theorists are likely to view themselves as striking a blow against corporate power and its abuses; they fashion themselves the black rather than the white knights of the corporate world. In fact, the blow they strike may have just the opposite effect. To see this paradoxical aspect of the present debate we must return to the first assumption underlying the Question, concerning the supposed unity of criminal liability. In contesting this assumption, I have distinguished a number of disparate factors that this practice ordinarily combines.

However, for present purposes we need focus only on two. One is the *sanction*—that is, the use of power to affect conduct. But as noted in Chapter 7, the practice of criminal punishment has an additional salient aspect: an unusually restrictive system of *constraints*—substantive, procedural, and evidentiary—to which the use of this power is subject. The debate concerning the punishment of corporations focuses on the first element, the sanction, whereas the second element, the constraints, is mostly taken for granted, and so remains invisible. An affirmative answer to the Question accordingly involves not only a recommendation that corporations be liable to sanction, but also a further and usually undefended implication that once the state imposes sanctions on a corporation, it is bound by the same network of constraints that tie its hands when punishing individuals.[4] Once we depart from the unitary notion of criminal liability, and specifically distinguish between sanctions and constraints, the Question divides in two. First, ought corporations to be sanctioned—that is, subject to the enforcement of criminal norms? Second, ought the sanctioning of corporations be bound by criminal law's strict restrictions?

These two questions can only be pursued in light of the answers to more fundamental ones: why does the criminal law impose sanctions? why does it employ constraints? Though this is a highly contested area, I will proceed with an approach to punishment that enjoys considerable support. According to this familiar story, criminal law's coercive threats are designed to promote some social goals or values, mostly through deterrence. But these goals and values set necessary but insufficient conditions for punishment. As mentioned earlier,[5] the reason is that we can imagine situations in which punishment would serve these purposes when imposed on someone who is innocent of any wrongdoing; yet, punishing the innocent even in those situations would be a moral outrage. But why? Seen in consequentialist terms, the answer is far from obvious; the opposition to punishing the innocent rests more securely on broadly Kantian grounds. Punishing the innocent, even in the service of some desirable goals, amounts to treating an individual as a means rather than as an end, and so is offensive to human dignity. To ensures that punishment be limited to the blameworthy thus requires restricting the consequentialist reasons that support sanctions in the first place by a system of dignity-based moral constraints.[6] Evincing this heightened anxiety lest an innocent defendant be punished, the substantive, evidentiary, and procedural strictures of the criminal trial erect on the road to conviction some formidable obstacles that exceed what pure consequentialist considerations would mandate.[7]

In order to apply this account to corporations and answer the two questions just distinguished, we accordingly need to inquire, first, whether corporations are proper objects of the consequentialist considerations served by sanctions, specifically deterrence; and second, whether they are proper objects of the deontological concerns that call for side constraints. Some writers treat these two questions as equivalent, but the distinction I drew in the previous chapter between *practical* and *moral* personhood implies that they are not. This leads to an affirmative answer to the first question and to a negative answer to the second. In the interest of keeping the promise (made at the beginning of this book) of maintaining each chapter as freestanding, I will summarize the considerations presented in the previous chapter that lead to these conclusions, and then raise some additional points that bear on the two questions at hand.

II. WHY SANCTION

The case for subjecting corporations to sanctions consists of two complementary claims: that sanctioning corporations is needed and that it is efficacious. Both the need and the efficacy depend on a dual distinction: between *distributive* and *global* corporate acts, and correspondingly, between *distributive* and *global* effects on the corporation. By distributive acts I mean acts that, though ascribed to the corporation, are performed by some identifiable individuals; nondistributive acts are corporate acts that are not traceable or reducible to the acts of particular individuals. Similarly in regard to effects on the corporation: actions that are putatively directed toward the corporation will have distributive effects when the effects are traceable to some particular individuals, and global effects otherwise. The existence of global corporate acts would create a gap between controlling the conduct of particular individuals on the one hand, and a modification of the corporation's conduct on the other, and so would provide corporate sanctions with a target and an objective. Without sanctioning the corporation, we would face an accountability and enforcement deficit. But this would be only half the case for sanctioning corporations. The fact that there is a gap does not mean that ways of filling it exist, and in particular that corporate sanctions would avail. The other half of the argument accordingly concerns the likely efficacy of imposing sanctions on the corporation. Here the notion of global effects comes into play. Corporate sanctions are distinguished precisely by the fact that they are designed to affect the corporation as such, rather than any particular individuals. This can be accomplished only if global, non-distributive effects on the corporation exist.

When the question of sanctioning corporations is posed in these terms, an affirmative answer seems quite straightforward, since despite the controversy regarding this question, it is not really clear whether the existence of global actions and effects that would support corporate sanctions are ever seriously contested. Although there is a wide range of approaches to what I have called in the previous chapter the corporation's *practical personhood*, they tend to converge in their relevant conclusions. To see this we need look a bit closer at the main division, mentioned in the previous section, between holistic views and reductionist views. The holistic views differ, but they all share two abstract and general philosophical tenets. One is the distinction between constitution and identity: whereas a corporation is constituted by a bunch of individuals, it is not identical with them. Where does the difference come from? Here, the notion that comes into play is that of emergent properties. The world is after all full of composites with global properties quite different from the properties of their components (e.g., water is wet whereas H_2O molecules are not). The same holds of human composites as well. In this vein, organization theory, broadly conceived, can be seen as carrying out a program of spelling out the various structural factors that mediate between what are seen as individual inputs on the one hand, and some global features or outcomes attributable only to the organization as a whole, on the other.

Although reductionists take a different ontological approach to collectivities, their conclusions regarding the corporation's practical personhood converge for the most part with the holists'. While insisting that an account of collective phenomena in terms of individual actors is *in principle* possible and desirable, few would deny the epistemological and other practical obstacles to actually performing the reduction and advocate eliminating the corporation as a unitary and independent factor. The upshot of these otherwise divergent views is that hardly anyone maintains that we can actually replace the name "the Ford Motor Company" in the statement "the Ford Motor Company manufactures the Mustang" with a list of all the individual contributions; nor is anyone likely to maintain that payment for the car could be made in the form of direct payments to all these people, prorated to their relative contributions. This broad agreement is sufficient to make the case that sanctioning corporations addresses a genuine need and has a viable target. For just as manufacturing a car is a global corporate action, and a buyer's paying for it a global effect, so also are, respectively, polluting the environment and a fine.

As I mentioned, the case for sanctioning corporations depends not only on the need for such sanctions but also on their efficacy. To glimpse the ways sanctions may bring about a change in the corporation's conduct it is useful to distinguish three possible mechanisms of deterrence: *direct, indirect,* and *mediated*. Direct deterrence designates the most common, garden-variety form of deterrence in which the sanction is designed to influence the decisions and so directly modify the conduct of the sanction's intended object; the target of the sanction and the object of control coincide. In the two other forms, these diverge. Indirect deterrence occurs when, due to some special relationship between the target of sanction and the object of control, addressing the threat of sanction to the one will influence the decisions of the other. Think, for example, of a radical group kidnapping a politician so as to put pressure on the government, not on the captured politician. In mediated deterrence, the target of the sanction holds a position of power over the object of control or is otherwise able to modify the latter's behavior. In this case, the sanction is intended to impact its immediate target, but only so as to induce actions by her that would in turn influence the ultimate object of control—for example, holding parents responsible for the misdeeds of their children, intended to induce parental control over the children's behavior. Evidently, all three mechanisms of control apply in the case of a corporation. Sanctioning the corporation involves direct deterrence when we envisage the sanction, in impersonal terms, as a setback to the corporation's goals and so as a "disturbing event" in the corporation's environment that serves to alert its decision-making process to the existence of a certain dysfunction, triggering some standard operating procedure into taking remedial action consisting in some structural or systemic changes.[8] Indirect deterrence takes place when, whether out of loyalty or self-interest, members of the corporation respond to the harm to the corporation represented by sanctions. Their response may amount to or bring about a change in the corporation's behavior. Mediated deterrence reverses this direction of influence, which in this case runs from the corporation to its individual members: a corporation may be expected to react to sanctions, imposed in response to some harmful results ascribed to the corporation, by putting in place internal systems of pressures and rewards designed to change some individuals' patterns of behavior, so as to prevent the recurrence of such harmful results.[9]

III. AGAINST CONSTRAINTS

Whereas for the reasons just given imposing on corporations a regime of sanctions is warranted, subjecting these sanctions to the full panoply of criminal law's constraints is not. On the conception of criminal punishment I have summarized, these constraints are designed to protect defendants' dignity. To ask whether corporations ought to be protected by these restrictions is accordingly to inquire whether dignity extends to corporations. And as I argued in the previous chapter, it does not. In a nutshell, the argument that leads to this conclusion consists of the following steps.

The notion of dignity (expounded in Chapter 6) applies to human beings by virtue of their autonomy, which makes them the origin of all value, and so endows them with worth. However, as explained in the previous chapter, we do not reach this conclusion by observing which beings happen to possess some abstractly conceived dignity-supporting traits, but rather by reflecting on what best accounts, from a first-person perspective, for one's own experience as a self, and by investigating the significance and contours of the "I" in terms of which this experience is available and expressed. As I have also argued, however, the road to ascribing dignity to collectivities is not entirely blocked, since some collective affiliations, those that can be broadly labeled as *communal*, are constitutive of self, effacing the distinction between the respect due to the individuals qua members and the respect due to the collectivity as a whole. The final step in the argument then invokes an instrumental conception of business corporations to deny that affiliation with them by such constituencies as shareholders and employees plays this constitutive role. Since the identity of these groups' members is not bound up with the corporation, nor is their dignity.

But even if affiliation with the corporation is not constitutive of the members' identities, sanctioning corporations will have predictably negative effects on various stakeholders all the same. Do not these effects call for reinstating on the stakeholders' behalf the battery of side constraints that punishing individuals requires? True, the nominal defendant in a corporate criminal trial is the corporation rather than any designated individuals. But isn't ignoring the individual ramifications of the sanction taking this formality way too seriously, and ascribing to the corporate veil magical powers? The view of criminal law's restrictions as designed to avert the special threat to human dignity that punishment poses implies a negative answer. As I have argued in Chapter 7,[10] this threat is posed by punishment since it is an instance of a kind of deprivation I call *mistreatment*, a deliberate singling out of an individual for the sake of a severe deprivation.* The battery of restrictions created by criminal law

---

* The elements in this definition can come in various versions and in different degrees. In particular, one can "single out" in the relevant sense a group of individuals when one targets an identity-fixing (e.g., ethnic or racial) property common to its members. It is significant

is designed to mitigate this threat by ensuring, as much as possible, that the defendant is justly treated rather than being the victim of the equivalent of a crime. Punishing the corporation, however, involves no one's mistreatment. None of the shareholders or other stakeholders who are made worse off by the corporate sanction are personally singled out for a deliberate deprivation. Consequently, the effects of corporate sanctions on shareholders and other individuals do not carry the invidious message of disrespect that mistreating them would have. For this reason, the corporate veil not only hides but morally shelters individuals from the effects of corporate punishment. The resulting individual deprivations must, of course, be taken into account in designing the system of corporate criminal liability. But the role that these "collateral harms" should play in our deliberations lacks the special urgency present when the mistreatment of individuals is at issue.

IV. CONCLUSION

Nothing I have said in this chapter bears directly on the desirable level of government control of corporate behavior or on the best means of exercising such control. I have made two related but different points. First, the corporation is a suitable object for the imposition of sanctions.* Second, insofar as the imposition of sanctions is deemed desirable, it need not be hampered by the same restrictions as those that tie the government's hands when dealing directly with individuals. This dual conclusion has wider repercussions, within criminal law and beyond. Let me briefly indicate what they are.

One such repercussion relating to criminal law was foreshadowed earlier in this chapter when I mentioned various ways, other than the distinction between sanction and constraint, in which criminal law can be

---

therefore that membership in a corporation (e.g., that of its shareholders) is not identity-fixing, nor is the membership defined in terms of some other identity-fixing characteristic.

* This does not by itself tell us when, if ever, the imposition of sanctions is warranted, or how it compares with other modes of control.

disaggregated. This implies potential additional ways in which the treatment of corporations within what we broadly conceive as the criminal law can be custom-tailored to suit them. Exploring these possibilities might eventually lead to a two-track system, with the tracks differing along the substantive, procedural, and evidentiary dimensions. These tracks need not, however, end at the boundary of criminal law. The considerations that shape them pertain to other legal areas as well, suggesting a two-track legal system throughout.[11] Though some steps in this direction have already been taken, they are spotty and sporadic.[12]

The considerations canvassed in this chapter also suggest a broader claim, that the corporate economy opens up an area in which government has greater moral leeway than when its coercive power is brought to bear directly on individuals. Interposing an intermediate entity between government and its citizens blunts some of the moral edge of coercion and mitigates the threat it otherwise poses to individuals' dignity and autonomy. This has two complementary implications. One is that in dealing with corporations, the government may legitimately pursue social goals more aggressively than when dealing with individuals. The second implication is that the greater moral license the government enjoys in regard to corporations may bolster greater circumspection on government's behalf in dealing with individuals. Shifting government's coercive powers from individuals to corporations, and letting the latter serve as the preferred vehicles for attaining policy objectives, may provide a way of promoting the social interest with a reduced moral toll.

10

Freedoms of Collective Speech

Few areas of law have occasioned such fierce disagreements and reversals of course by the Supreme Court as corporate free speech.[1] The area does indeed raise difficult issues. Although theories are not designed to decide cases, greater theoretical clarity is indispensable. However, in order to gain some insight into issues of corporate speech we cannot treat them in isolation; we must locate them instead in the broader context of collective speech. Drawing on the discussion in previous chapters of this book, I distinguish between two main types of collectivities, organizations and communities, and then subdivide organizations in terms of the nature of their communicative activities into *commercial, expressive*, and *protective*.* In addition, the last section of this chapter focuses on government speech, which raises some thorny issues of its own. This typology of collectivities is imbricated in turn with a typology of speech rights. As I argue in the next section, freedom of speech is a cluster of rights, reflecting different considerations that bear on the kind and level of protection due to any entity in regard to its communications. The upshot of the present chapter resembles the point made in the preceding chapter regarding corporate criminal liability: the respective rights involved in both cases provide individuals, and by extension communities, with a shield that is not directly available to corporations and other organizations. But due to the multiplicity of rights to free speech on the one hand, and to the

---

* These categories are meant to be neither exhaustive nor mutually exclusive.

multiple ways in which various collectivities relate to communication on the other, the overall shape of collective freedom of speech is quite complex. The best summary I can offer of my conclusions is provided in a table at the end of this chapter. Perhaps by way of a general orientation, the reader may want to take a glance at it now, though I fear that at this stage it may prove quite uninformative, whereas by the time it is reached in due course it may seem otiose.

I. RIGHTS TO FREE SPEECH

The normative backdrop to the following discussion of free speech is the same as the one that served us in other parts of the book: a juxtaposition between utilitarian consequentialism on the one hand and Kantian deontology on the other. But whereas various aspects of law and social policy are amenable to interpretation in terms of either approach, the concept of a right, at least in accordance with a prominent conception, arises out of the tension between the two. On this view, rights are designed to insulate certain aspects of persons and their lives from the demands of society's aggregate welfare, thus securing individuals' autonomy and respect for their dignity. In discussing freedom of speech, I focus exclusively on this "strong" meaning of right.[2] To carry the weight normally assigned to it, freedom of speech must be understood as what I call an *autonomy right*—that is, a right that protects some fundamental aspects of personhood vital to one's dignity and exercise of autonomy.*

Even within these somewhat artificial strictures freedom of speech remains a complex right. First, freedom of speech is supported by two sets of interests: those of the speaker, the *active* aspect of free speech,

---

* I don't accordingly pursue here the question whether corporate and other collective communications should get some protection on purely utilitarian grounds. Within the present scheme, the rights secured by such protections would be "weak," because they would be vulnerable to conflicting utilitarian policy considerations and liable to being defeated by them.

and those of the listener, the *passive* aspect. The active right to speak is linked to the ideas of self-expression and self-realization, whereas the passive right to listen emphasizes the importance of access to information, ideas, and points of view for one's ability to form independent, informed, and intelligent judgments. A second distinction that applies to freedom of speech is between two kinds of rights. A right may be recognized in P out of concern for P himself. In such a case, P has what I shall call an *original right*. A right may be also granted to P out of concern for someone else. In this case, P will be said to have a *derivative right*. A guardian, for example, may be given such rights as are necessary for the effective execution of her role. The reason for these rights would lie in the concern for the ward's interests, and only derivatively in the concern for protecting the guardian's interests.[3] By combining the two distinctions, we get the following typology of speech rights. In addition to the speaker's *original* right to self-expression, concern for the listener's autonomy-based right to listen implies a *passive derivative right* in the speaker not to be interrupted in her communications. First Amendment protection may also extend to someone other than the speaker if granting such protection to the other person promotes or protects the original speaker's self-expression. A publisher of a book, for example, may deserve such protection based on her contribution to the author's self-expression. In such a case the publisher would have an *active derivative speech right*.

Though all speech rights secure to their bearers a measure of protection, the scope and the weight of a speech right crucially depend on whether it is considered original or derivative, and in the latter case, on the primary interest from which the right is derived. An original speech right recognizes speech as an integral aspect of the speaker's autonomy; to respect the right is to respect that aspect of the right-bearer's dignity that is bound up with her self-expression. Infringing an original autonomy right is prima facie wrong even when done in order to enhance the enjoyment of a similar right in others, since doing so would amount to an impermissible act of sacrificing one person for another. In contrast, a derivative right is instrumental: its purpose is to safeguard or enhance the enjoyment of certain rights by others. And as all instruments, a derivative right is measured by its effectiveness. It may be limited or discarded in favor of better means to attain the same goals.

II. ORGANIZATIONAL SPEECH

Can Organizations Speak?

Before we discuss the protections due to organizational speech, we must address a threshold question: is organizational speech distinct from the communications of particular individuals? In other words, can organizations speak? Indeed, one line of opposition to extending First Amendment protection to corporate speech denies the existence of such speech, maintaining instead that only individuals can communicate. Talk of corporate speech in particular, and organizational speech more generally, is seen as a misleading way of referring to the views of those in control combined with their expending corporate or other organizations' resources to disseminate these views.[4] If the messages transmitted by an organization are always attributable to specific individuals, withholding First Amendment protection from such putatively organizational speech would result in no loss in communicative content. The same ideas and information would remain in circulation, with the additional advantage that their individual sources would be exposed rather than hidden behind an organizational veil.

To those, like myself, averse to extending to organizations full-fledged First Amendment protections, this line of reasoning is tempting, since it offers an easy way out from a normative conundrum. But the temptation must be resisted. Ascribing speech to organizations makes sense, and does not require resorting to anthropomorphism or spooky metaphysics. In considering the constitutional status of organizational and specifically corporate speech, we must accordingly grapple with the normative issues that arise once we recognize that such speech exists. The grounds for ascribing speech to the organization rather than to any particular individuals have been laid in previous chapters, specifically in our discussion of two pivotal notions: organizational decision-making and organizational roles.[5] As we have seen, one of the main, and indeed defining, features of formal organizations is a decision-making process geared toward the attainment of the organizational goals. Implicit in the notion of decision making are two other notions: information and preferences. And for reasons we have already mentioned, neither the information nor the preferences involved are reducible to the information and the preferences that are associated with particular individuals. An organizational communication, like other products and performances we ascribe to organizations, is the result of decision-making processes that combine preferences with information in ways that create an ineliminable gap between the individual inputs and the global, organizational output. Consequently, speech, no less than widgets, may be a global, nondistributive phenomenon, emanating from the organization without being traceable or reducible to individual utterances.

The foregoing description of organizational speech as the joint and undifferentiated product of complex decision-making processes does not, however, always apply. Sometimes, the speech we ascribe to the organization is uttered by a specific, identifiable individual. But even in this simpler case, the organizational perspective cannot be avoided and a constitutional analysis in terms of the individual speaker's own self-expression would not do. Statements made by organizational position-holders carry with them the understanding that they are made "from the organizational point of view" and in one's "official capacity." Such speech cannot be extracted from the organizational context and viewed instead as uttered by the speaker in her individual capacity and on her own behalf: the speaker may be neither inclined nor able to perform the same speech acts outside of her office hours, so to speak. Failure to recognize that such speech is made in the speaker's official capacity and is thus irreducibly organizational in nature, and the consequent failure to protect it as such, may result in this particular message being lost.

Organizational Speech and Individual Speech

Recognizing that organizations can speak seems to lead to the conclusion, unpalatable to many, that such speech deserves the same protection as individual speech. In an attempt to avoid this conclusion, especially in regard to business corporations, courts and commentators have appealed to "compelling state interests" that can supposedly override the legal protection due to such speech. These alleged interests vary, and they include such concerns as protecting the marketplace of ideas from domination by wealthy corporations, and making sure that investment opportunities not be affected by a corporation's controversial political views.[6] But as defenders of corporate free speech have been quick to point out, the same interests would justify what are generally believed to be impermissible restrictions on individual speech as well.[7] Recognizing that corporations and other organizations can speak seems to present a dilemma between restricting individual as well as corporate speech to promote the kinds of interests just mentioned, or else giving full protection to corporate as to individual speech, thus compromising these interests across the board. A way out of this dilemma is to deny the assumption that once an organization's activity qualifies as speech, it assumes the same constitutional status and is entitled to the same protection as a corresponding activity carried out by an individual. It is at this more fundamental level that the distinction between the legal treatment of individual and organizational speech must be drawn. Doing so, however, should not be too difficult, since the very same traits of organizations that warrant ascribing speech to them also mark their speech as distinctly impersonal, and so as lacking the expressive value of individual speech.

Seen as the products of the organization's decision-making processes, the organization's communications, no less than its operations in manufacturing widgets, are instrumentally oriented to some preconceived goals that provide the organization with its legitimacy and raison d'être. Such communications are at odds with the discursive universe projected by the First Amendment. At the heart of the First Amendment lies an ideal of uninhibited human communication driven by the belief that the meanings constitutive of human life are always in flux, amenable to indefinite modification, elaboration, and reinterpretation. Specifically, the goals we pursue are forever contestable and revisable. An instrument, designed to effectively pursue and realize a given set of goals, does not fit in this discursive universe. It is part of the instrumental conception of an organization that its goals are externally provided, and that its performance is geared toward the attainment of these goals. To be sure, organizations too can revise their immediate goals from time to time, but they can do so (ex hypothesi) only within the limits set by the broader and more abstract goals set for them, and as a way of improving the accomplishment of those goals. They are not meant to participate in the open-ended "conversation of humanity" that is oriented, at whatever level of generality or abstraction, toward the ends of human life.*

A similar conclusion applies to speech that is ascribed to an organization when uttered by specific individuals in their organizational capacity. To speak "on behalf" of an organization is to speak in one's capacity as the holder of a distant role and so engage in *detached speech*. As we have seen before (in Chapter 1), one marker of such speech is an exemption from the norm of sincerity that ordinarily links speakers to utterances and gives speech its expressive significance. I have illustrated this point by the example of the telephone operator who thanks callers for their patronage of the corporation. It would be odd for such an operator to affirm his sincerity by adding "and I (or, we) really mean it." The oddity results from the fact that this communication of gratitude is not designed to express the speaker's state of mind. Indeed, the explicit affirmation of gratitude would be just as inappropriate even if while speaking to the customer the operator did in fact experience a surge of gratitude. The operator is not in violation of the condition of sincerity, but rather this condition does not at all apply to him.

---

* This is not, of course, meant to imply that only speech that engages directly with ultimate questions regarding the meaning of life should be protected, nor do I enter the dicey issue of what type of behavior should count as speech. For example, the decision how to dress up for work, formally or casually, likely meets the criteria for First Amendment protection along both dimensions.

It might be objected, in response, that the condition of sincerity is not really suspended in this case at all, but merely displaced, since the operator does not speak on his own behalf but on behalf of someone else. He engages in *representative speech*. Given his representative capacity he is simply the wrong person in whom to search for the intentions that animate the speech in question. Now, as a general proposition, this suggestion is quite plausible. Take a simple example: Rhonda reads to Susan a thank-you note she received from Sam. If Rhonda were to interrupt the reading and add the words, "and I'm really grateful," referring to herself, we would think her deeply confused. But it would be altogether appropriate for her to interject the phrase, "and he is really grateful," referring to Sam, on the evidence, let us suppose, of the large bouquet that accompanied the note. Some speech situations, in other words, may present a question as to who is the real speaker whose intentions ought to control the interpretation of a given utterance. These situations need not be exempt from the condition of sincerity that ordinarily applies to speech acts. Once the real speaker is identified, the condition of sincerity would apply to her. However plausible as the suggestion is in this case, it does not apply to the operator. If we try to track down the origin of the operator's speech, we are most likely to be led to an AT&T public relations office or to an advertising firm. Someone in some such outfit must have come up with the idea that a standardized display of politeness on the operator's part would enhance AT&T's public image. The idea quite likely needed and received the approval of someone in the corporation's management, whereupon the appropriate instruction was inserted into the operators' manual. The most important aspect of this hypothetical scenario is that at no point does it involve anyone's actual gratitude that the operator's utterance might purport to express.[8]

In short, whether we view organizational communications as the undifferentiated product of a system of instrumentally oriented structures and processes, or as the detached production of the holders of some distant roles, such communications do not implicate the values of self-expression and self-realization that underlie an individual speaker's original First Amendment rights.

Organizations' Derivative Speech Rights

This negative conclusion does not, however, exhaust the possibilities of applying the First Amendment to organizations. Though organizations do not have active original speech rights, they may be the bearers of various derivative speech rights. But as we have seen, derivative rights provide their bearers a weaker protection than original rights, and so ascribing to organizations derivative speech rights qualifies the protection due to organizational communications compared to that extended to individual expression. In examining organizations' derivative speech right, I start with a right shared by all of them. This is the *passive* right, derived from the prospective audience's original First Amendment right to listen. Insofar as organizations are irreducible sources of communication to which the public is entitled to listen, it makes perfectly good sense to ascribe this kind of right to them.

What are the implications of ascribing to an organization this type of right? In order to assess the level of protection to which a derivative speech right entitles its bearer we need distinguish between "internal" and "external" concerns that stand in opposition to the right. By *external concerns* I refer to interests and values different from those protected by the derivative right itself. Take, for example, the argument mentioned earlier, that an economic reason exists for subjecting corporate political speech to a requirement of unanimous shareholder consent. Otherwise, the argument goes, the practice of "[a]llowing capital to be raised on the condition that its contributors permit management to use it for political purposes ... may increase the cost of capital."[9] The argument fails, since a derivative autonomy speech right is intended to protect the listener's autonomy interests precisely against such economic non–autonomy-based reasons. The opposite holds when a derivative right encounters an *internal concern*, by which I mean a concern for the same autonomy interests that the derivative right is itself intended to protect. Such, for example, is the argument that due to the wealth and the size of corporations, "their views may drown out other points of view."[10] In this case, both the derivative speech right and its proposed curtailment advance the same interest and so draw their normative strength from the same source: individual listeners' ability to form independent and informed judgments based on free access to information and ideas. Curtailing corporate speech for this reason is accordingly consistent with allotting them the passive derivative right by which their speech is protected.

As we have seen, ascribing to organizations passive derivative speech rights does not exhaust the range of speech rights that may apply to them, since they may also possess *active* derivative speech rights—that is, rights derived from the original rights of some speaker and based on the function the organization performs with regard to that speaker's communications. Here the picture is more complicated since greater variety among organizations exists in this regard. In canvassing this variety it will be useful to follow the tripartite division of organizations into *commercial, protective*, and *expressive* I've mentioned at the outset. I consider them in reverse order, starting with expressive organizations. This is a large and heterogeneous category that includes political organizations of various kinds, media organizations, trade unions, and many other nongovernmental organizations. By joining such organizations, the individual members delegate their self-expression regarding a range of issues to the organization and acquiesce in having their views represented by it. In doing so, each member must recognize that the organization's communications may distort the message that members themselves would like to convey. By delegating speech to the organization, individuals thus trade accuracy for volume. Given this implicit and often advantageous tradeoff, it makes good sense to ascribe to the organization's speech derivative value, and protect it by a right that is derived from the individual members' original right to self-expression.[11] Still, as in the case of an organization's passive derivative speech rights, a derivative active speech right does not endow an organization with unqualified First Amendment protection. Since the constitutional protection of expressive organizations' speech depends on the delegation, such protection is justified only as long as the organization fulfills the terms and purposes of the delegation. The internal structure and the decision-making processes of expressive organizations thus become matters of public, indeed constitutional, concern.

Communications produced by a bureaucratic structure that has become sufficiently entrenched and fossilized so as to lose connection with the members on whose behalf it purports to speak will have lost their claim to expressive value. The specter of the membership organization without any members is the limiting case.[12]

Similar considerations apply to *protective organizations*, which are designed to protect some individuals' self-expression, and so possess active derivative rights under the First Amendment. Consider the university. Characterizing the university as a protective organization draws on the view that academic freedom is an instance of self-expression,[13] and that protecting academic freedom is one of the university's central goals.[14] For example, universities allocate to their faculty members the resources needed for their research without at the same time imposing on them restrictions that would interfere with their academic pursuits. A certain degree of independence of the university's decision-making processes may be necessary in order for it to fulfill this function, thus endowing the university with an autonomy right that derives from the faculty members' original right to academic freedom. Adequately protecting this right requires that a similar protection be extended to those liberties and immunities of the university that are deemed necessary for securing researchers their original speech rights. Consequently, if utilitarian considerations are generally deemed insufficient to override a professor's right to academic freedom, the university's derivative rights necessary for protecting professors' academic freedom must also be immune to adverse utilitarian considerations.

However, determining the scope of a protective organization's derivative right is not a simple matter. No great difficulties would arise if the university were meticulously serving the single goal of protecting the faculty's freedom of speech. If this were the case, the university's derivative right would be coextensive with its entire activity. Any successful claim to "injury" made by such an organization (i.e., any successful claim that an event constitutes an impediment to the achievement of its goal) would ipso facto pose a threat to the organization's derivative right. In this case, the university's claim to autonomy would be fully supported by the faculty's underlying original right. But such alignment between an organization's derivative rights and the underlying original rights is in fact unlikely, for at least two reasons. One is the multiplicity of organizational goals. As is typical of large organizations, the university pursues a variety of goals, some of which are unrelated to anyone's academic freedom. In that case, the university may try to rely on its derivative rights to institutional autonomy in the service of any of those other goals, thereby trying to extend the derivative right beyond its legitimate scope as defined by the underlying original speech rights it is designed to secure.

The other source of discrepancy between the organization's derivative rights and the original speech rights is organizational goal displacement.[15] For example, subunits within the organization may engage in activities geared toward the accomplishment of their own subgoals in a way and to an extent that do not necessarily comport with the achievement of any of the organization's goals. These subunits may invoke the organization's rights in protection of the units' particular goals, even though the activities concerned do not in fact contribute to, and may even hinder, the original rights from which the organizational right is derived. The campus police, for example, and other disciplinary authorities may pursue their departmental subgoal of preserving "law and order" zealously and single-mindedly, and so in ways that are detrimental to academic freedom. And yet here too the university may invoke its institutional autonomy, expressed in the idiom of academic freedom, as an argument against judicial interference with a university's disciplinary proceeding that results, say, in the expulsion of a student who had participated in a demonstration on campus.[16]

Finally, these comments about the ways various organizations may acquire active derivative speech rights imply a negative conclusion in this respect for the first category of organizations we've distinguished. The goals or mission of *commercial organizations*, of which business corporations are by far the most prevalent specimen, concern the promotion of society's economic welfare through the production and distribution of goods and services. Since the goals that ground a business corporation's social legitimacy are of utilitarian value, so also is their speech. Like other corporate activities, their communications are not protected by the kind of strong, autonomy-based rights that are capable of overriding conflicting considerations of social utility. The mandate of a business corporation does not ordinarily include the protection of anyone's speech, nor does the corporation engage in representative speech. None of its stakeholders' affiliation with the corporation, in particular that of its shareholders and employees, includes a delegation of any speech activity to it with an understanding that the corporation may speak on their behalf.

III. COMMUNAL SPEECH

I have argued thus far that organizations can have various derivative First Amendment rights, but no original rights to self-expression. There is a perennial gap between organizational speech on the one hand and the source of its expressive value on the other. Even in the case of an expressive organization, authority regarding the expression remains vested in the individual members: their disparate communicative intentions provide the measure of adequacy for the collectivity's performance. Communal speech is fundamentally different. Since communal communication expresses an aspect of the members' identity defined by their collective affiliation, the distinction between collective speech and individual self-expression is effaced.

As we have seen, speech can be ascribed to organizations either when it is the undifferentiated product of organizational decision-making processes, or as the pronouncement of specific position-holders. The case of communities is parallel. Starting with position-holders, when we discussed organizational speech, we saw that the individual speaker, as illustrated by the telephone operator's profession of gratitude on the company's behalf, engages in detached speech, which involves no self-expression, nor does it implicate the individual speaker's autonomy. The opposite is the case in the communal context. Recall the contrasting example, given in Chapter 1, of a parent who thanks a stranger for helping a child cross the street.[17] Unlike the operator, the parent does not only avow gratitude but expresses it, since being, say, a father is simply the aspect of one's personal identity that pertains to the situation at hand. But whereas the gratitude the father expresses is personal, it is not his alone. Expressing gratitude as a parent in the imagined circumstances involves a judgment that what the stranger did is in the child's interest, and so advances one of the family's causes or missions. It is therefore to give expression to an attitude that is appropriately taken to be held by other family members as well. In this case, "I am grateful" is ipso facto said on the family's behalf and is the equivalent of "we are grateful."

To be sure, this unity of judgment and of attitude may not hold. For example, the other parent, the mother in this case, may view the stranger's act as a transgression. Had she been on the scene, she would not have thanked the stranger but would have chastised him, and in doing so, she too would have purported to convey the family's attitude in this matter. Even so, this possibility does not by itself vitiate the conception of communal speech I advocate. What each parent says purports to reflect the family's attitudes because of a shared commitment to the child's welfare. The difference between the parents' views reflects conflicting assessments of what under the circumstances would have been in the child's interest, thus affirming that the child's welfare sets the proper standard for assessing the stranger's behavior. Given this agreement, and a sufficient level of cohesiveness and trust, each parent may be authorized to speak on the family's behalf, even if what each might have said on a given occasion would have been different. Though the family be in this scenario of two minds, it still speaks with one voice. And this does not distinguish it from the case of an individual speaker. The norm of sincerity that applies to the individual speaker does not range over all the thoughts that occur to her. Speech, that is the public articulation of a thought, is a canonical way of owning up to the thought, taking responsibility for it, and so constituting it as one's own. To speak is in this sense to exercise with regard to a thought one's first-person authority.[18] The picture in the case of communal speech is similar. Both parents are authorized to speak on the family's behalf, and what they each say in their parental capacity has each other's implicit backing and is the articulation of a content to which they both own up and for which they take joint responsibility.

The other way of ascribing speech to a collectivity views its communications as the composite product of an undifferentiated, collective activity. Here, too, the communal picture differs significantly from the organizational. I can best make the point with the help of a familiar analogy: the orchestra or the choir. Like sports teams, these ensembles serve as stock examples for accounts of collective action. My present interest in them somewhat shifts the focus toward collective meaning.* Each player's or singer's contribution is in itself fragmentary and often musically (or in the case of the choir also linguistically) unintelligible; meaning here resides in the music (or text) that is collectively produced. The expressive value of these performances does not accordingly lie in the individual contributions taken separately. Rather, the medium of self-expression in these cases is the collective production as a whole. And yet this "global" production is a vehicle for the self-expression of each of the players and singers as well.†

It will be useful to contrast this conception of communal speech with communications by expressive organizations that in some ways resemble the communal case. One question that arises with regard to all collective speech, organizational as well as communal, is which utterances (statements, documents, etc.) count as the collectivity's and are properly ascribed to it. But in the case of expressive organizations, a second question arises: how do the organization's communications relate to the original individual speakers whose views these communications purport to represent? This second question has no equivalent in the communal case. Once the criteria for ascribing speech to a community are satisfied, there is no further question regarding the relation between this communal speech

---

* In terms of the ordinary use of "community," the family and the orchestra (or choir) are at most proto- or quasi-communities. But their relative simplicity makes them suitable heuristics for teasing out with some clarity important characteristics of what I call *communal speech* that are instantiated in many other social formations to which the label *community* is more aptly applied.

† It is noteworthy that one need not even produce any audible segment of the music in order to be a participant in the communal expression: the person who is usually thought to be the most prominent contributor, the conductor, does not.

on the one hand and the members' self-expression on the other; speech properly ascribed to the community is ipso facto also properly ascribed to each of the members in their collective capacity, that is qua community members.

IV. GOVERNMENT SPEECH

Although the present discussion of the main forms of collective speech does not purport to be exhaustive, no survey of this topic can afford to ignore speech by the most salient of collectivities, the state. However, in considering the application of the First Amendment to the state I do not mean to add a new category to the classification of forms of collective speech offered thus far. Rather, the question raised in this section is which of the preceding categories of collective speech apply to what in the constitutional context is loosely and somewhat imprecisely referred to as "government speech."[19] And the short answer is that they all do. This answer is not the conclusion of the discussion that follows but its methodological starting point: a decision not to treat the state as a sui generis phenomenon, but to find out instead what the general categories of collective speech we've distinguished can teach us when applied to the range of phenomena that the term *government speech* commonly designates.

Types of Government Speech

We can start by recalling an observation I have made earlier in the book, that our vision of the state and our attitudes toward it oscillate between the two poles marked by the community/organization distinction.[20] We often think of the state as a vast bureaucracy or, perhaps more accurately, as a conglomerate of impersonal, goal-oriented bureaucracies. The state is also the quintessential coercive collectivity, addressing us by means of threats backed by force. Reliance on such external motivation for compliance with the state's demands is at once a recognition and a consolidation of the fact that one's actual continued assent is not required or expected as a condition of one's playing a role in the collective enterprise. When we contemplate the state in these terms, we envision an organization.[21] But this is not the only way we think about the state. To be French, for example, is not only to stand in a certain relationship to the French bureaucracy and be subject to its coercive threats; "French" is also used to designate sharing important bonds, such as those of culture, language, and tradition, with many other people. When used in this way, *French* is a summary reference to a nondetached affiliation role that is a constituent of its bearers' identity. Seen in such terms, the state is the social union of these nondetached roles and, to that extent, a community. The label *government speech* tends to obscure this duality and draw attention to the organizational aspect of the state. And indeed, if one thinks of the state's communicative activity in organizational terms, it is natural to maintain that "communications emanating from such institutions do not vindicate individual self-expression and dignity."[22] Conceived as an organization, government is not a medium for self-expression associated with the values that give rise to original speech rights. However, such organizational speech need not exhaust the state's expressive activity. The state's communal aspect points toward the possibility of communications that do involve collective self-expression and so give rise to original active speech rights.

These conflicting images of the state and attitudes toward it are familiar and persistent. My aim is not to attempt a resolution but to point out that any discussion of government speech must acknowledge the conflict and come to terms with it. But not all the issues that commonly arise under the *government speech* umbrella implicate these conflicting attitudes to the state as a whole. By purporting to name a single, unitary subject of communication, *government speech* conjures up an image of government as a mammoth entity that speaks with a single, and allegedly deafening, voice. The label obscures thereby another salient feature of its subject matter: the fragmentation of government into numerous semi-independent and sometimes feuding organizations. A similar point applies, perhaps even more emphatically, to the communal aspect of the state as well. So-called government speech can be the product of a plethora of subcommunities of vastly varying structure and size, some related more loosely and others more tightly to the more inclusive entity. Consequently, a wholesale denial that government speech can be the exercise of a communal original right to self-expression goes beyond rejecting the communal aspect of the state as a whole or a denial that the communal aspect can be expressed through the state's political institutions. Instead, this negative position would also apply, for example, to each and every municipality, no matter how small, homogeneous, and closely knit it may be.[23]

When we combine the communal aspect of the state with the state's fragmentation, we arrive at a particularly suggestive version of communications that belong to the public domain and yet involve the kind of self-expression that is duly protected by original speech rights. Here are three examples of the ways recognizing this option would impact the treatment of those regions of "government speech" that belong in this category. First, advocates of full speech rights for municipalities sometimes equate municipal speech with corporate communications.[24] The analogy is designed to draw support for the protection of municipal communications from the Supreme Court's recognition of corporate free speech. But the pendulum of the Supreme Court's attitude to corporate speech keeps swinging, and at any rate, on the argument I have presented, corporate speech has a weaker claim to First Amendment protection than a municipality's communal communication. To base the case for a municipality's free speech on the analogy to corporate speech is to give up at the outset a claim for the municipality's more robust right tied to its communal aspects.[25]

A second implication of allowing that certain forms of government speech can give rise to active communal speech rights concerns the difficult, and crucial, issue of dissenters.[26] As we have seen in the relatively simple case of the family discussed earlier, procedural agreement in the face of substantive disputes may settle the question of communal expression for all the members involved. Absent such agreement, procedural as well as substantive, it becomes questionable that a community uniting the discordant parties still exists. Be this as it may, the situation regarding larger and more complex formations such as municipalities is more difficult. In particular, the formal boundaries of the municipality may not coincide with the boundaries of any single community within it. As a result, the municipal communication may be communal, while still leaving out some group of dissenters who are not part of the larger community, and perhaps form a de facto community of their own. The result is a genuine conflict between original speech rights. When the municipality purports to speak on everyone's behalf, it violates the dissenters' speech rights. But to curtail the municipality's communications would be to suppress self-expression and so offend against a genuine exercise of First Amendment rights. Earlier in this chapter I have discussed conflicts between original and derivative rights, but not conflicts in which original rights appear on both sides. Such conflicts raise difficult issues I will not enter here. But in the present case there is a way of avoiding the conflict, by protecting the municipality's communications while securing for the dissenters an appropriate opportunity to disassociate themselves from the municipality's message and voice their own, perhaps by requiring that adequate funds be allocated to the dissent for this purpose.

Finally, a common argument against protecting government speech arises from the fear of state propaganda.[27] The concern is that due to the government's control of large communicative resources, government speech will saturate the marketplace of ideas and drown out other voices. Controlling government speech would thus appear to be merely a matter of regulating the communications traffic in the listeners' interest. Here too the argument is least compelling in cases in which the two factors we're considering, community and fragmentation, are at play. First, when the speaker is a relatively small unit, the threat to communicative traffic posed by the amplitude of Leviathan sounding off does not arise. Second, as I have previously argued, a policy of curtailing some speech in the interest of improving communication traffic is least appropriate when it involves the curtailment of original active speech rights. Even though not all government speech implicates such a right, government speech that is a form of communal self-expression does. The argument based on the fear of propaganda is accordingly weakest in this case.

The picture on the organizational side of government speech parallels this picture of its communal side. Here, too, rather than ascribe speech to the government conceived as a single massive organization, we can disaggregate government into an array of units each of which performs different speech-related functions, so that the three categories of organizational speech that I have distinguished—commercial, expressive, and protective—would apply here as well. Perhaps most often government speech is performed by what are best seen as utilitarian governmental entities—agencies charged with promoting various aspects of society's aggregate welfare, and whose speech therefore has a similar normative status to that of commercial organizations we've considered. The discussion of government speech often seems to tacitly assume that all government communications belong in this category, and that the only individual speech rights at stake are listeners' rights. When speech is produced by such a utilitarian government entity, its constitutional treatment should indeed resemble the treatment of commercial organizations. But not all governmental units belong in this category. Like other organizations, government entities can also perform expressive or protective functions, and so be the bearers of the corresponding derivative speech rights.

Who Speaks?

Treating *government speech* as a unitary category has the appeal of simplicity. Disaggregating the state into a multiplicity of units and so of potential speakers, with a variety of quite different speech rights, considerably complicates matters. The problem is not just the multiplicity of categories from which we must choose in order to characterize any particular communication. The very contours of the speaking entity are often blurred and contested. Any attempt to ascribe a particular communication to a subdivision of the state is vulnerable to counterclaims based on a more unitary or a more fragmented view of the state. But the problem goes beyond complexity. Since people's attitudes and understandings are constitutive of the nature and boundary of a social entity, the controversy may amount to an "ontological" disagreement. The disputants may not just disagree about fixing the most adequate unit of analysis, but their disagreement may reveal that no such single entity exists: the source of the disagreement may be conflicting clusters of beliefs and attitudes that are the constituents of differing collective units to which the disputing parties relate.

So, for example, a city council's proposed resolution condemning the insensitivity of large corporations to the plight of laid-off workers can be for some the apt expression of a communal sentiment, provoked perhaps by a recent incident that occurred in the city. The city council's speech directly expresses these supporters' own frustrations and resentments. Others may perceive the council's proposed resolution in more detached, organizational terms, approving of the communication or acquiescing in it because they view themselves as having delegated to the council expression as well as action on matters such as these. Still others would, in effect, deny the council both original (communal) and derivative (delegated) speech rights. They could do so, for example, by invoking their *national* identity, arguing that only those who can speak on behalf of the country as a whole—a branch of the federal government, perhaps—are qualified to make pronouncements in their name in matters of social justice.[28] For these individuals, city council members are but low-level functionaries in the state's hierarchy and should not presume to exercise any authority that is not derived from that inclusive structure.[29] Now these conflicting views regarding the proposed communication can, in principle, all be valid. They express incommensurate but tenable social worlds. The social world inhabited by those who find an indispensable outlet of personal frustration in the council's proclamation contains an entity, the local community, that is absent in the world inhabited by those whose primary identification in the present context is with the country as a whole and for whom the locality has purely instrumental significance. In contrast, the latter group lives in a social world in which the state is a viable community, absent from the world of those with the local identifications.

These reflections strike what at this point in the book should be a familiar note. They echo the constructivist theme broached in Chapter 1 and pursued throughout this book. And as on other occasions, this theme also has special relevance here for the role of judicial decisions. In deciding a First Amendment case, a court does more than settle the constitutional issue at hand; it also implicitly decides who the speaking subject is, thereby contributing to fixing, in an authoritative manner, the underlying social ontology and decreasing the indeterminacy just described. But, of course, a court can perform this (or any other) function only when a sufficiently pervasive and robust agreement prevails concerning the conditions under which someone's pronouncements, such as on matters of collective speech rights, are made in one's "judicial" capacity, thus on behalf of a "court," so that when these pronouncements are made, all concerned rest assured that Government speaks!

V. CONCLUSION

It may be helpful to summarize the foregoing classification schema of collective speech rights in the form of a table. The table is self-explanatory, but in order for it to correspond fully to the preceding discussion, I should clarify that the collectivities listed in it and the speech rights assigned to them pertain to "government" or "state" entities as well as to those collectivities that belong in the private domain.

The table conveys in a graphic way, and so accentuates, a property of the discursive exposition that preceded it: it is the neatness of the typology of both collectivities and rights and of their interrelationships. Let me then sound a warning to which I have already alluded earlier. Any attempt to fit a substantial segment of social reality into a table forces such reality into a procrustean bed. The present case is no exception. Many collectivities will no doubt prove recalcitrant in the face of the sharp divisions

I propose, and the appropriate constitutional protections will often elude the schematic structure of rights that I have elaborated. Here, as elsewhere, theoretical clarity will be an aid rather than a hindrance only so long as the caveat regarding theory's limited ambition that I sounded at the outset is firmly kept in mind.

Type of collectivity \ Type of speaker's right	Original (expressive) right	Active derivative right	Passive derivative right
Commercial organization			+
Expressive organization		+	+
Protective organization		+	+
Community	+		+

NOTES

INTRODUCTION
1. By Pico della Mirandola in his *Oration on the Dignity of Man*, A. Robert Caponigri, trans. (Washington, DC: Regnery Gateway, 1956).

CHAPTER 1
1. As a prominent sociologist puts it, "persons are at once socially constituted and self-determining." Philip Selznick, *The Moral Commonwealth: Social Theory and the Promise of Community* [Berkeley: University of California Press, 1994], 219. I attempt to give some more precise content to this general outlook.
2. The dramaturgical perspective is most famously associated with the work of Erving Goffman, e.g., *Encounters: Two Studies in the Sociology of Interaction* (Indianapolis: Bobbs-Merrill, 1961), 85–152, and *Frame Analysis: An Essay on the Organization of Experience* (Chicago: Northwestern University Press). On narrative conceptions see, e.g., Charles Taylor, *The Sources of the Self* (Cambridge, UK: Cambridge University Press, 1989), and Marya Schechtman, *The Constitution of Selves* (Ithaca, NY: Cornell University Press, 1989). And see more generally, Norbert Wiley, *The Semiotic Self* (Chicago: University of Chicago Press, 1994).
3. For a further elaboration of this point see Chapters 5 and 6.
4. For a helpful overview of relevant literature see Seumas Miller, "Social Institutions," in *The Stanford Encyclopedia of Philosophy* (Fall 2012 Edition), Edward N. Zalta, ed. (http://plato.stanford.edu/archives/fall2012/entries/social-institutions/).
5. For another account that attempts to do justice to both the individual and the collective without being reductionist in either direction see Anthony Giddens, *New Rules of Sociological Method* (London: Hutchinson, 1976). See also Giddens' *The Constitution of Society: Outline of the Theory of Structuration* (Cambridge, UK: Polity Press, 1984).
6. There is a vast sociological literature on the concept of role. For some sources and references to the standard use of the term, see Bruce J. Biddle and Edwin J. Thomas, eds., *Role Theory: Concepts and Research* (Hoboken, NJ: Wiley, 1966). The approach I present is probably closest to that of Talcott Parsons, *The Social System* (New York: Free Press, 1951).
7. As reported by Margaret Mead in *Sex and Temperament* (New York: Morrow Quill, 1935, 1963) at 35.

8. My own view, for which I've argued elsewhere, is that there is an inherent tension between normativity and coercion. See my "In Defense of Defiance," *Phil. & Public Affairs* 23(1): 24–51; reprinted in my *Harmful Thoughts: Essays on Law, Self and Morality* (Princeton, NJ: Princeton University Press, 2002), Chapter 3.
9. See "Role Distance" in Erving Goffman, *Encounters*. The concept of role-distance is applied in Goffman's essay, "The Underlife of a Public Institution: A Study of Ways of Making Out in a Mental Hospital," in his *Asylums: Essays on the Social Situation of Mental Patients and Other Inmates* (New York: Anchor, 1961), 171, 318–320. Although I borrow the notion of role-distance from Goffman, I modify it for my present purposes and employ it in ways that depart from his own use.
10. John Searle, *Expression and Meaning* (New York: Cambridge University Press, 1979), 4–5; see also his *Speech Acts: An Essay in the Philosophy of Language* (Cambridge, UK: Cambridge University Press, 1969), 60–67.
11. *Reasons and Persons* (Oxford: Clarendon Press, 1984), 199–350.
12. See Ferdinand Tönnies, *Community and Society (Gemeinschaft und Gesellschaft)*, Charles Loomis, trans. (East Lansing: Michigan State University Press, 1957). For short surveys of related dichotomous typologies of social structure, see the essay by Charles Loomis and John McKinney, "The Application of Gemeinschaft and Gesellschaft as Related to Other Typologies," in the above-cited English translation of Tönnies' work, pp. 12–29; and Horace Miner's entry, "Community-Society Continua," in *International Encyclopedia of the Social Sciences* (New York: MacMillan and Free Press, 1968), vol. 3, pp. 174–180.
13. For more on this point, see Daniel Bell, *Work and Its Discontents* (Boston: Beacon Press, 1956).
14. See especially Chapters 5, 8, and 9.
15. This conclusion derives, by analogy, from Kant's observation that the strain we often feel in performing our moral duties results from their conflict with our inclinations. Even so, when we do follow morality, despite our inclinations, we act autonomously because we heed an internal call. See Immanuel Kant, *Groundwork of the Metaphysics of Morals*, Herbert James Paton, trans. (New York: Harper & Row, 1964), esp. 98–101.
16. See note 8.
17. Jean-Paul Sartre, *Being and Nothingness*, Hazel Barnes, trans. (New York: Washington Square Press, 1966, 1956).
18. Ibid., p. 101.
19. Ibid., pp. 102–103.
20. For a rich, book-length discussion of the metaphoric appeal of the theater see Bruce Wilshire, *Role Playing and Identity: The Limits of Theatre as Metaphor* (Bloomington: Indiana University Press, 1982).

CHAPTER 2

1. Delivered at Stanford University in 2008; published as Harry Frankfurt, *Taking Ourselves Seriously & Getting it Right*, Debra Satz, ed. (Stanford, CA: Stanford University Press, 2006).

2. Ibid., at 7.
3. Ibid., at 12.
4. 1 *W.L.R.* 317 (1955).
5. 79 *Idaho* 266, 313; *P.2d* 706 (1957). For a more complete juxtaposition of these two cases and a related discussion, see my "Responsibility and the Boundaries of the Self" *Harv. L. Rev.* 105 (1992): 959; a revised version appears as Chapter 7 in my *Harmful Thoughts: Essays on Law, Self and Morality* (Princeton, NJ: Princeton University Press, 2002).
6. That a defendant may not have been able to act otherwise than he did may actually be the ground of his responsibility. This would be the case were he impelled by *volitional necessity*, which is on Frankfurt's view the paradigm of free will and autonomy. Harry Frankfurt, "The Importance of What We Care About," in *The Importance of What We Care About* (Cambridge, UK: Cambridge University Press, 1988), 80, at 85–88.
7. Chapter 1, p. 13.
8. See Frankfurt, *Taking Ourselves Seriously*, at 16–17.
9. Ibid., at 23, 24.
10. Bernard Williams, "Internal and External Reasons," in his *Moral Luck* (Cambridge, UK: Cambridge University Press, 1982), 101.
11. Frankfurt, *Taking Ourselves Seriously*, at 19.

CHAPTER 3

1. This is the dominant view and clearly the paradigm case, but borderline cases sometimes arise, complicated by the occasional difficulty of establishing who counts as the victim of a wrongdoing. See, e.g., Trudy Govier and Wilhelm Verwoerd, "Forgiveness: The Victim's Prerogative," *S. Afr. J. Phil.* 21 (2002): 97.
2. It is quite common to view pardon as a form of official forgiveness. See, e.g., Joram Graf Haber, *Forgiveness* (Lanham, MD: Rowman & Littlefield, 1991), 60–61. The proximity between forgiveness and pardon is also suggested by the French word pardoner, meaning "to forgive," a usage that has a colloquial echo in the English expression "pardon me."
3. These correspond to the three types of reactive attitudes distinguished by Peter Strawson in "Freedom and Resentment" in his *Freedom and Resentment and Other Essays* (London: Methuen, 1973): personal, self-reactive, and vicarious.
4. The view of forgiveness as the overcoming of resentment probably originated with Bishop Butler; see Joseph Butler, "Upon Forgiveness of Injuries," in *The Works of the Right Reverend Father in God, Joseph Butler, D.C.L.*, Samuel Halifax, ed. (New York: Carter, 1846), 106–107, and has been reinforced by Strawson's influential paper ("Freedom and Resentment," see note 3), in which resentment is seen as the paradigm reactive attitude and thus the natural focal point of discussions of forgiveness. The moral significance of resentment is also discussed in Thomas Brudholm and Valérie Rosoux, "The Unforgiving: Reflections on the Resistance to Forgiveness After Atrocity," *Law & Contemp. Probs.* 72 (Spring 2009): 33. See

also on this point Norvin Richards, "Forgiveness," *Ethics* 99 (1988): 77, 79; and Robert Roberts, "Forgiveness," *Am. Phil. Q.* 32 (1995): 289.
5. See, e.g., Richards, "Forgiveness."
6. This is the gist of Jean Hampton's position: "The forgiver ... comes to see [the wrongdoer] as still *decent, not* rotten as a person, and someone with whom he may be able to renew a relationship." In Jeffrie Murphy and Jean Hampton, *Forgiveness and Mercy* (Cambridge, UK: Cambridge University Press, 1988), 83. On her view, repentance provides the main reason for such a change in the forgiver's conception of the wrongdoer, though Hampton also allows for forgiveness "for old times' sake."
7. Richards, "Forgiveness," at 88.
8. Murphy and Hampton, *Forgiveness and Mercy*, at 26.
9. Compare the "paradox of forgiveness" formulated by Aurel Kolnai. Unless forgiveness involves the offender's change of heart, "the wrong is still flourishing, the offence still subsisting: then by 'forgiving' you accept it and thus confirm it and make it worse; or the wrongdoer has suitably annulled and eliminated his offence ... and by 'forgiving' you would only acknowledge the fact that you are no longer its victim. Briefly, forgiveness is either unjustified or pointless." Aurel Kolnai, "Forgiveness," *Proc. Aristotelian Soc.* 74 (1973–1974): 91, 98–99.
10. The theme of the past as a heavy weight and of the yearning to shake free of it is captured well in Hannah Arendt, *The Human Condition* (Chicago: University of Chicago Press, 1958), §33. See also Theodor Adorno, "What Does Coming to Terms with the Past Mean?" reprinted in *Bitburg in Moral and Political Perspective*, Geoffrey H. Hartman, ed. (New Jersey: John Wiley & Sons, 1986), 115 ("One wants to get free of the past: rightly so, since one cannot live in its shadow, and since there is no end to terror if guilt and violence are only repaid, again and again, with guilt and violence"). Adorno talks about the "destruction of memory" as responding to this desire, and associates it with the devil's position in Goethe's Faust (p. 117). Others underscore the futility of attempts to escape the past: "[R]epentance consists in our setting ourselves against a past reality and absurdly attempting to efface that reality from the world" (Haber, "Forgiveness," at 94).
11. For a critical discussion of the change-of-identity approach in the case of individual wrongdoing, see Haber, "Forgiveness" 95–98; and Joanna North, "Wrongdoing and Forgiveness," *Philosophy.* 62 (1987): 499. Professor Ruti Teitel discusses decisions regarding reparations for past wrongdoing by a previous regime as involving a dialectic of continuity or discontinuity of identity in *Transitional Justice* (Oxford: Oxford University Press, 2000), 137, 146–147, 192–193.
12. See, e.g., Norman Klein, *The History of Forgetting: Los Angeles and the Erasure of Memory* (London: Verso; updated edition, 2008); Avishai Margalit, *The Ethics of Memory* (Cambridge, MA: Harvard University Press, 2002), 205 ("Total forgiveness entails forgetting"); and Robert Walker, "Sovereign Identities and the Politics of Forgetting," *Public* 9 (1994): 95. Some of those observing this way of escaping the past lament it: "[T]he worst distortion is willed amnesia, whether for the sake of self-exculpation or some sort of convenient reconciliation." Fritz

Stern, *N.Y. Times*, May 12, 1985 (reviewing Eberhard Jaeckel, *Hitler in History* [1985]), quoted in Donald Shriver, Jr., *An Ethic for Enemies: Forgiveness in Politics* (Oxford: Oxford University Press, 1995), 103. Teitel speaks of the amnesty granted in Spain to members of the Franco regime as "an agreement to forget the distant past." Teitel, *Transitional Justice*, at 53.

13. On the significance of "counting as" as fundamental to social phenomena in general, see John Searle, *The Construction of Social Reality* (New York: Free Press, 1995), 43–51.
14. This indeterminacy in subjects' temporal shape should be distinguished from Ian Hacking's well-known and controversial view that, because emerging new concepts issue in novel descriptions of past events, there is an indeterminacy regarding the past. See Ian Hacking, "An Indeterminacy in the Past," in his *Rewriting the Soul: Multiple Personalities and the Sciences of Memory* (Princeton, NJ: Princeton University Press, 1995), 234–257.
15. For a sensitive discussion of such temporal gaps seen as analogous to a "no man's land" situation in the spatial domain, see Teitel, *Transitional Justice*, at 69, 77, 183.
16. Cf.: "[territoriality] simplifies issues of control and provides easily understood symbolic markers 'on the ground,' giving relationships of power a greater tangibility and appearance of permanence." James Anderson and Liam O'Dowd, "Borders, Border Regions and Territoriality: Contradictory Meanings, Changing Significance," *Regional Stud.* 33 (1999): 593, 598. See generally Benedict Anderson, *Imagined Communities: Reflections on the Origin and Spread of Nationalism* (New York: Verso, revised ed., 1991). There is a surprising dearth of serious philosophical reflection on the territoriality of states. As a recent commentator testifies, "[C]ontemporary political philosophers, like their historical predecessors, have almost always begun with the idea of states as units with legitimate territorial dimensions, proceeding more or less immediately to questions about how such territorial states can be justly governed." A. John Simmons, "On the Territorial Rights of States," *Phil. Issues* 11 (2001): 300, 302.
17. Though I focus here on the state's temporal dimension, ignoring the two senses of both *spatial* and *temporal* has deleterious effects on the treatment of spatial conflict as well. Consider, for example, John Urry's claim that temporal and spatial relations "are asymmetrical. In particular, relations within space must exhibit a constant sum, while relations within time are not so constrained ... Hence, space is necessarily limited and there has to be competition and conflict over its organisation and control." John Urry, "Social Relations, Space and Time," in Derek Gregory and John Urry, eds., *Social Relations and Spatial Structures* (London: Macmillan, 1985), 20, at 30. To see the problem with this view, imagine a conflict between two neighboring states as to whose capital a particular city near the border should be. This would seem to present the kind of zero-sum spatial conflict manifesting the scarcity of space that Urry has in mind. But this conceptualization of the matter misrepresents the possibilities. In addition to the two exclusive, either-or solutions to the conflict, a third solution exists, namely that this city serve as capital of both countries. This option can take the form of indeterminacy—different parties consider the

contested city as the capital of one state or the other, without further resolution; or better yet, normative arrangements can make the city count as the capital of both contending states.

18. For an extended discussion of this point, see my "The Value of Ownership," *J. Pol. Phil.* 9 (2001): 404; reprinted in my *Harmful Thoughts: Essays on Law, Self, and Morality*, (Princeton, NJ: Princeton University Press, 2002), Chapter 9.

19. See also my "Responsibility and the Boundaries of the Self," *Harv. L. Rev.* 105 (1992): 959; a revised version appears in my *Harmful Thoughts*, Chapter 7.

20. Chapter 2, pp. 48–51.

21. John Locke, *An Essay Concerning Human Understanding* (Amherst, NY: Prometheus Books, 1995). The quotations are from pp. 245, 256, 252, and 251, respectively. In discussing Locke's position I benefitted much from the study by Galen Strawson, *Locke on Personal Identity: Consciousness and Concernment* (Princeton, NJ: Princeton University Press, 2011).

22. For a sample of the large literature, see Patrick Hutton, *History as an Art of Memory* (Hanover, NH: University Press of New England, 1993); Pierre Nora, "General Introduction: Between Memory and History," in *Realms of Memory: Rethinking the French Past*, Lawrence Kritzman, ed., and Arthur Goldhammer, trans. (New York: Columbia University Press, 1996); Noa Gedi and Yigal Elam, "Collective Memory—What Is It?" *Hist. & Memory* 8 (1996): 30; Wulf Kansteiner, "Finding Meaning in Memory: A Methodological Critique of Collective Memory Studies," *Hist. & Theory* 41 (2002): 179; Kerwin Lee Klein, "On the Emergence of Memory in Historical Discourse," *Representations* (Winter 2000): 127; Thomas Laqueur, "Introduction," *Representations* (Winter 2000), at 1; Allan Megill, "History, Memory, Identity," *Hist. Human Sci.* 11 (1998): 37; and Jeffrey Olick and Joyce Robbins, "Social Memory Studies: From 'Collective Memory' to the Historical Sociology of Mnemonic Practices," *Ann. Rev. Soc.* 24 (1998): 105.

23. The classical text that introduced the notion of collective memory is Maurice Halbwachs, *On Collective Memory*, Lewis Coser, ed. & trans. (Chicago: University of Chicago Press, 1992/1941). For some general discussions of the issues involved see, e.g., David Middleton and Derek Edwards, eds., *Collective Remembering* (London: Sage, 1990); Paul Connerton, *How Societies Remember* (Cambridge, UK: Cambridge University Press, 1989); Iwona Irwin-Zarecka, *Frames of Remembrance: The Dynamics of Collective Memory* (New Brunswick, NJ: Transaction Publishers, 1994); Susan Crane, "Writing the Individual Back into Collective Memory," *Am. Hist. Rev.* 102 (1997): 1372; Jeffrey Olick, "Collective Memory: The Two Cultures," *Soc. Theory* 17 (1999): 333 (juxtaposing what he calls "collected memory," which is an aggregate of individual memories, to genuinely "collective memory," tied to national narrative and identity); as well as sources cited in note 22.

24. For a survey of the issues and the literature concerning the relationship of individuals and collectivities raised by the notion of collective memory, see, for example, the section "Between Individual and Collective" in Kansteiner, "Finding Meaning in Memory," at 185–190.

25. On the connection between collective memory and such emotions as pride and shame, see, for example, Eviatar Zerubavel, "Social Memories: Steps to a Sociology of the Past," *Qual. Sociol.* 19 (1996): 283 at 290.
26. On this view, collective memory is a legitimate field of political contestation in a way that history is not. This is congruent with the spirit of Foucault's warning that "Since memory is actually a very important factor in struggle ..., if one controls people's memory, one controls their dynamism." Michel Foucault, *Language, Counter-memory, Practice: Selected Essays and Interviews*, Donald F. Bouchard, ed. & trans., Sherry Simon, trans. (1977), quoted in Olick and Robbins, "Social Memory Studies," at 126. Eviatar Zerubavel speaks in this context of the "[f]ierce mnemonic battles [that] are ... fought over what ought to be collectively remembered." Zerubavel, "Social Memories," at 296. My point is that all of this is to be distinguished from the acquisition of historical knowledge.
27. The process I advocate here of converting memory into history corresponds to what Halbwachs describes in terms of the loss of an organic relationship to past events. See Halbwachs, *On Collective Memory*, at 80. It can also be seen as the flip side of the process that Yerushalmi, in his classical study of Judaism, describes as the displacement of Jewish memory by historiography since the eighteenth century. Yoseph Hayim Yerushalmi, *Zakhor: Jewish History and Jewish Memory* (Seattle: University of Washington Press, 1982).
28. For related issues arising in connection with teaching history to children, see, e.g., Frances Fitzgerald, *America Revised: History Schoolbooks in the Twentieth Century* (Boston: Little, Brown, 1979); and Yael Zerubavel, *Recovered Roots: Collective Memory and the Making of Israeli National Tradition* (Chicago: University of Chicago Press, 1995).
29. See, e.g., Martin Golding, "Forgiveness and Regret," *Phil. Forum* 16 (1984–1985): 121–137, at 122.
30. This has led some to play down the psychological difficulties and to deny any limitation on forgiveness. See, e.g., Trudy Govier, "Forgiveness and the Unforgivable," *Am. Phil. Q.* 36 (1999): 59.
31. Despite the surface similarity, my point differs fundamentally from the position critiqued by Trudy Govier in "Forgiveness and the Unforgivable." Using the example of Pol Pot, Govier examines the possibility that "in such a case the moral person is defined by his acts over so much of his lifetime—that ultimately we cannot draw a moral distinction between these terrible things to which he committed so much of his life and the person that he is" (p. 68). Govier rejects this line of reasoning, arguing that "We go too far if we insist that some people have become so indelibly evil that there is no possibility of their moral change ... Many persons do change, and even some persons who have been guilty of appalling evil do change" (p. 69). But this is essentially the future-oriented conception of revisionary practices and, by implication, of the reactive attitudes, that I criticized earlier on. This approach does not take seriously enough the significance of the ongoing presence of the past atrocities in the person's life and identity quite apart from any subsequent changes in the person's attitudes or values.

32. Cf.: Berel Lang, "Forgiveness," *Am. Phil. Q.* 31 (1994): 105–117, listing this and some other factors as bearing on whether an action is in principle unforgivable. I am not quite clear what theory is supposed to unite these considerations in his view.
33. See Chapter 1, p. 13.

CHAPTER 4

1. Bernard Williams, "Moral Luck," in *Moral Luck* (Cambridge, UK: Cambridge University Press, 1982), 20. Unless otherwise indicated, all references to Williams in this chapter are to this text.
2. "D'où Venons Nous ... Que Sommes Nous ... Où Allons Nous?"
3. Williams, at 23.
4. Williams further clarified his intentions in this article in Bernard Williams, "Postscript," in Daniel Statman, ed., *Moral Luck* (Albany: State University of New York Press, 1993), 251.
5. Williams, at 20.
6. Williams, at 36.
7. The quotes in this paragraph and the next are from Williams, pp. 20–22.
8. Also referred to as *resultant luck* and as *outcome luck*. See, e.g., Margaret Urban Walker, "Moral Luck and the Virtues of Impure Agency," *Metaphylosophy* 22 (1991): 14, reprinted in Statman, *Moral Luck*, at 235; Ken Levy, "The Solution to the Problem of Outcome Luck: Why Harm Is Just as Punishable as the Wrongful Action that Causes It," *Law & Phil.* 24 (2005): 263.
9. Williams, at 35.
10. Williams, at 33, 34.
11. Bernard Williams, "Persons, Character, and Morality," in Williams, *Moral Luck*, at 1, 12–14.
12. Harry Frankfurt has objected, however, that making the willingness to go on contingent upon the execution of a project is the mark of the seriously depressed, suggesting instead that healthy people are propelled by the sheer love of life. Harry Frankfurt, *Taking Ourselves Seriously & Getting It Right*, Debra Satz, ed. (Stanford, CA: Stanford University Press, 2006), 27, 36–39.
13. Williams, at 35.
14. See Harry Frankfurt, "Identification and Externality," in *The Importance of What We Care About* (Cambridge, UK: Cambridge University Press, 1988), 58; "Identification and Wholeheartedness," in *The Importance of What We Care About*, at 159; and *The Reasons of Love* (Princeton, NJ: Princeton University Press, 2004). And see discussion of these issues in Chapter 2, pp. 46–49.
15. Williams, at 35.
16. Bernard Williams, "Internal and External Reasons," in Williams, *Moral Luck*, at 101.
17. Williams, at 27.
18. Parallel issues arise in connection with so-called wrongful life cases, in which the limits of intelligible counterfactuals in relationship to a person's identity

play an important role. For an especially illuminating discussion see David Heyd, "From Wrongful Life to Wrongful Identity," *Ann. Rev. L. & Ethics* 9 (2001): 173.

19. See John Locke, *An Essay Concerning Human Understanding*, Book 2, Chapter 21, Section 12; Harry Frankfurt, "Alternate Possibilities and Moral Responsibility," in *The Importance of What We Care About*, 1. For a related discussion see my "Conceptions of Choice and Conceptions of Autonomy," *Ethics* 102 (1992): 221, reprinted in Meir Dan-Cohen, *Harmful Thoughts: Essays on Law, Self, and Morality* (Princeton, NJ: Princeton University Press, 2002), 125.

20. Probably the most influential text here is Saul Kripke, *Naming and Necessity* (Cambridge, MA: Harvard University Press, 1972). Kripke maintains that an object's, including a person's, essential properties can be discovered empirically. He then asks rhetorically: "How could a person originating from different parents, from a totally different sperm and egg, *be this very woman?*" He concludes that "anything coming from a different origin would not be this object" (pp. 110–113). The constructive view need not deny this point, insisting, however, that in the case of persons there are additional properties that accrue over a lifetime, and are cumulatively necessary.

21. Williams, at 35–36.

22. His position would then resemble that of the swindler I discuss below in Part IV.

23. *Oxford English Dictionary* (Oxford, UK: Oxford University Press, 2d ed., 1989).

24. For a similar view, though one attached to a conception of human identity that differs from mine, see Nicholas Rescher, "Moral Luck," in Statman, *Moral Luck*, at 141, 155. For an argument that at least some versions of the idea of constitutive moral luck lead to absurdities, see Michael Zimmerman, "Luck and Moral Responsibility," in Statman, *Moral Luck*, 217, 222–224.

25. Williams, at 25.

26. Referring to the proposed view as *retrospective essentialism* is designed to signal one sense in which this view "splits the difference" in the essentialism/anti-essentialism debate concerning roles and other human categories. For a helpful overview and discussion of the issues involved, see Ron Mallon, "Human Categories Beyond Non-Essentialism," *J. Pol. Phil.* 15 (2007): 146–168.

27. For an elaboration of this point see my "Conceptions of Choice and Conceptions of Autonomy."

28. See Bernard Williams, "Resenting One's Own Existence," in Williams, *Making Sense of Humanity* (Cambridge, UK: Cambridge University Press, 1995), 224.

29. A similar distinction between regret and a critical judgment underlies Rüdiger Bittner, "Is It Reasonable to Regret Things One Did?" *J. Phil.* 92 (1992): 262. Professor Bittner deems all regret unreasonable because of the gratuitous suffering it involves, but believes that forswearing it is compatible with maintaining a critical attitude toward one's past actions.

30. See Thomas Nagel, "Moral Luck," in Nagel, *Mortal Questions* (Cambridge, UK: Cambridge University Press, 1979), 24.

CHAPTER 5

1. See Gerald Dworkin, *The Theory and Practice of Autonomy* (Cambridge, UK: Cambridge University Press, 1988); Thomas Hill, "The Kantian Conception of Autonomy," in *The Inner Citadel: Essays on Individual Autonomy*, John Christman, ed. (New York: Oxford University Press, 1989), 91–105; and Joseph Raz, *The Morality of Freedom* (Oxford, UK: Oxford University Press, 1988), Chapter 14.
2. Immanuel Kant, *Groundwork of the Metaphysics of Morals*, Herbert James Paton, trans. (New York: Harper & Row, 1964), Chapter 2.
3. John Rawls, *A Theory of Justice* (Cambridge, MA: Harvard University Press, 1971), 251–257. Cf.: Robert Taylor, *Reconstructing Rawls: The Kantian Foundations of Justice as Fairness* (University Park: The Pennsylvania State University Press, 2011), esp. Chapter 2.
4. Kant, *Groundwork*, Chapter 3.
5. Rawls, *A Theory of Justice*, at 12, 16, 21, 120.
6. See Michael Sandel, *Liberalism and the Limits of Justice* (Cambridge, UK: Cambridge University Press, 2nd ed., 1998).
7. See Henry Sidgwick, *The Methods of Ethics* (Indianapolis: Hackett, 1981 [1907]), 382, 386, 404; and Thomas Nagel, *The Possibility of Altruism* (Oxford: Oxford University Press, 1970), 58, 99–100.
8. Cf.: Pamela Johnston Conover, "Citizen Identities and Conceptions of the Self," *J. Pol. Phil.* 3 (1991): 133–165.
9. See also Chapters 8–10 below, and more generally, Meir Dan-Cohen, *Rights, Persons, and Organizations: A Legal Theory for Bureaucratic Society* (Berkeley: University of California Press, 1986).
10. See Robert Paul Wolff, *In Defense of Anarchism* (New York: Harper and Row, 1970).
11. See my "In Defense of Defiance," *Phil. & Public Affairs* 23 (1994): 24, reprinted in Meir Dan-Cohen, *Harmful Thoughts: Essays on Law, Self, and Morality* (Princeton, NJ: Princeton University Press, 2002), 94–121.

CHAPTER 6

1. See, e.g., R. M. Hare, "What Is Wrong with Slavery," *Phil. & Public Affairs* 8 (1979): 103.
2. The canonical discussion of this point is in John Stuart Mill, *On Liberty*. For a critical commentary of Mill's argument, see, e.g., Chin Liew Ten, *Mill on Liberty* (New York: Oxford University Press, 1980), 117–123.
3. Stephen Pinker, "The Stupidity of Dignity: Conservative Bioethics' Latest, Most Dangerous Ploy," *The New Republic*, http://www.newrepublic.com/article/the-stupidity-dignity.
4. See Remy Debes, "Dignity's Gauntlet," *Phil. Perspect.* 23 (2009): 45. Debes canvasses a range of different conceptions of dignity and concludes that "there is no single concept of 'dignity'" (p. 61). He nonetheless maintains that "a conscientious *metatheory* about what dignity is, might remedy the manifest ambiguity in

how we talk about it" (p. 47). I have no objection to such a project, but pending its successful completion one might prefer to reserve judgment.
5. Ludwig Feuerbach, *The Essence of Christianity*, George Eliot, trans. (New York: Harper & Row, 1957, 1841).
6. Karl Barth summarizes Feuerbach's view as holding "that man is not only the measure of all things, but also the epitome, the origin and end of all *values*." See Karl Barth, "Introduction," in Ibid., at x, xxviii.
7. A. Robert Caponigri, trans. (Washington, DC: Regnery Gateway, 1956).
8. Immanuel Kant, *Groundwork of the Metaphysic of Morals*, Herbert James Paton, ed. & trans. (New York: Harper & Row, 1976 [1948/1785]).
9. Ibid., at 90, 96–97.
10. For a particularly illuminating version of this strand, see Christine Korsgaard, *The Sources of Normativity*, Onora O'Neill ed. (Cambridge, UK: Cambridge University Press, 1996).
11. For an illuminating discussion of Kant's uses of "intelligible" in this connection, see Henry Allison, *Kant's Theory of Freedom* (Cambridge, UK: Cambridge University Press, 1990), 214–229.
12. See, e.g., Herbert Paton, *The Categorical Imperative: A Study in Kant's Moral Philosophy* (Philadelphia: University of Pennsylvania Press, 1971, 1947), 189.
13. Cf.: "To recognize persons as self-legislators in a Kantian sense *just is* to recognize a kind of authority that they bear." Colin Bird, "Status, Identity, and Respect," *Pol. Theory* 32 (2004): 207, 213.
14. Cf. Donald Davidson, "On the Very Idea of a Conceptual Scheme," in *Inquiries into Truth & Interpretation* (Oxford: Clarendon Press, 1984), 183.
15. See, for example, Jeremy Waldron, "Dignity and Rank," *Archives Européennes de Sociologie* 48 (2007): 201; *Dignity, Rank, and Rights: The Tanner Lectures by Jeremy Waldron*, Meir Dan-Cohen, ed. (Oxford: Oxford University Press, 2012).
16. Jeremy Waldron, "Dignity, Rights, and Responsibilities," *Ariz. St. L. J.* 43 (2012):1107, at 1121. The references in the following paragraph are additionally to pp. 1115 and 1125–1127 of Waldron's lecture.
17. Which is not to say that Waldron commits such a mistake, but rather that he employs a different category.
18. See Chapter 1, pp. 22–26.
19. Available at http://www.usccb.org/comm/Dignitaspersonae/Dignitas_Personae.pdf (2008).
20. Ibid., at 1.
21. *Human Dignity and Bioethics: Essays Commissioned by the President's Council on Bioethics* (Washington, DC: The President's Council on Bioethics, 2008); available at http://bioethics.georgetown.edu/pcbe/reports/human_dignity/human_dignity_and_bioethics.pdf.
22. See Pinker, "The Stupidity of Dignity."
23. This is not surprising in light of the composition of the Council, which, as Pinker points out, consisted for the most part of religious scholars. Ibid.
24. Compare Joseph Raz, *The Morality of Freedom* (Oxford: Oxford University Press, 1988), 380.

25. For a discussion of this notion in a different context, see ibid., at 35–37.
26. E.g.: "The body of a human being, from the very first stages of its existence, can never be reduced merely to a group of cells." *Instruction Dignitas Personae on Certain Bioethical Questions*, at 3.
27. For a general discussion of the issues involved, see, e.g., Margaret Jane Radin, *Contested Commodities* (Cambridge, MA: Harvard University Press, 1996).

CHAPTER 7

1. It should be clear that by proposing to reverse this trend I do not espouse the position associated with Lord Devlin and don't side with him as against H. L. A. Hart in their famous exchange. Patrick Devlin, *The Enforcement of Morals* (Oxford: Oxford University Press, 1965.); H. L. A. Hart, *Law, Liberty and Morality* (Stanford, CA: Stanford University Press, 1963). Put in Hart's terms, Devlin advocates enforcing by law a community's *conventional morality*, whatever its content. Hart contrasts this view with the utilitarians' insistence that law ought to promote social utility as a matter of *critical morality*, and so quite apart from whether any particular community subscribes to this moral perspective. The harm principle is the product or expression of this latter approach. My proposal is on the same plane as the utilitarian, substituting as a matter of critical morality (or moral theory), Kant's Categorical Imperative for Bentham's, or Mill's, or J. Austin's, utilitarian approach.
2. Bernard Harcourt, "The Collapse of the Harm Principle," *J. Crim. L. & Criminology* 90 (1999): 109.
3. The classical articles that sounded the alarm in this regard are by Professor Sanford Kadish: "The Crisis of Overcriminalization" and "The Use of Criminal Sanctions in Enforcing Economic Regulation", both in Sanford Kadish, *Blame and Punishment: Essays in the Criminal Law* (New York: Macmillan, 1987) at p. 21 and p. 40 respectively. For an instructive recent update see Jonathan Simon, *Governing Through Crime: How the War on Crime Transformed American Democracy and Created a Culture of Fear* (New York: Oxford University Press, 2007).
4. Cf.: Glanville Williams, *Criminal Law: The General Part* (London: Stevens, 2nd ed., 1961), 259; Kadish, "The Use of Criminal Sanctions," at 56–58.
5. The canonical texts are Ronald Dworkin, *Taking Rights Seriously* (Cambridge, MA: Harvard University Press, 1978), especially Chapters 4, 7, and 12, and Robert Nozick, *Anarchy, State, and Utopia* (New York: Basic Books, 1974), 26–53. For an illuminating overview, see Samuel Scheffler, *The Rejection of Consequentialism* (Oxford: Clarendon Press, 1982; rev. ed., 1994). For a book-length study of the application of this template to various areas of law, see Eyal Zamir and Barak Medina, *Law, Economics, and Morality* (Oxford: Oxford University Press, 2010).
6. 204 *Cal. App.* 2d 832; 23 *Cal. Rptr.* 92 (1962).
7. 364 *A.2d* 27 (N.J. Super. Ct. Law Div. 1976), aff'd, 381 *A.2d* 1231 (N.J. Super. Ct. App. Div. 1977).
8. For a related discussion of puzzles to which victims' consent can give rise see Leo Katz, *Ill-Gotten Gains: Evasion, Blackmail, Fraud, and Kindred Puzzles of the Law* (Chicago: University of Chicago Press, 1996), 145–157.

9. See Chapter 6, pp. 163–164.
10. Cf.: Charles Fried, *Right and Wrong* (Cambridge, MA: Harvard University Press, 1978), 32–42.
11. Courts are sometimes required to decide whether a form of government deprivation not explicitly labeled as punishment is in fact punitive and so subject to criminal law's strictures. For example, in concluding that the revocation of citizenship is indeed punitive, the criteria enumerated by the Supreme Court include "[w]hether the sanction involves an affirmative disability or restraint, whether it has historically been regarded as a punishment, whether it comes into play only on a finding of scienter, whether its operation will promote the traditional aims of punishment—retribution and deterrence, whether the behavior to which it applies is already a crime, whether an alternative purpose to which it may rationally be connected is assignable for it" (*Kennedy v. Mendoza-Martinez*, 372 U.S. 144, 168–69 [1963]). (For a slight variation of these criteria, see also *Kansas v. Hendricks*, 521 U.S. 346, 361–63 [1997].) These criteria roughly correspond to elements in my notion of mistreatment, but the notion of mistreatment gives the determination of punitiveness a unified theoretical basis that the Court's criteria lack.
12. For a classical version of this view, see H. L. A. Hart, "Prolegomenon to the Principles of Punishment," in his *Punishment and Responsibility: Essays in the Philosophy of Law* (Oxford: Oxford University Press, 1969), 1–27.
13. Immanuel Kant, *The Metaphysical Elements of Justice*, John Ladd, trans., (Indianapolis: Bobbs-Merrill, 1965), 102.
14. Herbert Morris, "Persons and Punishment," in *On Guilt and Innocence* (Berkeley: University of California Press, 1976), 31.

CHAPTER 8

1. See generally Lynne Rudder Baker, "Why Constitution Is Not Identity," *J. Phil.* 94 (1997): 599. Professor Baker extends this point to the case of human beings in *Persons and Bodies: A Constitution View* (Cambridge, UK: Cambridge University Press, 2000).
2. For the role and nature of information processing in organizations see, e.g., Robert Bonczek et al., *Foundations of Decision Support Systems* (New York: Academic Press, 1981).
3. See Daniel Dennett, "Conditions of Personhood," in *Brainstorms: Philosophical Essays on Mind and Psychology* (Montgomery, VT: Bradford Books, 1978), 267, 271.
4. See Harold Wilensky, *Organizational Intelligence: Knowledge and Policy in Government and Industry* (New York: Basic Books, 1967).
5. Even Professor Jeremy Waldron, who has recently advocated ascribing dignity to collectivities of various kinds, does not discuss business corporations in this connection. See Jeremy Waldron, "The Dignity of Groups," *Acta Juridica* 66 (2008): 74–90.
6. For widely ranging variants of this theme, see, for example, David Ozar, "The Moral Responsibility of Corporations," in *Ethical Issues in Business: A Philosophical Approach*, Thomas Donaldson and Patricia Werhane, eds. (Englewood Cliffs,

NJ: Prentice-Hall, 1979), 294, 294–299; Thomas Donaldson, "Moral Agency and Corporations," *Phil. in Context* 10 (1980): 54; and Peter French, "The Corporation as a Moral Person," *Am. Phil. Q.* 16 (1979): 207.

7. The general issue is sometimes referred to as that of "moral considerability." See, e.g., Mark Bernstein, *On Moral Considerability: An Essay on Who Morally Matters* (New York: Oxford University Press, 1998).
8. French, "The Corporation as a Moral Person," 207, 208.
9. E.g., Peter Singer, *Animal Liberation: A New Ethics for Our Treatment of Animals* (New York: Avon Books, 1975, 1990).
10. See Chapter 6, pp. 146–151 above.
11. See Immanuel Kant, *Groundwork of the Metaphysic of Morals*, Herbert James Paton, ed. & trans. (New York: Harper & Row, 1976 [1948/1785], esp. Chapter 2. Though Kant does talk about a seemingly broader category of rational beings, people are the only terrestrial beings it comprises.
12. Since if one is, by whatever standard, a human being at any time, then one is a human being, tenselessly, at all time. See, e.g., David Wiggins, *Sameness and Substance Renewed* (Cambridge, UK: Cambridge University Press, 2001).
13. Referred to by philosophers as "the argument from marginal cases." See, e.g., Daniel Dombrowski, *Babies and Beasts: The Argument from Marginal Cases* (Urbana: University of Illinois Press, 1997).
14. *Oration on the Dignity of Man*, A. Robert Caponigri, trans. (Washington, DC: Regnery Gateway, 1956).
15. Cf.: "all great and extraordinary wrongs done to particular persons ought to be considered as in a manner done to all the rest of the human race." Oliver Cromwell to the Speaker of the Parliament of England, 2 April 1650, in *The Writings and Speeches of Oliver Cromwell*, W. C. Abbott, ed. (Cambridge, MA: Harvard University Press, 1939), Vol. II, p. 234.
16. *Merriam-Webster Dictionary* (10th ed., 2002).
17. See Chapter 1, pp. 37–43.
18. See, e.g., Maurice Merleau-Ponty, *Phenomenology of Perception*, Colin Smith, trans. (New York: Humanities Press, 1962), esp. pp. 143, 145.
19. I elaborate such a theory more fully in *Rights, Persons, and Organizations: A Legal Theory for Bureaucratic Society*, (Berkeley, CA: University of California Press, 1986).

CHAPTER 9

1. For warnings to this effect, see, e.g., Robert Reich, *Supercapitalism: The Transformation of Business, Democracy, and Everyday Life* (New York: Knopf, 2007), 218–219; and John C. Coffee, Jr., "'No Soul to Damn: No Body to Kick': An Unscandalized Inquiry into the Problem of Corporate Punishment," *Mich. L. Rev.* 79 (1981): 386, 386 n.2, 390, 441, 448.
2. See, e.g., John Hasnas, "The Centenary of a Mistake: One Hundred Years of Corporate Criminal Liability," *Am. Crim. L. Rev.* 46 (2009): 1329; Joseph Francis, "Criminal Responsibility of the Corporation," *Ill. L. Rev.* 18 (1924): 305, 314–323; V. S. Khanna, "Corporate Criminal Liability: What Purpose Does it Serve?"

Harv. L. Rev. 109 (1996):1477; Eliezer Lederman, "Criminal Law, Perpetrator and Corporation: Rethinking a Complex Triangle," *J. Crim. L. & Criminology* 28 (1985):576; and Manuel Velasquez, "Debunking Corporate Moral Responsibility," *Bus. Ethics Q.* 13 (2003): 531, 538–540.

3. See, e.g., Lawrence Friedman, "In Defense of Corporate Criminal Liability," *Harv. J. L. & Pub. Policy* 23 (2000):833; Regina Robson, "Crime and Punishment: Rehabilitating Retribution as a Justification of Organizational Criminal Liability," *Am. Bus. L. J.* 47 (2010): 109; see also *N.Y. Cent. & Hudson River R.R. v. United States*, 212 U.S. 481, 494–96 (1909).
4. With occasional exceptions; see, e.g., *Doe v. United States*, 487 U.S. 201, 206 (1988) (privilege against self-incrimination does not apply to corporations).
5. Chapter 7, p. 173.
6. This account is sometimes referred to as the *mixed* or *hybrid* theory of punishment. See, e.g., Mitchell Berman, "Punishment and Justification," *Ethics* 118 (2008): 258, 258–259. An early, classical version is H. L. A. Hart, "Prolegomenon to the Principles of Punishment," in *Proc. Aristotelian Soc.* 60 (1959–60): 1. See also Jeffrie Murphy and Jules Coleman, *Philosophy of Law: An Introduction to Jurisprudence* (Boulder, CO: Westview Press, rev. ed., 1990), 117–124.
7. See, e.g., Herbert Packer, "Two Models of the Criminal Process," *U. Pa. L. Rev.* 113 (1964): 1, 27 ("[People] have to be prepared to pay a price for a regime that fosters personal privacy and champions the dignity and inviolability of the individual. That price inevitably involves some sacrifice in efficiency"); see also Peter Arenella, "Rethinking the Functions of Criminal Procedure: The Warren and Burger Courts' Competing Ideologies," *Geo. L. J.* 72 (1983): 185, 201–202 (noting the value of Fifth and Sixth Amendment protections apart from their contributions to producing efficient and accurate results in criminal trials); and Richard Saphire, "Specifying Due Process: Toward a More Responsive Approach to Procedural Protection," *U. Pa. L. Rev.* 127 (1978): 111, 117–125 (arguing that the dignity of the individual is a basic value underlying the due process required by the Fifth and Fourteenth Amendments).
8. This description draws particularly on the depiction of organizational behavior in Richard Cyert and James March, *A Behavioral Theory of the Firm* (Hoboken, NJ: Blackwell, 2nd ed., 1992).
9. This mechanism of deterrence is particularly emphasized in Brent Fisse and John Braithwaite, *Corporations, Crime, and Accountability* (Cambridge, UK: Cambridge University Press, 1993), 32–34.
10. P. 175.
11. For a precursor of a line of thought pointing in this general direction, see Christopher Stone, *Where the Law Ends: The Social Control of Corporate Behavior* (New York: Harper & Row, 1975).
12. Numerous laws tie various special obligations to corporate size. See, e.g., *Family and Medical Leave Act of 1993*, 29 U.S.C.A. §§ 2601–2654 (West 2010) (tying the right to take a leave of absence to care for certain family members to employees of corporations with fifty or more employees); and *Civil Rights Act of 1964*, 42 U.S.C.A. § 2000e (West 2009) (limiting the Act's prohibition on employment

discrimination to companies that employ fifteen or more employees). However, the suggested approach has recently suffered a severe setback in *Citizens United v. Fed. Election Comm'n*, 558 U. S. 310 (2010), in which the Supreme Court reversed previous decisions that had limited corporate First Amendment protections. I address some of these issues in the next chapter, as well as in *Rights, Persons, and Organizations: A Legal Theory for Bureaucratic Society* (Berkeley: University of California Press, 1986).

CHAPTER 10

1. The original article on which this chapter is based was written soon after the Supreme Court's decision in *Austin v. Michigan Chamber of Commerce* 494 U.S. 652 (1990). In this case the Court upheld a Michigan statute that prohibits corporations from using general treasury funds for independent expenditures in connection with state candidate elections. In doing so, the Court departed from its earlier holding in *First National Bank v. Bellotti*, 435 U.S. 765 (1978), the seminal case that had extended First Amendment protection to corporate political speech, reversing in this regard a previous holding, in *Buckley v. Valeo*, 424 U.S. 1 (1975). In yet another, more recent swing of this pendulum, *Citizens United v. Fed. Election Comm'n*, 558 U. S. 310 (2010), the Court put the issue back on the public and scholarly agenda by overruling in the relevant respects *Austin* and reinstating the *Bellotti* decision.
2. The most influential statement of this view is in Ronald Dworkin, *Taking Rights Seriously* (Cambridge, MA: Harvard University Press, 1977), esp. 188–192.
3. For this conception of rights and its application to organizations I draw on my *Rights, Persons, and Organizations: A Legal Theory for Bureaucratic Society* (Berkeley: University of California Press, 1986), Part II.
4. See, e.g., Charles O'Kelley, "The Constitutional Rights of Corporations Revisited: Social and Political Expression and the Corporation after *First National Bank v. Bellotti*," Geo. L. J. 67 (1979): 1347, at 1373 ("Corporate communication does not exist; only individuals can have ideas").
5. In Chapter 8, pp. 106–107 and Chapter 1, pp. 185 and 17–28, respectively.
6. For the first argument, see *Austin v. Michigan Chamber of Commerce*, 494 U.S. 652, 659–60 (1990); for the second, see Victor Brudney, "Business Corporations and Stockholders' Rights Under the First Amendment," Yale L. J. 91 (1981): 235 at 268.
7. For example, Justice Scalia points out that the fortunes amassed by wealthy individuals also give them political power that is "no reflection of the power of [their] ideas," a fact that would hardly make it "lawful to prohibit men and women whose net worth is above a certain figure from endorsing political candidates." In *Austin v. Michigan Chamber of Commerce* at 680.
8. This point is adapted from my "Interpreting Official Speech," in *Harmful Thoughts: Essays on Law, Self, and Morality* (Princeton, NJ: Princeton University Press, 2002), Chapter 8.
9. Brudney, "Business Corporations," at 264.

10. *Bellotti*, 435 U.S. at 789; see also Chevigny, "Philosophy of Language and Free Expression," *N.Y.U. L. Rev.* 55 (1980):157, 189–190.
11. Without getting into much doctrinal detail, it is worth mentioning that the present argument generally comports with the Supreme Court's position in *Federal Election Commission v. Massachusetts Citizens for Life, Inc.*, 479 U.S. 238 (1986), in which the Court articulated criteria for exempting some organizations (whether or not they have a corporate form) from the kind of speech regulation that would be permissible with regard to an ordinary business corporation.
12. See, e.g., James Wilson, *Political Organizations* (Princeton, NJ: Princeton University Press, 1995), 211 (claiming that for an increasing number of associations, "'members' exist only as an historical artifact, as symbols of 'private' legitimacy, or as grounds for claiming a representational function").
13. Academic freedom has in fact been recognized as a First Amendment right. See *Keyishian v. Board of Regents*, 385 U.S. 589, 603 (1967). See also Thomas Emerson, *The System of Freedom of Expression* (New York: Random House, 1970), 613–614.
14. See Edward Gross, "Universities as Organizations: A Research Approach," *Am. Soc. Rev.* 33 (1968): 518, 529–530 (finding in a poll of university administrators and faculty members that academic freedom is, and ought to be, first among universities' goals).
15. On the phenomenon of goal displacement in organizations see, e.g., Amitai Etzioni, *Modern Organizations* (Englewood Cliffs, NJ: Prentice-Hall, 1964), 10.
16. As the case of *NAACP v. Alabama ex rel. Patterson*, 357 U.S. 449 (1958) illustrates, classifying an organization as expressive or protective for First Amendment purposes may overlap. The National Association for the Advancement of Colored People (NAACP) objected to a state-compelled disclosure of its membership list. In determining that the association "is but the medium through which its individual members seek to make more effective the expression of their own views," the Supreme Court in effect recognized the NAACP as an expressive organization, and its standing to raise its members' speech rights (at 459). However, it is perhaps more accurate to view the NAACP as acting in this case as a protective organization. By securing its members' anonymity, the association protected their individual right to freedom of expression from the likely harassments and intimidations characteristic of the political atmosphere of the time. (As the Court noted, at 462–463, disclosing the identity of the NAACP's members would expose them to "public hostility.")
17. Pp. 23–25 above.
18. Compare discussion on pp. 75–76 above.
19. For a comprehensive study of this subject see Mark Yudof, *When Government Speaks: Politics, Law, and Government Expression in America* (Berkeley: University of California Press, 1983).
20. In Chapter 5, pp. 134–135 above.
21. For a similar conception of the state and its relation to the self, see Peter Gabel, "The Phenomenology of Rights-Consciousness and the Pact of the Withdrawn Selves," *Tex. L. Rev.* 62 (1984): 1563.
22. Yudof, *When Government Speaks*, at 43.

23. Cf.: Professor Lawrence Tribe's discussion of *Village of Belle Terre v. Boraas*, 416 U.S. 1 (1974). In *Belle Terre* the Court upheld an ordinance by which some two hundred families sought to preserve the character of their town by excluding, inter alia, groups of three or more persons unrelated by blood or marriage sharing the same household. Tribe suggests that assessing the associational rights of Belle Terre may call for an ascertainment of its genuine "communal" nature: "Belle Terre may not be a real 'community' or 'association' at all but simply a collection of persons ... because it has no organic life as a center of communal perceptions and common activities." Lawrence Tribe, *American Constitutional Law* (Mineola, NY: Foundation Press, 1978), §15–18, at 979.
24. E.g., Note, "The Constitutionality of Municipal Advocacy in Statewide Referendum Campaigns," *Harv. L. Rev.* 93 (1980): 535.
25. For a sustained argument in favor of a more communal conception of municipalities than we at present recognize, see Gerald Frug, "The City as a Legal Concept," *Harv. L. Rev.* 93 (1980): 1057.
26. Of course, the issue does not always arise, since there may not be any dissenters. So, for example, in *Anderson v. City of Boston*, the Court held that "the Commonwealth has no right to restrict [advocacy by a municipality on a referendum question] where there is no opposition from any affected citizen." 376 *Mass.* 178, 196, 380 *N.E.2d* 628, 639 (1978), *appeal dismissed*, 439 *U.S.* 1060 (1979).
27. Yudof, *When Government Speaks*, 20–37 and *passim*.
28. Compare Justice Burke's view that "[b]oards of supervisors and city councilmen are not 'representatives of local communities' on matters outside the scope of county and municipal affairs and certainly are not authorized in any *representative capacity* to express the will of the people on matters of national policy." *Farley v. Healey*, 67 *Cal. 2d* 325, 333, 431 *P.2d* 650, 656, 62 *Cal. Rptr.* 26, 32 (1967) (Burke, J., dissenting), with the view of Chief Justice Traynor: "As representatives of local communities, boards of supervisors and city councils have traditionally made declarations of policy on matters of concern to the community whether or not they had power to effectuate such declarations by binding legislation." *Ibid., Healey*, 67 *Cal. 2d*. at 328, 652, and 28 respectively.
29. This is the position taken by the Supreme Court in holding that "[a] municipality is merely a department of the State, and the State may withhold, grant or withdraw powers and privileges as it sees fit." *Trenton v. New Jersey*, 262 *U.S.* 182, 187 (1923).

INDEX

alienation, 37, 43–45
Anderson v. City of Boston, 250n26
animal rights, 187
Austin v. Michigan Chamber of Commerce, 248n1, 248n7
autonomy
  choice and, 160–162
  citizens and, 134–137
  criminal liability and, 170
  dignity and, 189, 205, 210–211
  Frankfurt on, 46
  Kant on, 120, 160–162, 189
  moral, 120, 126, 131–132, 135, 138–139, 189
  normative concerns regarding, 1, 11–12, 29–31, 74, 75, 133, 183
  noumenal self and, 152
  personal, 120, 126, 132–133, 135
  political, 122, 126, 132–133, 134–137
  prudence and, 126
  punishment and, 176
  responsibility and, 13, 50, 72, 177
  role distance and, 29–30, 34–36, 158
  the self and, 4, 12, 50–51, 72–75, 121, 135, 148, 152
  as self-government, 121
  slavery and, 139–141, 170–171
  speech rights and, 210–211, 217–221

bad faith, 37–45
Bentham, Jeremy, 1, 173–175

boundaries
  indeterminacy of, 52, 76
  normative considerations regarding, 69–70
  revision of, 64–73, 76–79, 85, 89–90
  roles and, 34, 158
  of the self, 1–5, 12–13, 25, 46, 48–52, 64, 72–78, 84, 89–90, 102, 158–159
  sovereignty and, 69, 72–73
  spatial forms of, 64–72, 74
  of the state, 46, 50, 64–72, 74–75, 79, 84–85
  temporal forms of, 5, 25, 56, 64–72, 75–79, 84–85, 89–90
Brown. See State v. Brown
Burke, Louis H., 250n28

categorical imperative, 146–147
Charlson. See Regina v. Charlson
citizens, 118, 131–137
collectivities. *See also* communities; corporations; organizations
  affiliation and, 192–193, 196, 206
  consequentialist norms and, 183, 184, 196
  construction of, 15–16, 18–19, 26–28
  dignity and, 6, 183, 186, 192–193, 196, 206
  identity and, 6, 85–88, 131, 192–193, 196, 206, 221–222
  individuals' relation to, 15

collectivities (*Cont.*)
  memory and, 84–88
  mission and, 19, 27, 186
  normative considerations regarding, 183, 186
  revision of, 56, 61–62, 89
  roles and, 18–19, 26–28, 34–35, 185–186
  speech by, 6, 209–210, 221, 223, 224, 230–231
communitarianism, 2–3, 14, 16, 36–37, 124
communities
  organizations contrasted with, 134, 223
  roles and, 26–28, 34–35
  speech by, 208, 221–224, 226–227, 229–230
constitutive decisions, 100–102
construction
  collectivities and, 15–16, 18–19, 26–28
  of identity, 100–103, 107, 111–114, 146, 155
  law and, 33–35
  modalities of, 11–17
  responsibility and, 48–49
  revision contrasted with, 91
  roles and, 17–26
  the self and, 2–5, 13–26, 29–33, 35–37, 42, 48–49, 56, 72, 73, 74–76, 91, 117, 126, 127, 129, 146, 155–156, 164, 191
  social, 14–16
corporations
  affiliation and, 194–195, 206
  consequentialist norms and, 196, 201–202
  construction of, 15
  criminal liability of, 6, 183, 198–201, 207, 209
  defining ethos of, 193
  dignity and, 6, 183, 186–189, 192–196, 206–207
  distributive acts of, 202
  emergent properties of, 184, 203
  global acts of, 202–203
  holistic views of, 184, 199, 203
  personhood and, 184–188, 196, 202
  punishment of, 197–208
  reductionist views of, 184–185, 199–200, 203–204
  role distance and, 194
  shareholders and, 195, 206, 217
  speech rights and, 209, 212–214, 217–218, 220–221, 226
crime
  dignity and, 175
  as mistreatment, 175
  utilitarian conception of, 169
criminal law
  boundaries of, 166–169, 201, 205–208
  corporations and, 198, 201, 206–207
  deterrence and, 201
  dignity and, 6, 165, 168–171, 176–178, 197, 205–206
  harm principle and, 165–167
  human life and, 169
  morality and, 165–169, 176
  punishment and, 165, 176–179, 201, 205–208

"defining projects," 100–103, 108–110, 113
deterrence, 32, 55, 175–176, 202–205
Devlin, Patrick, 244n1
dignity
  abstraction and, 192
  of animals, 187
  autonomy and, 189, 206, 210–211
  body and, 162–164
  choice and, 160–162
  collectivities and, 6, 183, 186, 192–193, 196, 206
  corporations and, 6, 183, 186–189, 192–196, 205
  crime and, 175
  criminal law and, 6, 165, 168–171, 176–179, 197, 205
  honor and, 151–154
  imago Dei as source of, 143–146
  Kant on, 6, 138, 141–144, 145–147, 150–151, 154, 157–160, 168, 173, 183, 188–189
  the law and, 154, 183

morality and, 132, 138–143, 146–149, 161, 165, 168–169, 183, 186, 197
of persons, 132, 138, 142, 147, 148, 159–164, 187–188, 191
price and, 146-148
punishment and, 6, 169, 173, 175–179, 201–202, 205, 207
religious cooptation and, 159–160
responsibility and, 13, 153–154
rights discourse and, 159
roles and, 153–154, 156–158
the self and, 1, 12, 143, 149, 155, 159, 188–191, 205, 225
slavery and, 141, 170–171
socially based conception of, 153–156
sources of, 143–146
universality and, 152–155, 157, 190
of victims, 177–179
Waldron on, 152–158
worth and, 142–143, 147, 152–153, 155–157, 159, 191

ethics
abstraction and, 131
the law and, 117–118, 129, 131, 138
morality and, 117, 129, 131, 138
prudence and, 117, 127, 129, 131, 138
essentialism, retrospective, 112, 241n26

Farley v. Healey, 250n28
Faust story, 130
Federal Election Commission v. Massachusetts Citizens for Life, Inc, 249n11
Feuerbach, Ludwig, 144
First Amendment rights. *See also* free speech
corporations and, 212, 226
individual right to self-expression and, 217
organizations and, 212, 217, 221
of the state, 224, 226
forgiveness
epistemology and, 77
limits of, 89–91

past-oriented nature of, 56–56, 60, 76–77
remorse and, 59
responsibility and, 90
temporal boundaries of the self and, 76–77
victim as focus of, 57
wrongdoer reassessed in, 58–59, 90–91
Frankfurt, Harry
on autonomy, 46
on alternate possibilities, 106
on harmony within the self, 51
on identification and the boundaries of the self, 102
on moral authority, 52–54
on responsibility, 46–50
free speech
active derivative forms of, 211
active rights to, 210–211, 217–220, 225–228, 231
autonomy and, 210–212, 219–221
collective actors and, 6, 209–210, 221, 223, 224, 230
corporations and, 209, 212–214, 217–218, 220–221, 226
derivative rights to, 211–212, 217–221, 228, 231
government's right to, 224–230
individuals and, 214–216
normative aspects of, 210, 218
organizations and, 209, 212–221, 223–225, 228
original rights to, 211, 217–221, 225–231
passive rights of, 211, 217–218, 231

government speech, 224–230
Govier, Trudy, 239n31

Hart, H.L.A., 244n1
History. *See* memory
honor, 151–154
Human Dignity and Bioethics report, 160

identity. *See also* self
  binary distinctions and, 25
  citizenship and, 134
  collectivities and, 6, 85–88, 131, 192–193, 196, 206, 221–222
  compositional, 25
  constitution contrasted with, 184, 203
  construction of, 99–103, 107, 111–114, 146, 155
  counterfactuals regarding, 104–110
  defining projects and, 101
  dignity and, 195
  Locke on, 81, 82
  luck and, 5, 111, 114
  memory and, 77–84
  nationality and, 225, 229
  noumenal self and, 100–101
  regret and, 93, 111–113
  repentance and, 61–62, 77
  revisions of, 65–67, 71–72, 77, 89–93, 101
  roles and, 4, 18, 25, 28, 31, 36, 39–39, 42–43, 130, 131, 157
  self-constitution and, 14
  temporal continuity and, 25
imago Dei doctrine, 143–146
Instruction Dignitas Personae on Certain Bioethical Questions (Vatican report), 160

Kant, Immanuel
  on autonomy, 120, 160–162, 189
  categorical imperative, 146–147
  on dignity, 6, 138, 141–144, 145–148, 150–151, 154, 157–160, 168, 173, 183, 189
  Kingdom of Ends, 123–124
  liberalism and, 160–161
  moral philosophy of, 95–96, 98–99, 111, 122–125, 138, 143–144, 146–148, 150–151, 154, 157–160, 168, 173, 183, 189
  noumenal self, 2, 111, 123–124, 143, 152
  on psychological inclinations *versus* rationality, 126
  on punishment, 176–179, 201
  Rawls compared to, 123–124
  on valuation, 146–148
  Williams on, 95, 111
Kripke, Saul, 241n20

ladder of abstraction, 6, 130
law. *See also* criminal law
  abstraction and, 127, 131–132
  citizens and, 131–132
  communal orientation of, 127
  construction and, 33–35
  dignity and, 154, 183
  ethics and, 117–118, 129, 131, 138
  government authority exercised through, 118
  morality and, 117–118, 127, 133, 154, 165–169
  normative grip of, 117
  obedience and, 135, 165
  prudence and, 117, 133
  roles and, 33–35
liberalism
  free will and, 160–162
  Kant's enduring influence on, 138, 160–161
  secularism and, 143
  the self and, 2
  slavery and, 139
Locke, John, 80–84, 106
luck
  consequential, 99, 110
  constitutive, 98–100, 110
  epistemic, 111
  identity and, 5, 111–112, 114
  incidental, 98–100
  moral, 5, 93–96, 98, 111, 114
  regret and, 93, 110–111, 114
  Williams on, 94–96, 98–100, 110–111

memory
  affective aspects of, 83–84
  cognitive aspects of, 83–84
  collective memory and, 84–88
  criminal liability and, 82

Index

history and, 84–88
identity and, 77–84
Locke on, 81–83
reflexivity of, 83, 87
responsibility and, 77–88
revision and, 80, 84
methodological individualism, 185
Minkowski. See State v. Minkowski
morality
  abstraction and, 122–125, 128, 131–132
  autonomy and, 120, 26, 132–133, 135, 138–139, 189
  communitarianism and, 125
  criminal law and, 165–169, 176
  deontological approaches to, 139–139, 146–147, 168 (*See also* Kant, Immanuel)
  dignity and, 132, 138–143, 146–149, 161, 165, 168–169, 183, 186, 197
  ethics and, 117, 129, 131, 138
  individual self-interest and, 122
  Kant on, 95–96, 98–99, 111, 122–125, 138, 143–144, 146–147, 150–151, 154, 157–160, 168, 173, 183, 189
  law and, 117–118, 127, 133, 154, 165–169
  noumenal self and, 123–124, 143
  persons and, 131–132
  prudence and, 126
  of punishment, 165, 174–179, 201–202
  slavery and, 139
  universal, 119–120, 125, 127
  utilitarian approaches to, 138–141, 166, 168
moral luck, 5, 93–96, 98–99, 111, 114
moral personhood, 186–187, 190, 202
Morris, Herbert, 177

NAACP v. Alabama ex rel. Patterson, 249n16
noumenal self
  abstract nature of, 2, 123, 127, 146
  autonomy and, 152
  dignity and, 155
  identity fixed by, 99–101
  Kant on, 2, 111, 123–124, 143, 152

morality and, 123–124, 143–144
rational will and, 123

Oration on the Dignity of Man (Pico della Mirandola), 146, 191
organizations
  commercial, 220–221, 228, 231
  communities contrasted with, 134, 223
  decision-making processes and, 185, 213–214, 221
  expressive, 218, 221, 223, 228, 231
  global acts of, 213
  missions and goals of, 27, 186, 213–215, 220
  protective, 218–219, 228, 231
  representative speech and, 216
  roles and, 26–28, 34–37, 185–186, 215, 221
  speech rights and, 209, 212–221, 223–225, 228

pardon
  limits of, 89
  past-oriented nature of, 56–56, 60, 76–77
  revision and, 5
  temporal boundaries of the self and, 76–77
Parfit, Derek, 25
the past
  fixity of, 55, 61–64, 93
  memory and, 62, 84–88
  reductionist approach to, 58–64, 63
  revision and, 5, 56, 60, 65, 66, 71–72, 76–79, 93
personal norms, 12–13, 29–31, 34–35, 72
personhood, practical and moral, 184–190, 192, 202–203
persons
  abstraction and, 130–132, 138, 192
  citizens and, 132–133
  corporations as, 184–188, 196, 202
  dignity of, 132, 138, 139, 142, 147–148, 159–164, 187–188, 191
  embodiment and, 162–164

persons (*Cont.*)
  individuals and, 130–131, 132–133
  moral personhood, 186–187, 190, 202
  practical personhood and, 184–190, 192, 203
  vegetative states and, 191–192
phenomenal self, 123–124
Pico della Mirandola, Giovanni, 146, 164, 191
Pinker, Stephen, 142, 160
"the political question"
  definition of, 118
  individualist challenge to, 125
  justification and, 119
  "the moral question" and, 123–127
  "the prudential question" and, 125–127
  Rawls on, 123–125
President's Council on Bioethics, 160
prudence
  abstraction and, 127, 131–132
  autonomy and, 126
  ethics and, 117, 127, 129, 131, 138
  individual self-interest and, 119, 127–128, 131–132
  law and, 117–118, 133
  morality and, 125
  the prudential question, 125–127
  the self and, 119, 126
  state enforcement of, 136
punishment
  autonomy and, 176
  constraints on, 201–202
  of corporations, 197–208
  criminal law and, 165, 176–179, 201, 205–207
  deprivations and, 174–176, 206–207
  deterrence and, 32, 55, 176–178, 202–205
  dignity and, 6, 169, 173, 176–179, 201–202, 205, 208
  distinctness of, 174
  of the innocent, 173–174, 201–202
  justification for, 173
  Kant on, 176–178, 201
  military force and, 168
  as mistreatment, 175–176
  morality and, 165, 174–179, 201
  payment compared to, 32
  responsibility and, 50, 177–178
  retribution and, 32, 176–177
  utilitarian approach to, 173–174

Rawls, John, 7, 101, 123–125, 128
Regina v. Charlson, 47–49, 51
regret
  agent-, 96, 103–105, 111
  identity and, 93, 111–113
  limitations of, 5, 110–111
  luck and, 93, 110–111, 114
  past-oriented nature of, 93, 104, 111–114
  Williams on, 102–105, 107, 108, 110, 113
repentance
  identity change and, 61, 77
  limits of, 89
  past-oriented nature of, 55–56, 60, 76–77, 93
  temporal boundaries of the self and, 76–77
representative speech, 216
responsibility
  autonomy and, 13, 50, 72–73, 177
  boundaries of the self and, 48–49
  criminal trials and, 48–51, 74–76
  dignity and, 13, 153–154
  forgiveness and, 91
  Frankfurt on, 46–51
  identification and, 46–51
  memory and, 77–88
  mental states and, 47–48, 73–76
  normative considerations regarding, 4, 12, 29–31, 50, 74–75
  punishment and, 50, 177–178
  responsibility rights, 153–154
  role distance and, 29–30, 34, 158
  the self and, 48–52, 73–77
  speech and, 222
  of stockholders, 194–195
  temporal boundaries and, 63

Index

revision
  of boundaries, 64–72, 76–79, 85, 89, 90
  limits of, 5, 89–91
  memory and, 80, 84
  of the past, 5, 56, 60, 65, 66, 71–72, 76–79, 93
  of the self, 5, 56, 60, 62–65, 72, 73, 76–81, 84, 89–93
  revisionary practices, 5, 56–57, 60–61, 63–84, 89–92
  contrasted with regret, 93
rights discourse, 159roles
  abstraction and, 130–131, 192
  affiliations and, 18, 26–28, 158
  alienation and, 37, 43–45
  atomism of, 18, 33, 38
  autonomy and, 29–3, 34–36, 158
  bad faith and, 37–45
  collectivities and, 18–19, 26–28, 34–35, 185–186
  compartmentalization and, 34
  definition of, 4, 17
  dignity and, 153–154, 192–193
  distance and, 4, 22–37, 44–45, 135, 158, 194, 215, 216
  distant or detached forms of, 4, 23, 28–28, 36–37, 45, 135, 158, 215
  enforcement of, 35
  formal aspect (script) of, 17–18, 33–34
  functional, 18
  identity and, 4, 18, 25, 28, 31, 36, 39, 42–43, 130, 157
  law and, 33–35
  love and, 30–31
  material aspect of, 17
  motivation and, 23–24, 31–33
  normative considerations and, 19–24, 27–33, 35, 37, 44
  organizations and, 26–28, 34–37, 185–186, 215, 216, 221
  parenthood and, 24, 26–28, 44, 221–222
  payment and, 25, 31–33
  proximate forms of, 4, 23, 26–33, 34–37
  representation and, 38–40

  self and, 4, 17–26, 29–30, 34–36, 42, 135, 158
  sincerity and, 23
  as social units, 19–20
  spatiotemporal framing and, 41–43
  telephone operator example of, 24, 27, 30–31, 45, 215–216, 221
  theatrical understanding of, 22, 38, 39–43
  waiter example and, 38–43, 45

Sartre, Jean-Paul, 38–45
Scalia, Antonin, 248n7
Searle, John, 24
self. *See also* identity
  abstract, 124, 127–133, 137–138
  alienation and, 44
  autonomy and, 4, 12, 50–52, 72–75, 121, 135, 148, 152
  the body and, 73
  boundaries of, 1–5, 12–13, 25, 46, 48–52, 62, 72–78, 84–85, 89, 102, 158–159
  communitarian views of, 125
  construction of, 2–5, 13–26, 29–33, 34–38, 42, 48, 56, 72, 74–76–77, 90–91, 117–118, 127, 129, 146, 155–156, 164, 191
  "core" of, 36
  dignity and, 2, 12, 143, 149, 155, 159, 188–189, 206, 225
  expression and, 211–213, 216–217, 218, 221–228, 231
  hermeneutical approach to, 2–3, 14, 38
  liberal tradition and, 2
  Locke on, 80, 83–84
  meaning-conception of, 2–3, 6, 44, 46, 72, 93, 107, 117, 129, 138, 191
  memory and, 85
  normative considerations regarding, 1–5, 12–13, 50–52, 74–75
  noumenal, 2, 100–101, 111, 123–124, 127, 143, 146, 152, 155
  phenomenal, 123–124
  property and, 73–74
  prudence and, 119, 126–127

self (*Cont.*)
   responsibility and, 48–52, 73–76
   revision and, 5, 56, 60, 62–65, 72, 76–81, 84–85, 89–93
   roles and, 4, 17–26, 29–30, 34–36, 42, 135, 157–158
   "topology" of, 35–37
   utilitarian approach to, 2
Shakespeare, William, 42
slavery, 139–141, 170–171
Snowden. See State v. Snowden
speech rights. *See* free speech
Spinoza, Baruch, 51
the state
   allegiance to, 118–120, 127–128, 135
   boundaries of, 46, 50, 62–73, 74–75, 79, 84–85
   citizens and, 118
   coercion and, 119, 135–136, 199
   communal aspect of, 225–227
   individuals and, 4, 63, 72–76, 119–123, 133
   memory and, 84
   normative concerns regarding, 118–122, 135
   ontology of, 67–72
   "the political question" and, 119–122, 127–128, 135
   propaganda and, 227–228
   sovereignty and, 69, 71–72, 121
   speech rights of, 223–230
State v. Brown, 170–173
State v. Minkowski, 169–170
State v. Snowden, 48–51, 75–76

Traynor, Roger J., 250n28
Trenton v. New Jersey, 250n29
Tribe, Lawrence, 250n23

value of valuation, 146–151
Village of Belle Terre v. Boraas, 250n23

Waldron, Jeremy, 152–158
Williams, Bernard
   on Gauguin, 94–100, 102–105, 107, 108, 110–113
   on internal reasons, 52
   on luck, 94–96, 98–100, 110–111
   on regret, 103–105, 107, 110, 113
worth. *See* dignity

www.ingramcontent.com/pod-product-compliance
Ingram Content Group UK Ltd.
Pitfield, Milton Keynes, MK11 3LW, UK
UKHW042006230426
12048UKWH00009B/580